Education and
Society in Africa

Education and Society in Africa

Mark Bray, Peter B. Clarke and David Stephens

Edward Arnold

First published in 1986 by
Edward Arnold (Publishers) Ltd
41 Bedford Square, London WC1B 3DQ

British Library Cataloguing in Publication Data

Bray, Mark
  Education and society in Africa.
  1. Educational sociology——Africa
  I. Clarke, Peter B. (Peter Bernard)
  II. Stephens, David
  370.19′096   LC191.8.A4/

ISBN 0-7131-8158-3

Typeset in 10/11 pt Compugraphic Paladium by Colset Pte Ltd, Singapore.

Printed and bound in Great Britain by Billings & Sons Limited, Worcester.

Contents

Contents

List of Tables

Introduction

This book focuses primarily on one question: what part does education play in the development of societies in sub-Saharan Africa? Although this is a short question, it requires a long answer. This is partly because of the complexity of the subject, and partly because we have defined both education and society broadly. The book is not only concerned with Western-type schools and universities but also with the Islamic formal system, structured out-of-school educational activities, and unstructured informal education. The societies we examine include nations as whole units, communities within nations, and schools themselves.

When it is also pointed out that education systems must be set in their political, economic and historical contexts it becomes clear that a detailed answer to the short question could have taken several books rather than just one. However, the essential issues can be brought out in one book, and we did not wish length to defeat the purpose for which the book was written. It is mainly intended for students in universities and teachers' colleges, for whom, at least when they begin their studies, a single comprehensive overview is often more valuable than an extensive library. At the same time, we do recommend readers to use the other literature in their libraries. We hope that they will relate the general discussion in this book to their own experiences and environments, and that they will be stimulated to follow up our references and read other material on specific topics.

Within Africa, of course, there is wide diversity in cultures, availability of resources, historical patterns of colonialism, types of government, and emphasis of official policy. However there are also considerable similarities. All the countries of Africa face comparable economic and social problems, all suffer tensions between the old and the new, and almost all have gained political independence only within the last thirty years. Comparison of educational issues helps both students and policy makers to see that many of their problems have been and are being suffered by others, and there is much for them to learn from events in other parts of the continent. To help make the general discussion concrete, several chapters include specific case studies which comment on the experiences of selected countries.

When choosing examples, it has not always been easy to decide which countries to focus on. Simply because this book is written in English, we expect its widest readership to be in English-speaking countries. Teachers should always relate their explanations to situations with which their students are familiar, and we felt it important for our readers to have a large number of examples from their own countries. However we are also unhappy about the fact that people in English-speaking countries often know very little about their non-English-speaking neighbours. We have therefore included examples from such countries as Togo, Guinea-Bissau, Mauritania and Senegal as well as from Lesotho, Zimbabwe, Tanzania and Sudan. We have allowed Nigeria to dominate our examples because it has the biggest population in Africa and because a high percentage of our readers are likely to be Nigerian, but awareness of the benefits of comparative analysis made us careful to include examples from other countries as well.

We also hope that this book will contribute to a more balanced appreciation of the role of Islamic education in Africa. The only formal schooling received by millions of people in Africa is in the Islamic system, and it has much older roots in the continent than does the Western system. In most West African states Muslims comprise the majority of the population and there are a significant number even in East African states such as Uganda and Kenya. Many other books ignore the Islamic system, and this we consider a serious omission.

We also have a chapter on the diverse forms of indigenous education, which have also been neglected in other books. The chapter permits us both to examine indigenous education systems in their own right and to discuss the influence of the Western, Islamic and indigenous education systems on each other.

The book treats its subject at four main levels. It begins by discussing education and development in an international context. The original models for the school systems in Africa were imported from outside, and even today decisions on education are influenced by past colonial links and by the structure of the international economy. Secondly, we examine developments at the national level, focusing particularly on the processes of nation building, employment, and social stratification. Thirdly, the book turns to the links between education and society at a sub-national and community level. This is of course linked to the national picture, but it deserves separate treatment. And finally, the book notes that schools are themselves societies, with their own rules and systems of control.

The last section of the book pulls strands together and comments on the prospects for educational reform. It does not reach any simple conclusions, chiefly because the links between education and society are very complicated and because policy makers must allow for the economic, political and social factors of their specific circumstances. Also, the last few decades have brought many disappointments and have highlighted the danger of making confident assertions. The book does show the likely consequences of different policies, however, and warns about potential pitfalls. Although it ends with a sober note on the obstacles to reform, by the time they reach the conclusion readers should at least have a better understanding of the forces in operation.

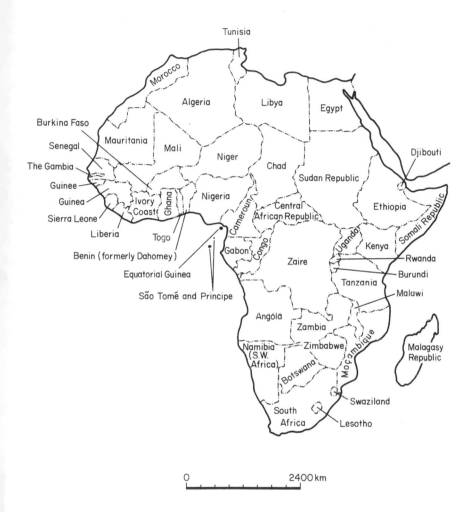

Africa, showing country boundaries in 1985.

Chapter 1

Education and development in an international context

Just as a full understanding of the forces governing urban and regional development within a country depends on a knowledge of relationships within the country as a whole, so the development of individual African nations cannot be fully understood without reference to world-wide relationships. During the colonial period there were obvious links between social, economic and educational changes in African countries and events in the home countries of the colonizing powers. With political independence, the nature of these relationships has changed; but international forces are still highly significant, and some have become even more important.

This chapter consists of three main parts. First it considers the nature of world-wide economic relationships, since they strongly influence the pattern of development. Secondly it examines the educational relationships established during the colonial period. Thirdly it discusses the changing nature, but continuing existence, of these relationships since independence.

Development in an international context

Our general ideas about the nature of development and underdevelopment have changed: during the 1950s and 1960s, underdevelopment was usually seen as a socio-economic situation in which a society simply lacked industry, capital, technology and an educated workforce. According to this interpretation, underdeveloped countries merely had to acquire the 'missing' elements – perhaps from the rich countries in the form of aid – in order to become developed. Now development and underdevelopment are seen as dynamic processes which can only be fully understood in a world context.[1] The rich countries became rich because they exploited and actively underdeveloped the poor ones. Despite some transfer of resources and a general increase in educational levels, this process continues today, and international economic relationships are heavily biased in favour of the rich countries.[2] The Brandt Report, published in 1980, stressed the need for rich countries to assist poor ones not merely for altruistic reasons but to ensure world peace and stability.[3] However, its recommendations have not been widely heeded.

Countries were colonized in order to exploit their resources. European

1

powers exported their own systems of administration, and promoted development of a cash economy based on export crops such as cocoa, coffee, sisal and cotton. The process did involve a form of economic development for the colonies. However, the principal justification for the investment of capital and human resources was not the well-being of the indigenous peoples of the colonies but that of the peoples of Europe. There were, of course, some colonialists who were concerned with the outlook and welfare of peoples in the colonies, and they were also keen to spread 'civilizing', European values, partly through Christian missionary work and education. But they were more interested in education as a means to supply clerks and skilled labour, and the whole economy was geared towards the export of raw materials. Look at the railway map of any African country: lines were built from the ports to the produce-growing areas. The railways were designed to transport goods rather than people, and they took little account of population distribution. To the colonial powers, development was mainly perceived in economic rather than social terms, and measured by such indicators as the volume of exports.

In the post-colonial era, and particularly in the early years, inde-pendent governments also perceived development mainly in economic terms. They saw it as a process through which the material standards of living of their peoples were improved, and most commonly used Gross National Product (GNP) per head as the main indicator of development.

Over the last two decades, however, governments and other observers have increasingly realized that measurement of GNP per head gives a poor indication of development, and that economic growth is just one goal. Statistics of GNP per head are only averages, and hide variations within the country. Thus even a rise in GNP per head conceals the fact that incomes for some groups may have fallen. Moreover, GNP per head gives an index only of economic growth, whereas development is a much broader concept. Dudley Seers was one influential figure who argued that three essential parts of development are reductions in poverty, unemployment and inequality.[4] Governments have become increasingly concerned with the social aspects of development,[5] and seek to ease the pains of transition from subsistence agriculture and traditional economic activities to those of the cash economy. Some leaders also attached con-siderable importance to political processes and the extent to which people can participate in the political decision-making. Others pay little more than lip-service to these concepts, and are anxious to preserve existing power structures even if it involves oppression. The South African government is an obvious example of the latter, but the élites of many other countries also give little more than lip-service to democracy and the welfare of the poorest.

The achievement of political independence for most African countries did not fundamentally alter the nature of international relationships. Agricultural raw materials still comprise the bulk of exports for the majority of African countries, and most of these products are consumed by Europe and North America. Domestic economies are still dominated by small-scale subsistence agriculture, which contributes little more than the basic diet of the peasants who are engaged in it. The principal strategy for change therefore involves a reorganization of the means of production and an injection of capital. This capital, mostly in the form of machines and expertise, comes from the developed world, and is either purchased with the earnings from raw material exports or comes in the form of aid. The terms of trade, however, remain unbalanced. The prices of raw materials have risen little and remain low, and those of machines are high and have risen faster. Both sets of prices are broadly determined by the richer developed countries rather than by the poor developing ones. The bulk of aid is also tied to specific projects, many of which also only benefit the donor country. Very little aid comes in the form of freely usable grants rather than loans which have to be devoted to projects showing a return large enough to satisfy the lender. Thus, dependence on the developed countries continues. In one respect, the dependence is mutual, since neither trading partner can do without the other, but because the conditions of trade are set in developed countries and are heavily biased in their favour, the interdependence is far from equally balanced. Many developing countries are therefore politically independent but economically still very dependent on the US and Europe.

Moreover, the status of élites in Africa is to a large extent based on external rather than internal factors: they are maintained by their position within the world capitalist system; their power derives from local control of the forces of production; and sometimes their position is specifically engineered by interests in the developed world. France, for example, deliberately created economic élites during the colonial period, and plays a continued major role in the economic and political affairs of all its former colonies. Both the West African and the Central African (CFA) francs are directly tied to the French franc; major financial changes in the African territories are made only with the approval of the French central bank; France has a large number of trading agreements with its former colonies; and on occasions France even deploys military forces to maintain or depose African governments.[6] Although the connections between France and her former colonies are the most blatant, similar links remain between all the other European powers and their former colonies. And while America did not formally colonize any part of Africa, dependency on the US is maintained through aid relationships and through the operation of national and transnational companies.

It is because of these relationships that colonialism is widely said to have been replaced by neo-colonialism. It is argued that nothing fundamental has changed since independence. The process of underdevelopment continues, it is suggested, and the rich countries are becoming still richer, at the expense of the poor ones.[7] Moreover, although some groups within developing nations are undoubtedly more prosperous than they would have been in the absence of relationships with the developed countries, the idea that wealth necessarily 'trickles down' to poorer groups has long been disproved.[8] Thus, most African countries are experiencing increasing inequalities of wealth, which lead to further discontent on the part of the majority and are arguably an additional form of underdevelopment.

These changing views on the process of development may be illustrated by the debate which followed publication of W.W. Rostow's book, *The stages of economic growth*, in 1960.[9] The book was subtitled 'A non-communist manifesto', and presented a strongly capitalist view of development, which was seen as a linear process. After comparing the experience of a large number of countries, Rowtow identified five stages which, he suggested, almost all developed countries had gone through and which, he implied, the underdeveloped countries would go through before they became developed. His five stages were: traditional, transitional, take-off, maturity, and high mass consumption.

The most fundamental critique of Rostow's theory has been put forward by André Gunder Frank, who has pointed out that Rostow totally ignored the international nature of development processes. Frank has stressed that the present underdeveloped countries have in some ways become more underdeveloped over time, and that this has been caused by the demands of other nations. India, for example, had a long history of sophisticated government and complex economic development, but was effectively de-industrialized by colonialism. In Africa, the slave trade undermined society before colonialism did so again, and in Latin America the Inca and Aztec civilizations were wiped out altogether.[10]

First of all, one must object to the suggestion, which is implicit in Rostow's theory, that the goal of all developing nations is, or should be, to imitate Western European or North American economic and social conditions. These developed nations waste considerable resources and suffer many social problems which the Third World would do better to try to avoid. Secondly, even if that were a desirable goal, its achievement for the majority of nations would be impossible. The present developed countries reached their position in large measure by exploiting other parts of the world. This option is not open to the developing countries. They have no colonies to exploit, and, except for the minority who are oil producers, the markets for their exports are both limited in size and controlled by the developed world.

Finally, while Rostow suggested that the rate of investment should be the principal stimulus for take-off, he neglected to ask who should reap the fruits of that investment. During the period 1955–62 in Ghana, for example, the rate of investment reached a level – 21 per cent of Gross Domestic Product – which according to Rostow's analysis should have substantially exceeded the necessary threshold. No take-off occurred, however, firstly because most investment was in construction, public works and other items rather than in directly productive processes, and secondly because a high proportion of profits were removed from the country.[11]

The processes through which the poor countries are, to their disadvantage, linked to rich ones are the principal focus of what is known as 'dependency theory'.[12] The main agents through which wealth is extracted are national and multinational companies. Because of the operation of international capitalist forces, Frank argues, 'countries such as Argentina, which Rostow claims to be taking off into development, are becoming ever more structurally underdeveloped . . . [I]ndeed, no underdeveloped country has ever managed to take off out of its underdevelopment by following Rostow's stages.'[13]

While such criticism should have effectively demolished Rostow's model and relegated him to obscurity, his influence has persisted in some quarters.[14] To cite just two examples, the 1976–80 Togolese Development Plan began with a quotation from President Eyadema in which he referred to the need for economic take-off, and a book published in 1980 on education in Nigeria made a similar statement.[15]

The model remains popular partly because of its simplicity. Its supporters often lack the time or inclination to investigate its validity more thoroughly and realize the deceptiveness of this simplicity. In part it is also an indication of the time-lag between the present, when politicians and planners are in positions of influence, and the period when they were in full-time education and became familiar with what was then up-to-date thought. Most importantly, however, the model is popular because it is conservative and does not threaten the status quo. The alternatives to Rostow's model present a situation of unequal development and exploitation which can only be rectified by considerable political change of a type which those at present in power are unwilling to contemplate.

A similar analysis holds for the equally deceptive concept of modernization, which was particularly popular in the 1960s and early 1970s. On a political level, 'modernization' implied replacement of a large number of traditional, religious, family and ethnic authorities by a single, secular, national authority, and the development of democracy. On an economic level, it embraced the growth of industries, use of capital-intensive technologies, concentration of decision-making, and high specialization and interdependence of labour. On an individual level, it implied the acceptance of occupational and geographical mobility and of a meritocracy, tolerance of impersonal working conditions, an outlook oriented more to the present and future than to the past, and a greater desire for a nuclear rather than an extended family.[16]

With the broadening of concepts of development, it has increasingly been realized that much of the content of modernization theory may be inappropriate. Although the boundaries of all African countries were determined by colonial powers and paid little heed to pre-existing kingdoms or ethnic groups, at independence it was felt necessary to maintain these boundaries, and one main task of governments has been to promote allegiance to the nation rather than to ethnic groups or regions. However, parliamentary democracy, which is basically a Western concept, is not necessarily the most suitable form of government for developing nations. Examples of exploitation which has arisen through dictatorships are easy to cite, but it is arguable that in some circumstances leaders in a military dictatorship or a one party state are better able to tackle development issues because they are less distracted by the need to win votes.

In the economic sphere also, industrialization and incorporation into the international capitalist system are not necessarily desirable goals for the majority of people in developing countries. Industrialization does indeed provide high incomes for some communities. But when one recalls that development also embraces the factors of inequality and employment, it is easier to see the dangers of assuming industrialization to be the only or even the major objective. Those developing countries which have begun to industrialize on a large scale have also experienced increased inequalities of wealth, and thus in one way have become *less* developed. They are cases in which the 'rich have got richer and the poor poorer'. Capital intensive technologies generate few employment opportunities and when machines replace people, they render some workers unemployed. Moreover, economically successful industries need large international and home markets. Successful industries in the developed world rely on access to both local and Third World markets. Developing countries may establish industries to produce goods locally that would otherwise be imported, but they often find it difficult to compete with developed-country products both in quality and price even in local markets. It is also extremely difficult for them to break into the developed-country markets.

On a cultural level, the last decade has witnessed strong criticism of the suggestion that nuclear families and Western lifestyles are 'better' than extended families or lifestyles in developing countries. Inkeles and Smith adopt a very narrow, one-sided and ethnocentric view when they refer to 'the binding obligations of powerful extended kinship systems' from which men and women have to 'assert their rights as individuals'. Such people, they suggest:

> . . . have sought to replace a closed world, in which their lives tread the narrowest of circles, with a more open system offering more alternatives and less predestination. From a desperate clinging to fixed ways of doing things, some have moved toward readiness for change. In place of fear of strangers and hostility to those very different from themselves, some have acquired more trust and more tolerance of human diversity. . . They now seek to break out of passivity, fatalism, and the subordination of self to an immutable and inscrutable higher order, in order to become more active and effective. . . [17]

Unfortunately, many people in Africa consider that the main task of development is to achieve an economy and society closely imitating that of Western Europe and the US. Others reject the suggestion that African values are inferior to Western ones. To them, development strategies must be oriented to the society for which they are intended, and for them *greater* emphasis must be placed on family and community rather than the reverse. Their philosophies are particularly strong in view of the major social problems currently experienced in the West which arise from the extent of individualism, competitiveness, materialism and narrow personal horizons. The ultimate objective of development must be the welfare of people. Quite apart from the theory's economic limitations, modernists have a tendency to forget this, and to lose sight of spiritual and social needs in their quest for material gain.

In conclusion, we emphasize the need for a broad understanding of the meaning and factors leading to development. Here we have indicated the international forces contributing to development and underdevelopment, and later we shall show that similar forces, whereby the rich become and remain rich at the expense of the poor, often operate within national boundaries. Dudley Seers' suggestion that development involves a reduction of poverty, inequality and unemployment is a useful contribution, and highlights the fact that it is possible to have economic growth without development (if the fruits of growth are not well distributed) and also that there can be development without economic growth (if existing resources are distributed more evenly). Education can play a useful role in all three of Seers' aspects of development. Later in this book we shall stress that it will not necessarily do so, however. Education is a vehicle for change rather than an independent force, and the direction which the vehicle takes depends very strongly on who is driving and where the driver wants to go.

International educational relationships during the colonial era

The first formal schools in most African countries were opened by Christian missionaries during the nineteenth century. They formed the nucleus of the formal education system, and only later did governments either support or supplement mission efforts. The models for the education systems were taken from the countries from which the missionaries and colonialists came, and are a clear example of the importation of non-African ideas to the continent.

Formal education was seen by most missionaries as an essential part of evangelism, and they established schools very soon after arrival in Africa. The first English speaking missionaries in Nigeria, for example, arrived in 1842 and opened a school almost immediately. A similar pattern was followed in Kenya, when an Anglican missionary arrived in 1844, in Uganda after 1877, in Congo-Leopoldville after 1878, and in a large number of other territories.[18]

One reason why the missionaries were concerned with education arose from the connections they considered it had with religion. 'Christianity is a religion of the book', Abernethy has commented. 'It was not sufficient for a preacher or a priest merely to proclaim the Gospel; his congregation must literally see the Word as well as hear it.'[19] Protestant missionaries in particular felt that people who could read the Bible for themselves did not have to rely on others to expound it for them, and would therefore more thoroughly understand the teaching of the church.

Education was also a means by which the missionaries extended their preaching, for in their schools they trained Africans to spread the message. Thirdly, educational provision improved relations between the missionaries and the colonial authorities, since both were concerned to 'civilize' Africa by promoting European values among the local peoples. Finally, education was a valuable means to gain local confidence. The links between schooling and economic and political advance were rapidly perceived by some African groups, and from the beginning there was a considerable demand for education.

In the early years, the role of colonial governments in education was generally confined either to assisting missionary efforts or to operation in areas in which, usually because they did not wish existing social structures to be radically undermined by new values, missionary activities were discouraged. The latter policy was particularly important in those areas administered by indirect rule, and led, for example, to the Saint-Louis school in former French West Africa. It was opened in 1855 for the sons of Muslim chiefs whose families the colonial authorities wished to influence, but whose religious affiliations and values they did not wish to be upset by Christian teaching.[20] For similar reasons, Christian mission activities were also carefully controlled in British Northern Nigeria.[21]

The colonial authorities' motives for educational development in the Sudan, which were generally representative of the rest of the continent, were summarized by the Director of Education at the beginning of the century. The authorities aimed, he said, at 'I. The creation of a competent artisan class. II. The diffusion among the masses of the people of education sufficient to enable them to understand the merest elements of the machinery of Government. . . III. The creation of a small administrative class. . .'[22]

However, although the basic principles were the same throughout Africa, the details of the imported philosophies and policies varied. Missionaries of different denominations and from different countries gave different emphasis to the use of vernacular languages in education, for example, and the extent to which they considered a mixture of indigenous and European lifestyles acceptable. In general, Protestant missions were more enthusiastic than Catholic ones about using vernacular languages in education. But both placed strong emphasis on such matters as hygiene, the wearing of certain kinds of clothes and monogamous marriage, and the Catholic Church, in line with European practice, also insisted on the celibacy of all those who joined the priesthood.

The educational policies of colonial governments also varied. In the sphere of language policy, the French and the Portuguese generally favoured use of the colonial language as the only medium of instruction. The British were more inclined to use vernaculars, especially at lower educational levels, and the Belgians took an intermediate position.[23] The French, Portuguese and Belgians also developed an education system more closely based on their home country models than did the British. The latter permitted greater local adaptation, and the directives issued by the Colonial Office in London allowed a relatively high degree of flexibility. This itself reflected dominant ideas in Britain, for as Lord Hailey noted, the British have had a 'traditional disinclination . . . to subject education or any other intellectual movement to state control'.[24]

Although differences can be identified, the similarities between the education systems which developed in Africa and those which existed in Europe were much greater. Ironically, this occurred largely because of

African demands rather than European ones. For example, Gifford and Weiskel identify three distinct periods in French colonial educational policy. During the second half of the nineteenth century, the dominant policy was one of assimilation, and schools sought effectively to produce 'black Frenchmen'. Between 1895 and 1945, policies were more in favour of adaptation to local conditions. The schools operated for French children in Africa closely followed home-country practices, but those for Africans were more related to local conditions. In the post–1945 period, Africans rebelled against this duality, and demanded the same type of education as the colonialists gave their own children. Consequently, in Gifford and Weiskel's words: 'In the post-war political context the French administration could not afford to resist African demands . . . [and] began to create in West Africa strict copies of French metropolitan schools. . . By 1960 African students could feel confident that their schools offered the same curriculum available in any French town'.[25] Children in these colonies studied Voltaire, Molière, Victor Hugo and other French authors, and sat the Baccalaureat examinations. Their counterparts in British colonies may not have attended schools that were quite such strict copies of those in Britain, but they studied Shakespeare, Dickens, Wordsworth and other British authors, and sat the School Certificate examinations.

As well as these clear links between educational practices in Europe and those in Africa, there were others between America and Africa. Connections were particularly strong with Liberia, which had been founded as a home for freed slaves with strong American support.[26] The principal component of American educational practice that was considered relevant to Africa was the type of provision for children of freed black slaves. In 1868, the Hampton Institute was opened in Virginia to give black people a combination of academic and technical training and to prepare them as model teachers, craftsmen and cultivators in their own communities. In 1881, a sister institution, called Tuskegee, was opened at Alabama. The institutions had a major local and international impact, and in the early twentieth century led to significant technical assistance projects in Togo and the Sudan.[27] Their impact was further increased in the 1920s by two investigative commissions which toured the whole of Africa and produced major reports.

The first expedition, in 1920–1, visited West, South and Equatorial Africa, and the second, in 1924, visited East, Central and South Africa. They were known as the Phelps-Stokes Commissions, since they were financed from a fund bequeathed by a philanthropist of that name. Their membership was principally American, but they were headed by a Welshman named Thomas Jesse Jones, and included in their number a Gold Coaster named J.E.K. Aggrey.[28]

The Phelps-Stokes reports had a major impact in Africa. The British Colonial Office issued a memorandum in 1925 in response to their recommendations,[29] and colleges were opened in East and Central Africa to implement some of their ideas. They were called Jeanes schools, after another American philanthropist, and sought to relate education more closely to local conditions and needs. They particularly emphasized use of readily available local materials and 'education for life' rather than mere certification. The staff, once trained, were given responsibility for groups of rural schools around which they travelled to support and advise. The first Jeanes school was opened in Kenya in 1925. Shortly after, two more were opened in what was then Southern Rhodesia, one was started in Northern Rhodesia, and a fifth was opened in Nyasaland. In non-settler British colonies and in non-British colonies, the impact of the American model was not so great. However, there is evidence that during the 1920s and 1930s it did have some influence on Belgian and French policy makers.[30]

Another mechanism through which educational ideas were disseminated was the transfer of officers to different colonies and from the overseas territories to the metropolitan centre. For example, in the first decade of this century, the educational models proposed by Cromer in the Sudan and Lugard in Northern Nigeria were heavily influenced by the Indian experience and a desire to avoid mistakes made there. In particular they hoped to avoid the divisive effects of religious education and the subsequent growth of nationalism that had caused the British Government so many problems in India.[31] Lugard left Nigeria in 1906 to go to Hong Kong. He returned in 1912, and again his thinking on education was strongly influenced by his experiences while he had been away.[32] Similarly, A.G. Fraser, who in 1925 had founded Achimota College in the Gold Coast to operate on similar lines to the Jeanes schools, had grown up in India and Uganda, and had previously served in Ceylon.[33] And Hanns Vischer, who had been given the responsibility to establish the Northern Nigerian education system in 1908, later moved to the Colonial Office in London, and was a member of the second Phelps-Stokes Commission. Currie (who had served in the Sudan), Lugard and Vischer were all members of the committee which drew up the 1925 Colonial Office memorandum, and had a strong influence on educational development throughout Africa.

To a lesser though still significant extent, there was also some cross-fertilization of ideas between colonies of different powers. In 1906, for example, the Director of Education in Senegal returned to Dakar with a plan to reorganize the Ecole Normale after visiting a Madras school in India. Again, in 1934, the Director of Education for what was then French West Africa remodelled the Ecole William Ponty with specific reference to Achimota College and to British accomplishments in Nigeria.[34] Pan-African studies by R.L. Buell, Victor Murray and Lord Hailey were also influential.[35]

Similar cross-fertilization of ideas among missionary educators resulted from formal and informal contact. At the 1910 World Missionary Conference in Edinburgh, for example, all the major Protestant missions were represented. Educational issues were discussed, including the significance of American models, and some general principles were enumerated. A major place in the conference was taken by J.H. Oldham, who later became Secretary to the International Missionary Council, and who wielded considerable influence in African educational policy formation. He also was a member of the committee which drew up the 1925 British Colonial Office memorandum, and played an important role at the second major international missionary conference at Le Zoute, in Belgium, in 1926. Among Roman Catholic missionary educators some directives and exchange of ideas occurred through Rome. Their cooperation with Protestant bodies tended to be slight, though there is evidence of some exchange of viewpoints through an International Institute of African Languages and Culture which was established in 1926 with Lugard as its head.[36]

It must be stressed, however, that cross-fertilization of ideas was slight bearing in mind the tendency for practitioners to adopt the educational models and ideas of their own home countries. There was nearly always a gap between policy articulated in official circles and the way in which programmes were implemented locally. Practitioners tended to fall back on their own educational experiences, in part simply to economize on effort in conditions of uncertainty.

The nature of education in schools was also strongly influenced by demands at university level. The oldest Western-type university in Africa was founded at Fourah Bay, in Sierra Leone, in 1827. It was affiliated to the British University of Durham in 1875, and was strongly influenced by British traditions. Not until after the Second World War did higher education expand rapidly, however. British, French and Belgian authorities adopted similar strategies for promoting development, and institutions in their colonies were affiliated respectively to the University of London, the Universities of Paris or Bordeaux, and the University of Louvain. The metropolitan universities provided guidance with operation and implementation of syllabuses, and set out to maintain standards of instruction. This conferred international recognition on the degrees from the African institutions. However, it also strongly limited curricular adaptation, and, as Ashby noted with reference to the British pattern, the University of London was 'uncompromising in resisting any departure from the pattern of the degree'.[37] Entry requirements were strict, and had a strong influence on the operation and development of secondary and even primary schools.

We may conclude, therefore, that some international links in education during the colonial period were very strong. They were principally those between the colonizing powers and their colonies. Ideas were predominantly transmitted in a one-way direction, and it cannot be said that practices in Europe were influenced at all by those in Africa. There was some cross-fertilization of ideas between territories, but it was subordinate to the flow from the metropole to the colonies.

International educational relationships since independence

Educational change in former European colonies is still influenced by changes in the European countries themselves. American ideas have a stronger influence than they did before, but the flow of ideas from the developed to the developing world remains as strong as ever. Within the developing world, cross-fertilization of ideas exists but is relatively slight.

The degree of change was so modest mainly because of persistent ideas about the nature and quality of education. In 1973, President Senghor of Senegal told a reporter that he was 'very proud of the 1,000 bacheliers who graduated this year from the *lycées* of his country and of the four [Senegalese] students who passed the mathematics *agrégation* – the French *agrégation* because, he told me, he does not want diplomas "on the cheap"'.[38] This is an extreme example of continued adherence to the traditions of a former colonial power. In the rest of Africa such ties may be less obvious and are loosening with time. However, throughout the continent they remain strong. A battle continues between those who want to relate education more closely to local needs and lifestyles, and those who wish to maintain 'standards', as they put it – which usually means close adherence to the formal system bequeathed to African countries by the colonial powers.

One way in which these 'standards' and international ties are maintained is through the examination system.[39] In 1981 the main secondary school examinations of seven Anglophone countries were still set by Cambridge University in Britain.[40] West African English-speaking countries have an independent, single examining body,[41] and former Belgian and French colonies now set examinations locally. However, the operations of these local bodies still display strong colonial legacies. In the 1980 West African Examinations Council 'A' level English Literature syllabus, for example, only six of the 39 authors specifically named were African, and only three were West African. Students were obliged to study a Shakespeare play, and among their options was fourteenth-century poetry by Chaucer (to be studied in the original – which even British students find very difficult) and seventeenth-century poetry by John Donne and George Herbert.[42] Similarly, the Senegalese Baccalaureat offered examinations in ten languages; but not one of them was Senegalese or even African.[43] The history section concentrated principally on Europe and Russia, and when it did refer to Africa it was only with an implied image of inferiority.[44]

Other evidence of strong international links may be seen in the number of expatriate teachers employed in African countries. Education is one sector in the economy in which indigenization has been relatively rapid, and the situation is still changing fast. However, there has remained a substantial gap between demand and supply of local staff in many countries, and at post-primary levels this has usually been bridged by expatriates. In Botswana, for example, as many as 74 per cent of secondary teachers in 1976 were expatriates.[45] The proportion was among the highest in Africa, but in Kano State of Nigeria, to cite another example, 30 per cent of secondary teachers in the same year were expatriates.[46] Employment of expatriates is not only expensive, but also they usually have only a limited knowledge of local languages and pupils' home background conditions.

International links of this type are diverse, for expatriates are recruited from many different countries. The Kano State expatriates mentioned above included large groups from India, Pakistan and the Philippines as well as from Britain, Canada and the US; the Nigerian authorities have also employed a significant number of teachers from other African countries, Ghana in particular. Of the expatriate teachers in Botswana in 1976, 17 per cent were Zimbabwean, and 5 per cent were South African. It is essential for a teacher to be a fluent speaker of the official medium of instruction, and because it helps if expatriates are familiar with the type of education system in which they have to work, a large percentage are recruited either from the former colonizing country or from other colonies of the same power. Many staff are also sent through bilateral aid programmes. Consequently, many more British teachers go to former British colonies than to former French, Belgian, Spanish or Portuguese ones, and a similar pattern applies to the other territories.

At the university level, ties of this kind are even stronger. Local staff shortages tend to be even more severe at this level, and universities also make conscious efforts to become members of a world-wide academic community. Ties with the formal colonial countries are maintained through former and informal links with European universities, and some administrative organizations established during the colonial era have continued with similar functions in the post-colonial era. For example, the University of London Institute of Education has links with Kenyatta University in Kenya, which involve exchange of staff each year, and with Ahmadu Bello University, Nigeria. Dakar University, in Senegal, still has a formal arrangement under which a substantial proportion of its staff are seconded from France, and in a large number of countries a network of external examiners from developed countries still operates.

At the university level, clear international links also exist in relation to the local staff, a large proportion of whom have themselves studied abroad. Again because of linguistic and historical ties, many Africans study in the former colonial countries, and while doing so gain experience of educational and other ideas which dominate there. Table 1.1 shows the number of Africans studying abroad in 1982, and indicates that students from former French colonies went in particularly high numbers to France. Similarly, Belgium hosted the largest groups from Burundi and Zaire, and Portugal hosted the largest groups from Angola and Mozambique. Students from former British colonies now tend to go to the US rather than to Britain, a trend which was reinforced in the early 1980s following a reduction in British aid and a sharp increase in British overseas student fees. Relatively few African students attend universities in communist countries.

There is much contact with the US and UK because English-speaking African students have fewer language problems when studying in these two countries. More importantly, however, it reflects deliberate American foreign policy, and from Table 1.1 we can see that there is also a large number of French-speaking students in the US. American policy-makers have recognized both Africa's resource potential and its political significance in the world context, and have used educational and other

Table 1.1   African students in foreign tertiary educational institutions, by country, 1982[17]

Host country	AFRICA	Angola	Benin	Botswana	Burundi	Chad	Congo	Ethiopia	Gambia	Ghana	Guinea	Ivory Coast	Kenya	Lesotho	Liberia	Malawi	Mali
								Country of origin									
US*	33,342	27	24	178	15	17	10	1,407	163	1,468	18	363	1,671	84	863	100	74
France**	60,308	—	1,174	—	—	—	1,195	—	—	—	—	2,673	—	—	—	—	—
Germany (Federal)	4,402	7	29	6	26	33	15	238	1	278	23	69	88	1	20	8	43
UK*	11,811	2	1	134	6	5	5	88	55	442	1	14	741	52	17	235	24
Canada	4,266	2	9	39	4	1	12	38	6	249	13	269	356	22	16	27	38
Italy**	1,620	—	—	—	—	—	—	159	—	—	—	—	—	—	—	—	—
Saudi Arabia*	3,795	—	—	—	—	106	—	125	—	—	28	—	—	—	—	—	89
Switzerland	1,079	10	16	—	26	3	5	11	—	18	14	17	8	—	2	1	14
India***	4,740	1	—	—	—	—	—	98	—	15	—	—	1,010	1	—	17	—
Belgium	4,046	4	15	—	160	7	24	5	—	10	7	61	11	1	—	—	43
Czechoslovakia	542	41	12	—	2	—	31	210	—	14	26	—	—	—	—	—	—
Senegal*	2,461	2	170	—	28	55	36	5	10	17	57	66	—	—	—	—	293
Cuba	1,397	23	52	—	—	—	58	531	—	5	40	—	—	8	—	—	59
Ivory Coast*	1,738	8	431	—	2	87	19	3	1	41	90	—	6	—	42	—	143
Portugal***	673	87	—	—	—	1	1	—	—	—	—	—	1	—	—	—	—
Others	22,507	46	68	4	69	118	206	396	12	255	128	16	177	18	27	24	188
Total (45 countries)	158,727	260	2,001	361	338	433	2,337	3,314	248	2,812	445	3,548	4,069	186	987	412	1,008

* 1981   ** 1980   *** 1979

Table 1.1   continued

Host country	Mozambique	Nigeria	Senegal	Sierra Leone	Somalia	South Africa	Sudan	Swaziland	Togo	Uganda	United Republic of Tanzania	Zaire	Zambia	Zimbabwe	Others and Unspecified
US*	4	15,651	110	504	314	1,063	658	87	52	401	483	177	299	520	6,537
France**	—	—	2,188	—	—	—	—	—	1,261	—	—	1,468	—	—	49,629
Germany (Federal)	2	366	45	42	62	113	83	3	85	83	82	135	14	25	2,377
UK*	11	4,306	12	165	57	327	785	74	1	172	525	29	484	820	2,221
Canada	2	533	74	27	10	100	21	10	43	52	169	101	70	48	1,905
Italy**	—	263	—	—	192	15	—	—	—	—	—	93	—	—	899
Saudi Arabia*	—	256	30	—	258	—	883	—	—	—	—	—	—	—	2,064
Switzerland	1	6	22	1	3	7	9	—	13	9	4	142	1	2	714
India***	7	852	—	—	115	336	68	—	—	95	231	—	163	—	3,008
Belgium	1	49	88	—	3	10	17	—	11	6	13	1,545	8	—	1,947
Czechoslovakia	9	16	5	1	4	4	43	—	1	5	—	2	7	8	101
Senegal*	—	12	—	4	1	—	—	—	183	—	—	27	—	3	1,492
Cuba	5	11	—	17	—	57	—	1	—	24	54	3	—	52	397
Ivory Coast*	—	72	65	9	1	—	2	—	93	4	5	29	1	—	584
Portugal***	39	—	—	—	—	—	—	—	—	—	—	11	1	—	532
Others	17	1,322	267	87	142	211	7,953	2	84	160	259	249	93	102	9,807
Total (45 countries)	98	23,715	2,906	857	1,162	2,243	10,522	177	1,827	1,011	1,825	4,011	1,141	1,580	84,214

* 1981   ** 1980   *** 1979

Note 1: Data are to be considered indicative rather than precise. Foreign students registered in these countries represent approximately 90% of the total. The USSR has not been included because recent figures were not available. It had a total of 30,563 foreign students (from all continents) in 1971.

2: The table refers to 45 countries in the whole continent and is not restricted to sub-Saharan Africa.

programmes to promote ties between the continents. Berman has gone further to assert that even the supposedly neutral and philanthropic American foundations – Carnegie, Ford and Rockefeller – have actively promoted this link, and have bound the newly independent African nations to the US. They did this, he continues:

> . . . primarily by funding programs linking the educational systems of the new African states to the values, *modus operandi*, and institutions of the United States. In public pronouncements, foundation officials have stressed the nonpolitical, technocratic natures of their involvement in African education, noting that the foundations' interests lay solely in the provision of educational models and institutional support designed to help the developing African nations modernize and thereby provide more benefits for their peoples. Internal foundation policy documents and correspondence, interfoundation memoranda, and personal reminiscences of foundation personnel suggest that this public rhetoric of disinterested humanitarianism was little more than a façade behind which the economic and strategic interests of the United States have been furthered.[48]

Not unexpectedly, representatives of the foundations have stoutly denied this accusation.[49] Whether or not we consider American programmes to have been deliberately fostered to promote US political objectives, however, it is quite clear that American educational links with Africa have increased markedly over the last three decades. The American foundations played a major role in funding tertiary institutions in Nigeria, Ethiopia, Zaire, and in a combined university for Kenya, Uganda and Tanzania;[50] a large number of African students study in the US; and recent major Nigerian educational restructuring has been explicitly based on American methods and philosophy.[51]

The role of international agencies in educational development should also be examined. They have acted as independent initiators and catalysts of major educational policy changes. One notable example of this was the shift of emphasis from higher to elementary education in the early 1970s. This change was accelerated by the World Bank, and its own thinking was made explicit in its 1974 *Education sector working paper*.[52] The change in emphasis was accompanied by interest in nonformal education, and World Bank and other international agency funding and expertise stimulated an unprecedented number of studies and projects concerned with nonformal learning. Now, the fashion has partly moved on, and international agency attention is focusing on ways to integrate formal and nonformal learning under the heading of 'basic education'.[53]

Like the Carnegie, Ford and Rockefeller foundations, the international agencies should not be assumed to be neutral institutions responding to requests from developing countries and without their own ideologies. Rather, they are heavily dominated by capitalist ideology, and it is significant that although their work principally concerns the developing world, all the major agency headquarters are in developed capitalist countries. For example, the headquarters of Unesco and the International

Institute for Educational Planning (IIEP) are in Paris; the International Bureau of Education (IBE) and the International Labour Office (ILO) are based in Geneva; and the World Bank is based in Washington. This is not coincidental. On one level, it reflects the state of world development when the organizations were founded; they were located at centres of international finance and communication. On another level, it reflects the ideological outlook of the most powerful individuals and nations associated with the organizations.[54] The international agencies do employ staff from developing nations. For example, in 1984 8.6 per cent of Unesco staff were from sub-Saharan Africa, and 33.1 per cent were from developing countries, and 63.0 per cent of new recruits to the World Bank were from developing countries.[55] However the organizations are heavily dominated by staff from Western developed nations, and individuals from any country are only likely to be recruited if their general attitudes correspond to those of the employing agency.

Another dimension of international relationships concerns the origin of research data. A high proportion of research in Africa is still conducted by non-nationals. This is partly because the number of Africans with higher degrees and research training is still fairly low, and governments have given other aspects of development a higher priority. The other main reason is that research is very time-consuming and laborious, and talented Africans who are suited to research often occupy posts dealing with more urgent administrative or developmental matters. Even university lecturers often do not conduct as much research as is commonly expected of them, partly because they are required for more important leadership and developmental functions. It is not unusual for a university professor to be called upon to serve in an important government ministry. For example, Professor Galadanci of Sokoto University became a close advisor to President Shagari of Nigeria after the elections of 1983.

Moreover, even Africans who publish their research findings frequently do so through companies of the developed world. This is usually because the established publishers carry more prestige and have better distribution services, and because the publishing industry in Africa is still small. Further, a writer's audience is still limited, for the circulation of knowledge is restricted by the language in which it is written. This book itself illustrates several of these points: its authors have wide experience in Africa but are Europeans; it is published in London; and because it is written in English, it is unlikely to be widely read in non-Anglophone countries, even though it adopts a comparative perspective and has material useful to other countries. It should be noted, however, that the publishing industry in Africa is growing rapidly, and is stimulated by population growth and the increased availability of education. In 1978 Nigeria, the country with the most developed publishing industry, had nearly 200 indigenous publishers. They played a particularly important role in encouraging books specifically produced for Nigeria and in promoting work written in local languages.[56]

Most of Africa's intercontinental links are with Europe and North America, and connections with other continents are less strong. Some examples are worth noting, however. For instance, Tanzanian policies have been heavily influenced by the Chinese experience,[57] and developments in Guinea-Bissau have been partly shaped by the Brazilian educator, Paulo Freire.[58] Though recent Russian and Cuban influence in Africa has been more concerned with military strategies, Marxist–Leninist political education, using Russian materials, has been a significant feature of schooling in Mozambique, Angola, Guinea, Ethiopia and Benin. In 1982, 1,397 post-secondary African students were reported to be resident in Cuba, and several thousand Angolan and Mozambiquan children, together with a few others from Namibia, Ethiopia, São Tomé, Guinea-Bissau and Congo, have been reported to receive schooling there.[59] Finally, Islamic parts of Africa have important ties with the Arab world. After the 1973 oil price rise, Saudi Arabia and neighbouring states became very wealthy. Some of this wealth has been dispersed to poorer Arabic-speaking countries, and in the mid-1970s the Arabic League Educational, Cultural and Scientific Organization provided funds for major Sudanese child and adult basic education programmes.

Within Africa itself, international educational links have operated through informal channels, and have not been strong. During their struggle for independence, the liberation forces of Mozambique and Zimbabwe operated schools in neighbouring friendly countries. Many universities also enrol students from other countries. Over 5,000 non-indigenous African pupils were recorded in Senegalese, Togolese and Ivory Coast tertiary institutions in 1982, and the University of East Africa and the University of Bechuanaland, Basutoland and Swaziland were specifically created to operate on a common basis. However, both the University of East Africa and the University of Botswana, Lesotho and Swaziland have now split into their national parts. The former British colonies are members of the Commonwealth, which holds education conferences at which ideas are exchanged. However, neither the former French nor the former Portuguese, Belgian or Spanish colonies have such an organization. Nor is there a formal arrangement, through the Organization of African Unity or any other body, to provide an educational forum for all African countries.

In conclusion, we may note that some formal and informal international ties in education are strong. They are greatest between Africa and Western developed nations, and still to a large extent follow the old colonial lines. The flow of personnel and ideas between France and French-speaking Africa is much greater than, for example, the flow between France and English-speaking Africa. This is partly because of the forces of tradition and the power of established links, but it also reflects the importance of language itself. Where expatriates are recruited from developing countries, they are frequently from former colonies of the same power, and it is significant that Paulo Freire, who is the only obvious educational link between South America and Africa, himself comes from one former Portuguese colony and has been working in another.

Contrasting with these links, which arise from colonial history, is the role played by the US. Over the last three decades, the US has become increasingly influential, through both American and international agencies. In part, the strong role of the US can be attributed to the fact that English is spoken there. China and Russia benefit from no similar coincidence, and since they also had no imperial links with Africa, their languages are barely spoken on the continent. The main reason for the different roles of the US and China and Russia, however, arises from deliberate policy decisions. In the period following the Second World War, the Americans perceived strategic advantages from links with Africa, and acted accordingly. The Chinese and Russians have not operated to anything like the same extent, though the last decade has witnessed increasing involvement, and there are signs that it may expand further in the future.

Finally, it is worth noting that the transfer of ideas remains very strongly a one-way process. Specialists from the developed countries travel to Africa to advise governments on how to organize their education systems. But no Africans travel to Britain, France or the US to advise their governments on how to organize *their* education systems! Similarly, specialist courses still exist in developed countries to train African educators, and involve, for example, Tanzanian officers examining Scottish schools to gain ideas for improving Tanzanian schools. But no one seems to suggest that Scottish educators should go to Tanzania to gain ideas for improving Scottish schools.

Nevertheless, aspects of this predominantly one-way transfer of ideas are beginning to change. African countries are increasingly training their own personnel, and decreasingly sending them overseas. Educational innovations are coming from within African countries rather than being imported. The number of expatriates in African secondary schools and universities is declining, and the number of African publishing houses, producing work written by Africans, is increasing. These trends must be welcomed, and will perhaps one day lead to a situation where Africa is not only importing new ideas and specialists but also exporting them much more widely as part of a fairer, more balanced system of international exchange.

Questions and project work

1 'The nature of present educational structures in Africa guarantees the continuing underdevelopment of Africa.' Present the arguments for and against this statement.

2 Outline how formal education in your country has changed since independence and, with reference to international links, discuss the obstacles to further change.

3 Look at the recommended book list for the main subjects you are studying. Note how many authors are (a) nationals of your country, (b) nationals of another African country, (c) Americans, (d) British, (e) French, (f) other nationalities. Similarly, note where each book was published. Discuss the reasons for your findings.

4 Find out the dates and the original founders of all the primary schools in your town/district established before independence. How many were opened by Christian missionaries, how many by the government, and how many by other voluntary organizations? If possible, examine the different philosophies and objectives of those who founded the schools, and discuss the impact of the schools on the local community.

Notes

1 Hoogvelt, A. *The Third World in Global Development*. Macmillan, London 1982.

2 See Rodney, Walter *How Europe Underdeveloped Africa*. Bogle-L'Ouverture Publications, London 1972, *passim*; and Hoogvelt, A. *The Sociology of Developing Countries*. Macmillan, London 1978, pt. II.

3 Brandt, Willy *et al*. *North-South: A Programme for Survival*. Pan, London 1980.

4 Seers, Dudley 'What are we Trying to Measure?' in Nancy Baster (ed.) *Measuring Development*. Frank Cass, London 1972.

5 See Hardiman, M. and Midgely, J. *The Social Dimensions of Development*. Wiley, London 1982; also Conyers, D. *An Introduction to Social Planning in the Third World*. Wiley, London 1982.

6 French interest in Chad in 1983 and their desire not to offend the Libyans was based very much upon their economic interests in both Libya and Chad, rather than any desire to see Chad as a viable political entity.

7 See Hoogvelt 1978, op. cit., pp. 74–88; and Amin, Samir *Neo-Colonialism in West Africa*. Penguin, Harmondsworth 1973.

8 Thirlwall, A.P. *Growth and Development*. Macmillan, London 1974, pp. 120–8.

9 Rostow, W.W. *The Stages of Economic Growth*. Cambridge University Press, Cambridge 1960.

10 Frank, André Gunder *Sociology of Development and the Underdevelopment of Sociology*. Pluto Press, London 1971, pp. 18–27.

11 Amin, op. cit., pp. 242–3.

12 For two reviews of the literature on this theory, see Palma, G. 'Dependency: A Formal Theory of Underdevelopment or a Methodology for the Analysis of Concrete Situations of Underdevelopment?' *World Development*, Vol. 6, Nos. 7–8, 1978; and 'Is Dependency Dead?' *IDS Bulletin*, Vol. 12, No. 1, 1980. An alternative Marxist view is presented in Warren, Bill *Imperialism: Pioneer of Capitalism*. Verso, London 1980. For a summary of the debate between him and the dependency theorists, see Hoogvelt (1978) op. cit., pp. 78–85.

13 Frank, op. cit., p. 24.

14 See Bauer, P.T. *Equality, the Third World and Economic Delusion*. Methuen, London 1981 for a 'conservative reappraisal' of colonialism and the relationship of developing countries to the developed.

15 République Togolaise *Plan de Développement Economique et Social 1976–1980*, Ministère du Plan, Lomé 1976, p. 1; Thakur A.S. and Ezenne, A.N. *A Short History of Education in Nigeria*. National, Delhi 1980, p. 94.

16 Inkeles, Alex and Smith, David H. *Becoming Modern*. Heinemann, London 1974, pp. 4, 16. See also Long, Norman *An Introduction to the Sociology of Rural Development*. Tavistock, London 1977, pp. 9–40.

17 Ibid., pp. 4–5.

18 See Anderson, John *The Struggle for the School*. Longman, Nairobi 1970, p. 10; Scanlon David G. (ed.), *Church, State and Education in Africa*. Teachers' College Press, Columbia, New York 1966, pp. 63, 141, 200.

19 Abernethy, David B. *The Political Dilemma of Popular Education*. Stanford University Press, Stanford 1969, p. 31.

20 Gifford, Prosser and Weiskel, Timothy C. 'African Education in a Colonial Context: French and British Styles', in Gifford, Prosser, and Louis, Wm. Roger, (eds.) *France and Britain in Africa*. Yale University Press, New Haven 1971, p. 672.

21 Crampton, E.P.T. *Christianity in Northern Nigeria*. Geoffrey Chapman, London 1976, p. 98 ff.

22 Currie, Sir James 'The Educational Experiment in the Anglo-Egyptian Sudan, 1900–33, Part I'. *Journal of the African Society*, Vol. 33, 1934, p. 364.

23 Lord Hailey *An African Survey*, Oxford University Press, London 1957, pp. 1226–8.

24 Ibid., p. 1222.

25 Gifford and Weiskel, op. cit., p. 694. See also Clignet, Remi 'Damned if you do, damned if you don't – the dilemmas of colonizer-colonized relations'. *Comparative Education Review*, Vol. 15, No. 3, 1971, pp. 291–312.

26 Marmelli, Lawrence A. *The New Liberia*. Pall Mall, London 1964.

27 King, Kenneth James *Pan-Africanism and Education*. Clarendon Press, Oxford 1971, p. 14.

28 Jones, Thomas Jesse *Education in Africa*. Phelps-Stokes Fund, New York 1922; Jones, Thomas Jesse *Education in East Africa*, Phelps-Stokes Fund, 1924. For a critical commentary on this subject, see King, ibid., passim.

29 Great Britain, Colonial Office *Education Policy in British Tropical Africa*. His Majesty's Stationery Office, London 1925.

30 Buell, Raymond Leslie *The Native Problem in Africa*. Macmillan, New York 1928, Vol. 11, p. 594; Gifford and Weiskel, op. cit., p. 696.

31 Gifford and Weiskel, op. cit., p. 687.

32 Perham, Margery *Lugard: The Years of Authority*. Collins, London 1960, p. 489.

33 Ward, W.E.F. *Fraser of Trinity and Achimota*. Ghana Universities Press, Accra/Oxford University Press, London 1965.

34 Gifford and Weiskel, op. cit., p. 696.

35 Buell, op. cit.; Murray, A. Victor *The School in the Bush*. Longmans Green, London 1929; Hailey, op. cit.

36 Oliver, Roland *The Missionary Factor in East Africa*. Longman, London 1965, pp. 272–3.

37 Ashby, Eric *Universities: British, Indian, African*. Weidenfeld and Nicolson, London 1966, p. 238.

38 Fontaine, A. quoted in Gillette, Arthur Lavery *Beyond the Non-Formal Fashion*. Center for International Education, Amherst 1977, p. 11.

39 See Dore, R. *The Diploma Disease*. Allen and Unwin, London 1976.

40 They were Botswana, South Africa, Lesotho, Swaziland, Zimbabwe, Malawi and Zambia (though Zambia operated its own examinations from 1982 and Malawi has also embarked on changes.)

41 The West African Examinations Council was established in 1951 to serve The Gambia, Gold Coast, Sierra Leone and Nigeria. Liberia joined it in 1974.

42 The West African Examinations Council *Regulations and Syllabuses*. Academy Press, Lagos 1980, pp. 149–51. The 'O'-level Literature in English syllabus was more oriented toward Africa, with 13 of the 27 named authors from the continent. However, for it also, Shakespeare was compulsory (ibid., pp. 212–3).

43 The languages were French, English, German, Arabic, Greek, Latin, Spanish, Portuguese, Russian and Italian.

44 For example, one of the few questions in 1980 referring to Africa was: 'After summarizing the stages of the French conquest of West Africa, indicate the causes of the final failure of the African armed resistance.'

45 Republic of Botswana *Education for Kagisano*. Ministry of Education, Gaborone 1977, Vol. I, p. 267.

46 Kano State of Nigeria *Education Statistics for Kano State 1976-77*. Government Printer, Kano 1977, pp. 48, 50.

47 Unesco *Unesco Statistical Yearbook 1984*. Paris, Table 3.15.

48 Berman, Edward H. 'Foundations, United States Foreign Policy, and African Education, 1945-1975'. *Harvard Educational Review*, Vol. 49, No. 2 (May), 1979, p. 146.

49 'Responses to Edward H. Berman', ibid., pp. 180-4.

50 Berman, op. cit., p. 159.

51 Onabamiro, Sanya 'The Place and Role of Education in the Evolution of an Egalitarian Society' in *Nigeria in Transition*. Federal Government Printer, Lagos 1980, p. 92.

52 The World Bank *Education Sector Working Paper*. Washington 1974.

53 See for example, Botti, M., Carelli, M.D. and Saliba, M. *Basic Education in the Sahel Countries*. Unesco, Hamburg 1978; and The World Bank *Education Sector Policy Paper*. Washington 1980.

54 See Carnoy, Martin 'International Institutions and Educational Policy: A Review of Education-Sector Policy'. *Prospects*, Vol. X, No. 3, 1980.

55 Unesco 'Questions and Answers' (mimeo) Paris 1985, p. 5; The World Bank *1984 Annual Report*. Washington 1985, p. 27.

56 Zell, Hans (ed.) *African Books in Print*. Mansell, London 1978.

57 Morrison, David R. *Education and Politics in Africa: The Tanzanian Case*. C. Hurst, London 1976, pp. 260-6.

58 See Institution of Cultural Action (IDAC) *Guinea-Bissau: Reinventing Education*. Nos. 11-12, Geneva, 1975-6; and Freire, Paulo *Pedagogy in Process: The Letters to Guinea-Bissau*. Writers and Readers Publishing Cooperative, London 1978.

59 Information from Mozambique, Angola and Guiné Information Centre, London.

Chapter 2

Education and nation building

The boundaries of most African countries were determined by European colonial powers in the last century. In most cases, the Europeans paid little attention to ethnic territories or the boundaries of African kingdoms, and countries were formed from arbitrary amalgamations of peoples. In other cases, peoples were deliberately split in a policy of 'divide and rule'. To give just two examples, the Yoruba live in present-day Benin Republic and Nigeria; and the Wolof are divided between The Gambia and Senegal. The arbitrary nature of many African boundaries can be seen just by glancing at a map: a high percentage of them are straight lines as if drawn with a ruler.

Although these arbitrary boundaries were not necessarily appropriate to the needs of independent countries, one of the first pronouncements of the Organization of African Unity, in 1964, was that international colonial boundaries should remain intact.[1] That decision was made to reduce claims by neighbouring territories to each others' land and to avoid the breaking up of African countries. In the period just before independence, many nationalist leaders found that one major factor binding peoples together was opposition to colonial rule. With the achievement of independence, that common goal no longer existed, and in many countries the threat of internal divisions increased.

Because of these factors, the fostering of a national identity has become one of the most important tasks of African governments, and education is seen as a major instrument for doing this. Both the formal school system and adult education campaigns are often explicitly geared to this end, while informal education plays at least as significant a part. Before discussing the ways education can promote unity, however, we should note some important theories about the organization of society.

Theories of social organization

Many different types and levels of social organization exist, and many different sociological theories have been developed to explain them. It is useful, first, to notice a distinction made by Emile Durkheim, a French sociologist, at the end of the last century.[2] Durkheim distinguished between societies of the 'mechanical' and the 'organic' type. Those of the first type, he suggested, are simple and undifferentiated, and their

23

members have similar attitudes, skills and lifestyles. A small nomadic group of hunters with very little specialization of labour is an example of this type of society; each person masters the same basic skills of hunting, and the society survives because no single member is indispensable.

Organic societies are much more complex, and are organized on the basis of difference rather than similarity. This type of society is increasingly dominant in Africa, and is the one which concerns us at the national level. There is considerable specialization and division of labour, and most individuals and groups have specific attitudes, skills and lifestyles that are not common to the whole. In these societies, there is considerable interdependence, for specialization usually means that individuals gain skills in one task at the expense of skills in others. If one group breaks away or dies, the whole society is liable to collapse because it is unable to replace their knowledge and expertise. Education plays a role in maintaining this type of society not only by providing individuals with skills but also by providing them, particularly during childhood, with attitudes which permit the whole society to function. Laws are made to regulate the way each individual behaves for the benefit of all. Sometimes individuals threaten society by breaking these laws. In these cases society controls them by sending them to prison or regulating their behaviour in some other way.

In this description of an organic society, it will be noticed that society itself has an identity independent of the identities of its individual members. This idea has been further developed by Talcott Parsons and the 'functionalists', who compared society to a living organism. An organism has its own identity, but is composed of such mutually dependent parts as the head, eyes, legs and so on, each of which performs a separate function. Organic societies, these theorists suggest, are similarly composed. Just as a body can die, so can a society; and just as a body can do without a few of its parts, so can a society.[3]

The functionalist approach to sociology is often identified with 'consensus theory'. This theory assumes that each part of society shares common values, and that there is consensus, or agreement, between the parts. The approach may be contrasted with 'conflict theory', which examines society from a different angle. Consensus and conflict theorists both view society as a system of interrelated parts, but the point at issue is the extent to which members of society benefit, equally or unequally. The conflict theorists are chiefly inspired by the work of Karl Marx. They feel that Parsons paid too much attention to the beneficial aspects of social organization, neglecting the extent to which established social arrangements operate to the disadvantage of some groups. Again, education plays a role in this process. As we shall see in Chapter 4, education is an agent of social stratification – assigning social roles to different groups and by distributing greater rewards to some groups than to others.

The Marxist model provides a theory to explain the changing nature of society: economic changes, it suggests, are the basis of social ones, and they themselves arise from conflicts between social groups and alterations in power structures. Thus, whereas the consensus theorists imply that all parts are mutually and more or less equally interdependent, the conflict theorists suggest that some parts are more important and more powerful than others. In political terms, the consensus theorists have come to be viewed as basically right-wing and capitalist, while the conflict theorists are basically left-wing and socialist. Socialists also generally seek change whereas consensus theorists generally support the status quo.

While these theories are introduced at the beginning of this chapter on national development, they are also applicable to the discussions in other chapters. Thus, at the international level, a functionalist interdependence may be identified, though we have pointed out that the benefits of inter-dependence are not evenly distributed. For example, it was pointed out in Chapter 1 that most African countries receive low prices for their agri-cultural exports but have to pay high prices for manufactured imports. Similarly, a form of functionalism exists in a school, where the head-master, the teachers, the prefects and the other pupils all have assigned roles and are part of a common body. A knowledge of these theories is useful because it enables us to understand how individuals and groups relate to each other in a wider context.

The goals of nation building and the role of education

The principal goal of nation building in Africa is to promote the evolution from simpler and more localized forms of social organization to wider and more complex ones. Mechanical societies of the hunting type are being threatened by a wider process of economic development and social change, and ultimately will be displaced by organic societies. Similarly, in some parts of Africa organic societies headed by kings, emirs or chiefs and involving considerable specialization of labour but usually with fairly local allegiances, are being replaced by wider organic societies with a national focus.

It is useful at this point to distinguish between two types of integration. Horizontal integration describes the unification of ethnic, racial, religious and linguistic groups, many of which inhabit distinct geographical areas. Vertical integration describes the relationship between rulers and ruled in a common network of communication, so that ideas and demands can flow 'upward' and 'downward'.

Education can promote horizontal integration in four main ways. The first concerns the curriculum, in which the importance of language must be emphasized. Nations composed of many ethnic groups have a cor-responding multiplicity of languages. Formal education usually promotes a common language, which permits communication between members of different ethnic groups. Most African countries have chosen to use a European language for official purposes. This is because internal rivalries prevent use of an indigenous language, and French, English, Portuguese and Spanish are considered 'neutral'. In sub-Saharan Africa, only in Tanzania and Somalia has a local language been sufficiently widespread for it to become the principal official one. Many governments encourage schools to teach several widely spoken local languages, in order to promote communication. However, they usually place stronger emphasis on the international, former colonial language. Governments also seek to promote unity through other aspects of school curricula and through adult education programmes. For example, in geography lessons pupils learn about different parts of their country, and in social studies or civics they learn about such national symbols as the flag and the national anthem and about official government policies in an international context. The material of adult literacy classes and of general public enlightenment is also frequency directly towards national issues, and informs the public about the policies of the head of state and other members of government.

Secondly, some countries have educational institutions in which pupils are selected by equal quota from different parts of the country. This policy is based on the idea that if pupils grow up together, they will become acquainted on a personal basis with people from other ethnic, racial, religious and linguistic groups, and the fears and ignorance which underlie much discrimination will be avoided. This is the principle on which Nigeria's Federal Government Colleges are based, for example.

Thirdly, several African countries, including Ghana, Nigeria, Zambia, Guinea, Chad, Tanzania, Kenya, Botswana, Malawi and Sierra Leone, operate national service schemes for school leavers. These schemes may be either voluntary or compulsory, but strong emphasis is always placed on national identification. Participants usually perform some community service, often outside their home areas. These schemes have a strong educational function, even though they are not always organized by the Ministry of Education. The Zambian and Tanzanian schemes, for example, operate under the Ministry of Defence, while the Kenyan one comes under the Ministry of Labour.

Finally, educational projects often attempt to reduce regional imbalances, which frequently correspond to imbalances between ethnic and religious groups. This policy is often manifested in universal primary education schemes, for it is argued that 100 per cent enrolments by definition eliminate numerical imbalances, at least at the bottom level. All individuals from all regions, it is suggested, are then able to compete for employment on a more equal basis. Botswana, Cameroon, Congo and Gabon have almost reached universal primary education, and major campaigns were launched in Nigeria in 1976 and in Tanzania in 1977.

Turning to vertical integration, it is worth noting two main ways in which education can promote unity. Firstly, extension of literacy makes it possible for more citizens to read newspapers, books and reports. This may mean that the population becomes better informed about local and national issues. Governments may inform the governed about the intentions of their policies, and individuals and groups have a medium through which they can make their feelings known.

Secondly, as education becomes more widespread, the basis on which individuals can complete for employment becomes more equal. Where education reaches only a small group, it may encourage élitism. But as it is expanded so that more or all groups receive some education, then a greater proportion of the population can be brought into the cash economy, and all groups can be placed on a more equal footing. In this instance, the functionalist role of education in creating a unified society is evident.

Constraints on the extent to which education promotes nation building

Although the mechanisms that we have just mentioned may promote horizontal and vertical integration, it cannot be assumed that they necessarily will do so. A large number of other factors, usually beyond the control of the Ministry of Education and sometimes beyond the control of the government, must be considered. They include political rivalries between individuals and groups, trends in employment, and the general level of economic prosperity.

Taking first the impact of schools on the attitudes of their pupils, it must be stressed that there is no such thing as a 'politically neutral' education system. All systems transmit and foster values, though in some cases the process is more obvious than in others. Some observers express considerable concern about what they describe as the indoctrination existing in some educational systems, particularly in socialist countries. But in every society the school system transmits values. In so far as this is not made explicit in some countries, or is unrecognized, it could be considered even more dangerous than in cases where it is more open.

Policies which deliberately set out to shape pupils' attitudes will only be wholly successful if the message communicated is clear, consistent and emphatic. We must distinguish between the formal and informal aspects of education, for they do not necessarily complement each other. Although the official curriculum may emphasize a national orientation rather than local or ethnic ones, this is not always similarly stressed by the *actions* of teachers, pupils and others taking part in the education process. There is a substantial difference between teaching or learning a subject such as civics for examination purposes and actually employing the principles in one's life outside the classroom. Pupils often enter what they see as a different world with different rules when they move into the school compound, and when they return home. When they leave school they often do not or cannot apply the 'theories' they have learned in the classroom.

Because of its importance, many studies have been made of the political outlook of school children. Fischer's Ghanaian work indicated a clear relationship between national identification and amount of schooling. He pointed out that some of the changed perceptions were due to age rather than schooling, and that many older primary pupils still had no clear attachment to the nation or its relevant symbols.[4] Nevertheless, the importance of education itself was evident, and has been supported by other researchers.[5]

At higher educational levels, however, the national orientations of students are less clear. Sawyer's work in Liberia, which is likely to be typical of African countries in this respect, suggested that while the national outlook of pupils tended to increase until secondary school level, it decreased again at the university level.[6] This, he indicated, arose partly from the students' greater interest in politics and partly from the specific political situation. Many politicians have found that the best way to compete in the national arena is to secure a strong regional or ethnic base, and they try to gain the support of students as much as others. In some cases the power of an individual derives from his ability to threaten national unity.

Aside from the purposes of education, the school system is itself often the focus of regional and ethnic disputes. Because formal education is a major route to wealth, status and economic security, individual and regional competition for schools is frequently intense. Politicians are therefore usually sure of gaining support from the regions and groups which benefit from allocation of educational institutions. Kenya's Harambee Institutes of Technology are one example of establishments opened more for political reasons, arising out of inter-ethnic rivalry, than for economic or educational ones. Twelve institutes were opened during the 1970s, chiefly because politicians demanded establishments for their own areas and refused to cooperate in common organizations. There were serious doubts about whether some institutes were economically appropriate, and it has been argued that they caused misallocation of national resources as well as being a focus for ethnic discord.[7]

One way in which governments seek to reduce ethnic, racial and religious educational imbalances is through the use of quotas. These also tend to become a focus for discord, however, for positive discrimination in favour of less educated groups can only be provided at the expense of more educated ones. The latter, usually backing their arguments with a desire to avoid declining academic standards, generally oppose the quotas. To the advantaged groups, the concept of equality implies that all individuals should compete within the existing education system without external intervention to assist some groups. But the quotas are based on the idea that the system itself is unequal – that it favours some groups at the expense of others, and that unless the disadvantaged groups are assisted, educational imbalances will be perpetuated. The two different sets of assumptions lead to conflict, for attempts to change the nature of the system inevitably threaten the position of those who benefited from the old arrangement.

Another way in which governments attempt to remove regional development imbalances, and therefore to avoid inter-ethnic tension, is by launching universal primary education campaigns. However, this strategy works only in the long term, for even if universal primary education is achieved, imbalances usually persist at post-primary levels. Different areas are also likely to experience qualitative variations, which partially negate the value of quantitative advances. Indeed, because schools in the disadvantaged areas have to expand most to achieve universal enrolments, they tend to experience the greatest qualitative problems. Also as enrolments expand, students of a different type are increasingly brought into the system.

When the school system is small, strongly motivated students comprise a greater proportion than when it is larger; particularly if they are also paying fees, these pupils tend to be more receptive to the values imparted by the authorities. Thus, even if the education system has had a strong impact on pupils' attitudes in the past, it does not necessarily follow that an expanded system will have the same impact on every child. Finally, development imbalances involve much more than education, and universalization policies must be complemented by other economic and political measures if they are effectively to promote equality. Even when qualitative imbalances have been reduced or eliminated, access to jobs often remains strongly influenced by non-academic criteria, and some groups still experience discrimination because of their ethnic identity.

Turning to the matter of vertical integration, we must note first that although the use of a common national language may permit members of different ethnic groups to communicate, if the language chosen for official business is not an indigenous one, it is likely to extend the gap between rulers and ruled. The rulers usually conduct their business in a European language, and because only rarely are proceedings translated into vernaculars, most of the ruled cannot understand them. When education systems reach only a minority they can be instruments for division, not for bonding.

Secondly, Western education has brought a new set of values which has destroyed, rather than reinforced, much of the old societies. Kofi Busia, who was Prime Minister of Ghana from 1969 until 1972, has strikingly related the impact of schooling on his own outlook.

> At the end of my first year at the secondary school I went home to Wenchi for the Christmas vacation. I had not been home for four years, and on that visit, I became painfully aware of my isolation. I understood our community far less than boys of my own age who had never been to school. I felt I did not belong to it as much as they did. It was a traumatic experience.[8]

In this quotation, the divisive effects of Western education are made very clear. The divisions go further than this, however, for there is often a gulf within the educated group. B.S. Kwakwa, building on Busia's point, has gone further to suggest that:

> . . . the effect of the western type of education has been to produce . . . three nations in the country, each unable to communicate effectively with the other. Many of those who have passed through the formal education system do not understand the ways of the 'educated'. In many circumstances the two do not understand each other. Then there is even a third group, the 'half educated', who understand neither the ways of their own indigenous society nor those of the 'highly educated'.[9]

In some ways, this is not an educational but an economic problem. African societies are experiencing a transition from 'traditional' economies based on self-employment in the rural areas to 'modern' ones based on wage employment in the towns. Each type of economy has its own requirements and set of values, and education is merely the bridge over which individuals cross from one economy and society to the other. Schooling is frequently seen as a passport to escape from the village. In their desire to reach the other side of the bridge, individuals sometimes consciously reject the values of the society they hope to leave behind.[10]

Social dislocation is often particularly acute when individuals have not succeeded in completely crossing the bridge from one society to the other, and when they are unemployed. The last two decades have witnessed increasing unemployment in Africa, and corresponding disillusion among school leavers. Problems have been particularly acute when the unemployed have received many years of education and have had high expectations, as has increasingly been the case. In many countries widespread unemployment leads to political instability and threatens the cohesion of the nation. Major political crises were exacerbated by the educated unemployed in Congo in 1964 and Tanzania in 1966, to cite just two examples.[11]

However, although unemployment causes strong disillusionment and is a destructive experience for the individual, it must not be assumed that it always results in political instability. Gutkind has pointed out that the unemployed are frequently poorly organized, and that their leadership is often 'bought off' by governments in times of disturbance.[12] Moreover, schooling often trains the individual to feel that if he fails, it is his own fault rather than that of the system.[13] Countries such as Kenya and Zambia have in the past experienced quite high levels of unemployment without being threatened by political instability.

The education system may thus be compared to a vehicle which carries people from one place to another. The people reach their destination more rapidly than they would if they were walking or bicycling, but the vehicle is not independent, and the direction in which it moves is mainly controlled by the people inside it. The driver is the person with the greatest control, but he is unlikely to choose a road without consulting at least some of his passengers. The passengers who will have the greatest influence on the driver are those nearest to him, those able to shout loudly, and those who can promise the greatest rewards if the vehicle goes where they want it to (or threaten the greatest problems if it does not). But even if the driver ignores all his passengers and chooses his own destination, he is still restricted by the capacity of his vehicle, the skill of those who maintain it and the availability of roads, and he may still find it impossible to reach his goal.

In the same way, education should not be considered an independent or even a flexible force for change. The direction in which the educational vehicle takes society depends firstly on the intentions of the government and other members of society, and secondly on the resources available. Even then, policy makers are restricted by the nature of the vehicle and, if resources are abundant, by the time it takes to adapt the vehicle or build new roads.

Thus, knowledge of a common language, for example, may be promoted through the education system, and may permit members of different ethnic groups to communicate with each other. But it does not necessarily follow that they will communicate, or that what they communicate will lead to unity rather than division. Similarly, literacy may promote vertical integration by providing a means for communication between governors and governed. But, while literacy provides them with another vehicle, it should not be assumed that illiterate people are always unable to make their feelings known, and therefore that education will necessarily make possible something that was previously impossible. Also, it should not be assumed that extension of literacy will ensure that the governors and governed will communicate. Newspapers and books are often not available in rural areas, and if they are, only a minority of people buy them. Much literature is written in complicated language, and many books – especially official reports – are boring. Finally, for information to flow both from governors to governed and vice versa, each side must be willing to listen as well as to talk. People in authority often do not wish to listen to the opinions of those they govern, and are only concerned with implementing their own ideas.

Case study: Education and nation building in Nigeria

To build a single nation out of the multitude of cultures and interests encompassed within Nigerian boundaries is no small objective. In the pre-colonial period, a number of cohesive units, such as the Sokoto Caliphate, the Benin and Songhai Empires and the Kingdom of Oyo, operated independently, albeit with some economic, religious and cultural links. But the existence of these units had little influence on colonial boundary determination, and kingdoms were grouped together or divided entirely arbitrarily. Today, with over 90 million citizens, Nigeria is by far the most populous country in Africa. Within her boundaries are over 250 ethnic groups, and though no precise figure is known (which is itself indicative of Nigeria's problems), nearly 400 languages are spoken.[14] In addition, most of the sects of Christianity are represented, as are the major Islamic brotherhoods and a wide diversity of indigenous religions.

During the last three decades, Nigerian politics have been characterized more by division than by unity. The political parties of the 1950s developed along ethnic and religious lines, and, as recognized even in an official publication, 'the only common factor that united them was the struggle for independence'.[15] Once independence had been achieved in 1960, this common objective no longer existed. During the years that followed, regional and ethnic disputes became increasingly serious, and in 1967 the country was plunged into civil war following the secession of the self-styled Republic of Biafra. The war was won by the federal forces, and the military continued to form the government until 1979. Some observers have suggested that the political parties which came to power that year were little different in their membership and outlook from those of the 1950s and 1960s. In 1983 the civilian regime was overthrown again.

The memory of the civil war has caused the Nigerian authorities to be highly conscious of the need for horizontal integration, and they have placed considerable faith in the ability of education to promote it. The *National policy on education*, for example, identified unification as one of the five basic objectives of the education system.[16] School curricula strongly emphasize the role of national institutions, and children learn about the flag, the national anthem and the geography of other parts of the country. Each day, children are required to recite:

> I pledge to Nigeria, my country
> To be faithful, loyal and honest,
> To serve Nigeria with all my strength,
> To defend her unity
> And uphold her honour and glory;
> So help me God.

The widespread knowledge of a common language, which is taught in schools, is also considered a major factor in horizontal integration. Although Hausa, Igbo and Yoruba are each spoken by over 10 million people, it has proved impossible to choose any one of them as the official national language because such a selection would encounter strong opposition from speakers of the other two languages. Consequently English, which is considered politically 'neutral', has been made the main official language.

Programmes for vertical integration in the last two decades have been weaker than those for horizontal integration. A major adult education campaign was launched in the north during the 1950s, but since that time adult education has been neglected, and in 1980 only 30 per cent of adults were estimated to be literate. Official emphasis on communication between the governors and governed, particularly during the period of military rule between 1966 and 1979, was one-sided. The government has been more concerned to inform the people about its programmes than to listen to their opinions. The late 1970s saw increased emphasis on local government participation, however, and a major adult literacy campaign was launched in 1982.

The Nigerian authorities have been very conscious that much strife has been caused by unbalanced development, of which wide variations in school enrolment have been both a cause and a symptom. Because of this, they have launched a number of educational projects which seek to reduce imbalances. The most obvious of these was the Universal Primary Education (UPE) scheme initiated in 1976.

Although the UPE scheme has encountered major difficulties, there were indications in the late 1970s that quantitative regional gaps at the primary level were being reduced.[17] Qualitative regional gaps were more difficult to close, however, and because they remained at least as great as before, the UPE scheme did not make so great a contribution to unity as had been hoped. Moreover, quantitative imbalances remained at the post-primary level, and the south had many more secondary schools than the north, despite having approximately the same population.

At the university level, the federal government has established institutions in every state. Its calculation has taken no account of the fact that some states have many more people than others, and has clearly been motivated more by political than by economic or educational considerations. However, even at a quantitative level, imbalances have remained, for states have been permitted to open their own universities. Oyo State in the south already had two, Anambra State opened its own in 1980. Further, although admissions are supposed to reflect Nigeria's federal character and embrace students from all states, some universities manage this better than others. There are very few northern students in the south, whereas there are many southerners in the north.

The education system of any country reflects society as well as shapes it, and despite the strong official emphasis on horizontal integration, the Nigerian experience exemplifies the limitations of educational strategies when they are not supported by other economic and political forces. One case in which this was apparent during the 1960s concerned Ibadan University. This institution, as Eleazu has remarked, was at one time a place where Nigerians met as Nigerians. They came in from parochial secondary schools such as Igbo Anglican, Igbo Roman Catholic, Yoruba Methodist, Yoruba Aladura, Hausa Muslim, Tiv, Sudan Interior Mission and so on, but they re-emerged as Nigerian. In the early years, however, this nationalizing process was mainly the result of events outside the walls of the university and the desire for independence. During the 1960s, regional conflicts became more marked. The opinions of the student body at Ibadan also polarized, presenting the same picture as the outside political scene.[18]

By contrast, the experience of a different body, the National Youth Service Corps (NYSC), has been more encouraging. The NYSC was initiated in 1973, and involves one year's obligatory service for all university graduates. The majority of graduates who do not have another specific skill become teachers, and all have to perform some kind of community service such as road construction. Corpers are required to serve in a state other than that of their origin. The majority of participants acquire more positive attitudes towards fellow Nigerians, and the NYSC has reduced educational imbalances by permitting the less developed northern states to benefit from the greater number of southern graduates.[18]

Questions and project work

1   What is meant by 'horizontal integration'? Discuss the extent to which the education system of your country has promoted horizontal integration, and the obstacles to the achievement of further integration.

2   Do you consider your own home area to be educationally advanced or educationally backward? Outline the historical reasons for this situation, and support your answer with current educational statistics.

3   Discuss the view that education is one of the least important factors in national building.

4 Find copies of the recommended primary and secondary school social studies and history textbooks in your home area. Examine the ways in which they discuss matters of national and ethnic identity. Comment on the impact you think these books have on the way pupils perceive issues and on the attitude of teachers towards these subjects.

Notes

1 Cervenka, Zdenek *The Organisation of African Unity and its Charter*. C. Hurst, London 1969, p. 94.

2 Durkheim, Emile *The Division of Labor in Society*. Free Press, New York 1964 (first published in French in 1925).

3 Parsons, Talcott *The Structure of Social Action*. Free Press, New York 1949 (first published in 1937). A useful summary of this and other theory is contained in Worsley, Peter *et al. Introducing Sociology*. Penguin, Harmondsworth 1980, Chapter 9.

4 Fischer, Lynn F. 'Student Orientations toward Nation-Building in Ghana' in Paden, John N. (ed.) *Values, Identities and National Integration: Empirical Research in Africa*. Northwestern University Press, Evanston 1980, p. 276.

5 Klineberg, O. and Zavalloni, M. *Nationalism and Tribalism among African Students: A Study of Social Identity*. Mouton, The Hague 1969; See also other papers in Paden, ibid.

6 Sawyer, Amos 'Social Stratification and National Orientation: Students and Nonstudents in Liberia' in Paden, ibid., p. 297.

7 Godfrey E.M. and Mutiso, G. 'The Political Economy of Self-Help: Kenya's Harambee Institutes of Technology' in Court, David and Ghai, Dharam (eds.) *Education, Society and Development: New Perspectives from Kenya*. Oxford University Press, Nairobi 1974, p. 254 ff.

8 Busia, K.A. *Purposeful Education for Africa*, quoted in Kwakwa, B.S. 'Formal Education and Conflict in Ghanaian Society'. *Legon Observer* 23/7/73, p. 125.

9 Kwakwa, ibid.

10 Many novels in the Heinemann African Writers Series (HAWS) deal with this theme. See e.g. Conton, W. *The African*, HAWS No. 12; and Dadie, B. *Climbié* HAWS No. 87.

11 Hanf, Theodor *et al*. 'Education: An Obstacle to Development? Some Remarks about the Political Functions of Education in Asia and Africa'. *Comparative Education Review*, Vol. 19, No. 1, 1975, p. 84; Morrison, op. cit., p. 195 ff.

12 Gutkind, P.C.W. 'The Unemployed and Poor in Urban Africa' in Jolly, Richard *et al*. (eds.) *Third World Employment*. Penguin, Harmondsworth 1973, p. 131 ff.

13 See Carnoy, Martin *Education as Cultural Imperialism*. David McKay, New York 1974, pp. 12–13, 344–5.

14 Federal Republic of Nigeria *Nigeria: A Guide to Understanding*. Federal Ministry of Education, Lagos, n.d., p. 6; Hansford Keir *et al*. 'A Provisional Language Map of Nigeria'. *Savanna*, Vol. 5, No. 2, 1976.

15 Federal Republic of Nigeria *The Struggle for One Nigeria*, Nigerian National Press, Apapa 1967, pp. 2–3.

16 Federal Republic of Nigeria *National Policy on Education*. Federal Ministry of Information, Lagos 1981, p. 4. This document was originally published, in slightly different form, in 1977.

17 Bray, Mark *Universal Primary Education in Nigeria: A Study of Kano State.* Routledge and Kegan Paul, London 1981, pp. 82–4.
18 Eleazu, Uma O. *Federalism and Nation Building: The Nigerian Experience.* Arthur H. Stockwell, Ilfracombe 1977, pp. 124–5. See also van den Berghe, Pierre L. *Power and Privilege at an African University.* Routledge and Kegan Paul, London 1973, p. 222 ff.; and Beckett, Paul and O'Connell, James *Education and Power in Nigeria.* Hodder and Stoughton, London 1977.
19 Marenin, Otwin 'National Service and National Consciousness in Nigeria'. *Journal of Modern African Studies,* Vol. 17, No. 4, 1979, p. 653 and *passim.*

Chapter 3

Education and employment

The links between education and employment have both economic and social significance. Education is a costly enterprise, and it is important that it should equip its recipients with skills that will be used by the economy. If school leavers are unable to find work for which they have been trained, the resources invested in them will have been at least partially wasted. Unemployment also has severe social consequences, for the unemployed often feel bored, have small or non-existent incomes, and do not feel that they are contributing to society. When unemployment reaches high levels, nations may experience problems of crime and political instability.

Over the last two decades, there have been significant changes in ideas about the links between education and employment. In the early 1960s strong emphasis was placed on manpower planning. It was felt that officials could make accurate assessments of future economic needs, and, in order to make the best use of scarce resources, should ensure that educational output was related to these needs. However, it is now realized that it is much more difficult to forecast demand than was earlier assumed. In the time it takes to train a person, technologies may change significantly. A new invention may put large numbers of people with a particular skill out of work, and may lead to demands for people with new skills. A country may also be significantly affected by unpredicted economic changes. For example, the 1973 oil price rise was of great benefit to such petroleum producing countries as Nigeria and Gabon, and led to rapid economic growth and manpower demand. For non-oil producing countries, however, it had a very serious effect, and economic growth was far less than had earlier been predicted.

Just as it is difficult to forecast demand, it is also difficult to forecast supply of educated manpower. It often happens that technicians, teachers, nurses and so on do not enter the profession for which they have been trained, or only do so for a short time. Some countries also suffer from emigration of skilled manpower. This problem is particularly acute for Sudan, which loses much educated manpower to Saudi Arabia, and for many West African countries, which in the past have lost personnel to Nigeria.

The last decade has also witnessed a significant change in what are considered the most fruitful forms of educational investment. Whereas manpower planning during the 1960s was concerned almost exclusively with supplies of secondary and post-secondary educated labour, a strong body of evidence now suggests that higher returns on investment are generally provided by primary education. In addition, extension of primary education can have social benefits, and can promote equality within the nation.[1] It must be recognized, however, that there usually remain strong political pressures for expanded secondary and higher education, and the strength of these demands may outweigh economic arguments.

This chapter will therefore take account of economic, social and political factors. It will also consider different types of education. Before turning to these, however, we need a clearer understanding of the different forms of employment and unemployment.

Definitions of employment and unemployment

The first point to note about employment is that its meaning is not restricted to wage-earning jobs in the formal sector, but also covers peasant farming, which employs over three-quarters of the labour in most African countries, and a large group of workers in the so-called 'informal' sector. The informal sector embraces a wide range of petty traders and small-scale entrepreneurs such as shoe-shine boys, carpenters, tailors and taxi drivers. Many of them are self-employed, though some work for a person who organizes the enterprise. Because the activities of informal sector workers are not always strictly legal, especially since a large number do not pay tax, workers often avoid being counted and it is difficult accurately to assess their number. However, in all African countries this sector is important: according to one survey in Kenya, for example, it accounted for nearly 40 per cent of adult non-agricultural employment.[2]

The nature of unemployment is more complex, and has several different forms. A person is usually described as unemployed when he or she is actively seeking work but is unable to find any. However, because it is rare for a person to be completely idle, many people are considered underemployed rather than unemployed. Underemployment also takes several forms and may be defined either in terms of output or in terms of time spent working. To clarify this, we shall distinguish between five types of underutilization of labour.

1 *Open unemployment* refers to the situation where labour resources are idle. It may be voluntary (if people exclude from consideration some jobs for which they are qualified, perhaps because they have a private income from other sources) or involuntary.
2 *Underemployment* refers to those working less (daily, weekly or seasonally) than they would like to work.
3 *The visibly active but underutilized* covers those who would not normally be described as unemployed or underemployed by the above definitions, but who have found alternative ways of occupying themselves.

    (a) *Disguised unemployment* covers people who seem occupied on farms or employed in government on a full-time basis even though the services they provide may actually require much less than full time. (If available work is openly shared among those employed, the disguise disappears and underemployment becomes explicit.)

(b) *Hidden unemployment* embraces those who are engaged in 'second choice' nonemployment activities, such as education and domestic activities, principally because work is not available at their level of education or because they are women who are not expected to take jobs.

(c) *The prematurely retired* are particularly common in the civil service. In many African countries, civil servants are permitted and sometimes obliged to retire between the ages of 45 and 55, even though they could remain productive for many years. This rule is partly a colonial legacy, and was originally introduced to enable Europeans to return to their home countries before they got too old. It also helps younger personnel to gain rapid promotion.

4 *The impaired* covers those who work full-time, but whose productivity is seriously reduced through malnutrition or lack of common preventive medicine.

5 *The unproductive* covers those who can provide the human resources necessary for productive work, but who struggle long hours without enough complementary resources, such as fertile land or simple tools, to make their work yield even the essentials of life.[3]

All these forms of underutilization of labour are common in Africa. However for convenience and to keep discussion brief, the remainder of this chapter will be concerned principally with open unemployment and underemployment.

The extent and nature of unemployment and underemployment

Because of problems of definition and the lack of accurate statistics, it is difficult to estimate the percentage of those unemployed or underemployed. However, we can distinguish certain characteristics and make some assessments.

First, we should note that in all developing nations high population growth has led to rapid expansion of the labour force, but expansion of job opportunities has been unable to keep pace. Table 3.1 shows projections for several continents for the years 1960 to 1990. It indicates that unemployment and underemployment are more serious in Africa than in Asia or Latin America, and that unemployment is increasing. Open unemployment is particularly serious in the towns, where it often affects 15 to 25 per cent of the labour force.[4]

The disparity in open unemployment between the villages and towns is increased by rural-urban migration, particularly of young people with some education. Modern sector opportunities, which generally yield much higher and steadier incomes than traditional sector opportunities do, are usually much more numerous in the urban areas. This fact, coupled with a wish for a more desirable lifestyle, attracts migrants from the villages. The low level of open unemployment in rural areas is thus an indication of the lack of opportunities there rather than the reverse.

Table 3.1 Employment and unemployment in developing countries, 1960–90[5]

Year	1960	1970	1973	1980	1990
*All developing countries**					
Employment (000)†	507,416	617,244	658,000	773,110	991,600
Unemployment (000)	36,466	48,798	54,130	65,620	88,693
Unemployment rate (%)	6.7	7.4	7.6	7.8	8.2
Combined unemployment and underemployment rate (%)‡	25	27	29		
Africa	31	39	38		
Asia	24	26	28		
Latin America	18	20	25		
All Africa					
Employment (000)†	100,412	119,633	127,490	149,390	191,180
Unemployment (000)	8,416	12,831	13,890	15,973	21,105
Unemployment rate (%)	7.7	9.6	9.8	9.8	9.9

*   excluding China
†   including underemployment
‡   not calculated for 1980 and 1990

Not everybody who migrates to the towns in search of work actually finds it, especially in the short run, and migrants therefore swell the pool of open unemployment. Research indicates that the majority of migrants are aware of the probablity of unemployment, at least for some time, and thus of the possibility that they will have to face even harder living conditions in the towns than at home. So great are the differences in income and conditions of work between modern and traditional sector employment, however, that it is usually considered worth facing unemployment in the hope of a lucky chance arising, especially for those who have some education. It is often more expensive to live in towns because of the costs of food and rent, but work requiring an education is more abundant in urban areas, and even individuals with no education are better off in the urban areas if they are able to secure a job. Hinchliffe's study in Nigeria, for example, showed that even after adjustment for costs of living and hours of work, unschooled labourers in urban areas earned 5 to 40 per cent more than those in the villages.[6]

Over the last two decades there has been a general increase in the educational qualifications of the unemployed. This is mainly because the number of school leavers is increasing faster than the number of job opportunities at the level to which they aspire. At the university graduate level unemployment is not yet widespread, though some countries are beginning to experience problems, especially in relation to arts graduates.

It was estimated in 1980 that there were formal sector opportunities for only 25 per cent of the 15-year-old age group in Africa, and the proportion was not expected to improve greatly in the near future.[7] Many of this age group work in the informal sector, but many others are openly unemployed.

Unemployment is particularly high among persons aged 15 to 24, for three main reasons.

1 The population structure is shaped like a pyramid. Because of rapid population growth over the last few decades, there are more people in the 15 to 24 age group than in the 25 to 34 age group, more in the 25 to 34 age group than in the 35 to 44 age group, and so on. Also, because in most African countries nearly half the total population is aged under 15, we can expect the 15 to 24 age group to expand further. (In fact, there may be many people aged less than 15 who are seeking work, but official statistics, perhaps wrongly, consider them too young and do not usually count them as unemployed.)

2 This is the age at which many people are seeking their first job. There is often a time lag in finding the first job, but once a person finds employment, that person is likely to become unemployed again or will spend only a short time between jobs.

3 This is the age at which a large number of people leave full-time schooling. Often they leave school with high aspirations and it takes time for them to be 're-educated' when confronted by the difficulties of the labour market.

What is relationship between education and employment?

We should begin by looking at ways of generating employment. In so far as education equips individuals with skills for self-employment, it can improve the employment situation. For example, through formal, non-formal and informal education, people may acquire skills in carpentry, welding, photography, trading and so on, which permits them to establish their own enterprises. Similarly, some studies have shown that basic education is likely to improve agricultural productivity by creating awareness of new techniques, providing the ability to read extension literature and instructions on fertilizer packets, improving the recipients' receptivity to change, and generally by teaching how to learn.

One series of studies recorded by the World Bank compared the output of unschooled farmers with others who had received four years' schooling.[8] In some cases output was also increased by other inputs, such as improved seeds, irrigation and transport to markets, but in other cases it was possible to examine the productivity increases resulting just from education. As expected, the studies showed high productivity increases where there were complementary inputs. But even where allowance was made for these inputs, the increase in productivity resulting from four years of schooling was, on average, 8.1 per cent.

These studies are significant, but it must be stressed that such evidence is incomplete. There was a wide variation in returns recorded, and in some cases negative returns apparently resulted from the changed inputs (Table 3.2). To reach a firm conclusion on the usefulness of schooling it would be necessary to take account of the costs of education, which are often high. Evidence about a group of farmers at one point in time, when the population may have been relatively low and land relatively abundant, should only be used to predict the situation in the future if account is taken of probable changes. In communities where land is not available in such abundance or where there are poor marketing facilities and other constraints on development, the effects of schooling on productivity may be low. We need much more research information before we can state with confidence that education necessarily improves agricultural productivity either in general or in specific places.

Table 3.2   Farmer education and farmer productivity[9]

Study	Estimated percentage increase in annual farm output due to four years of primary education rather than none
With complementary inputs[a]	
Brazil (Garibaldi), 1970	18.4
Brazil (Resende), 1969	4.0
Brazil (Taquari), 1970	22.1
Brazil (Vicosa), 1969	9.3
Colombia (Chinchina), 1969	− 0.8
Colombia (Espinal), 1969	24.4
Kenya, 1971–72	6.9
Malaysia, 1973	20.4
Nepal (wheat), 1968–69	20.4
South Korea, 1973	9.1
Average (unweighted)	13.2
Without complementary inputs	
Brazil (Candelaria), 1970	10.8
Brazil (Conceicao de Castelo), 1969	− 3.6
Brazil (Guarani), 1970	6.0
Brazil (Paracatu), 1969	− 7.2
Colombia (Malaga), 1969	12.4
Colombia (Moniquira), 1969	12.5
Greece, 1963	25.9
Average (unweighted)	8.1
No information on availablity of complementary inputs	
Average of eight studies (unweighted)	6.3

[a] Improved seeds, irrigation, transport to markets and so on.

Neither must it be assumed that increased productivity in one sector will improve its attractiveness relative to other sectors. Certainly, improved productivity might encourage individuals to embark on self-employment in the agricultural and informal sectors. But it must also be noted that improved productivity will only raise incomes and increase employment if there is sufficient demand for the products. One result of increased agricultural output could be a fall in prices and the maintenance of cash incomes at the same level. And if one mechanic is able to perform the work that formerly occupied two, then another mechanic could be made unemployed. Further, the attractiveness of one sector is relative to the potential earnings of others. The fact that basic education has improved individuals' potential productivity in agricultural and informal sector self-employment may not make them any more enthusiastic about work in those sectors if still higher earnings are available in formal employment.

It must be recognized, therefore, that the extent to which education actually creates employment is relatively small, and many school leavers are less interested in self-employment than in wage-earning jobs, in which the employment-generating potential of education is much less. Indeed, in so far as education both gives individuals access to jobs for which they were formerly unqualified and creates awareness of the opportunities available in the cash economy, it could promote open unemployment. For example, individuals working in agriculture but underemployed, might receive some education and then migrate to towns where they might fail to find work. In this situation education may be considered to have converted rural underemployment into urban open unemployment. Schools may provide jobs for teachers and suppliers of school equipment, but they should not be expected to create other jobs in the productive sectors of agriculture and industry. Training may provide the skills to be used in a job, but it does not usually provide the job itself.

Since there is now large-scale open unemployment among both primary and secondary school leavers, it must be asked why both pupils and governments continue to invest so heavily in education. Three principal reasons explain why pupils do so.

Firstly, there is a divergence between private and social costs. An individual thinking about beginning a course usually makes some assessment of the costs and benefits to him. The costs will include fees and the 'opportunity cost' of the income he could have received if he had not been studying. The benefits will include the greater income he is likely to obtain as a result of his education. It is rare, however, for a pupil to pay the whole cost of his schooling, especially at lower levels. For social and political reasons, governments usually subsidize education and often provide it free. Yet there is no such thing as free education in the sense that it does not have to be paid for by somebody. In practice, education is paid for by taxes whether the taxpayer has children in school or not. The effect of this system is usually to reduce the costs of education to the individual (but not to the society as a whole) while leaving the benefits as large as before. Thus it may still be worth the individual 'investing' in education because the private costs are low.

Individuals who seeks education in order to improve their subsequent income and status may be taking a gamble if there is high unemployment. The second reason for pupils' investment in education is that the difference between the incomes of those who do secure jobs and the incomes of those with no education is often so great that it is worth being unemployed for several months and perhaps for several years. This is why high aspirations are sometimes justified, and why people may be economically wise not to take lower paid, 'inferior' jobs.

Thirdly, students also recognize that education is often desirable in itself; they are often interested in the consumption aspects of education as well as in its production aspects. At the lowest levels, pupils acquire literacy because they perceive its non-economic uses as well as its economic uses, and at higher levels they may take courses because they enjoy the experience of learning.

On their part, governments principally continue to invest in education for a number of reasons. They hold a notion, which is often not critically examined, that education is a good investment in itself. It is widely noted that differences in general educational levels are a major factor which differentiate developing countries from developed ones, and it is often felt that greater educational provision of almost any kind will permit developing nations to 'catch up' with developed ones. We have noted that education can, under the right conditions, increase productivity in agriculture, and considerable emphasis is put on this. But the costs and quality of education are considerations usually pushed into the background. Education, especially at secondary and higher levels, is expensive, and costs seriously reduce the overall return from investment. At all levels, the provision of education is often inefficient, and the anticipated skills are frequently not learnt by the pupils. Because of this, drop-out rates from primary schools are often very high, and in a large number of cases pupils do not permanently acquire the skills of basic literacy even after six years' schooling.[10]

Education projects are launched by governments for social reasons as well as economic ones, and the former frequently take priority. Schemes to universalize education are often geared more to provision of education as a human right and to reduction of regional inequalities than to the labour market situation. Governments are often aware that education projects are likely to make unemployment worse, but they consider that the social benefits outweigh this disadvantage.

Governments also often launch educational programmes because in the short term it is easier to do so than to embark on radical restructuring of the economy, which might provide employment but would also threaten powerful interests. For example, unemployment among primary leavers can be reduced in the short run by increasing the number of secondary school places. But a few years later the pupils will graduate from secondary schools and will still seek work. The solution is no more than temporary and may make the situation worse since the pupils will have higher expectations and since the schools will have used resources which could have been devoted to other employment-generating projects. Nevertheless, it is often attractive to governments needing relief from immediate problems.

Governments also initiate education projects because it is politically desirable to do so. Because of the links between schooling and access to jobs, education projects are usually very popular. From a national perspective, it is frequently possible to identify considerable over-production of school leavers and waste of resources. But individuals are rarely willing to sacrifice their own futures for national ends. They are aware that they are competing with many other individuals for a small number of jobs, and that one of the most important criteria for success in obtaining a job is possession of a certificate. Indeed in this respect, unemployment and stronger competition for jobs *increase* the demand for education rather than reduce it.

Finally, we should stress the need for caution when comparing earnings between more and less educated individuals and attributing the difference to the productivity of education itself. When employers recruit workers, they are often less interested in the actual knowledge and skills the applicants have gained during their educational career than in the fact that the applicants have demonstrated intelligence and tenacity in studying. In other words, although individuals with higher educational qualifications are likely to obtain better paid jobs, their certificates have been used as indicators of general ability rather than as proof of possession of particular forms of knowledge. This sorting function of education may be a useful one, but the education itself has added little to the worker's productivity.[11]

What can educational planners do about unemployment?

We are suggesting that the role of education in creating or reducing unemployment is a minor one. Although schooling may be a vehicle for transforming disguised rural unemployment into open urban unemployment, education did not create labour surpluses and should not be expected substantially to reduce them. The fact that a high percentage of the unemployed are school leavers and that there is a general increase in their educational qualifications is largely a coincidence rather than an indicator of causation. Economic factors are more important causes of unemployment, and they will be discussed in the last part of this chapter. Nevertheless, it is useful to examine three ways in which educational planners can help to reduce unemployment. The first involves the costs of education, the second concerns links with manpower needs, and the third involves the nature of education.

We pointed out above that one reason why individuals are not dissuaded from gaining more formal education despite the major possibility that unemployment will render it of little use arises from the fact that they do not pay the full cost of education. Because of the divergence between private and social costs, individuals receive benefits from education that they do not directly have to pay for. Therefore, if educational planners increase private costs so that they are closer to social ones, individuals will be less likely to embark on courses, especially those which may not lead to employment, and the supply of school leavers will no longer exceed demand by so large an amount.

However, we must also note the political, social and economic reasons for government subsidy of education. Free and subsidized schooling is popular among parents and pupils, and contributes to political support.

Governments also recognize that poor families cannot afford to send their children to school, and this both discriminates against them and makes it difficult to identify the children's potential talents. Thus in order both to promote equality and to make best use of the nation's human resources there is a tendency to reduce school fees or abolish them entirely. Consequently, the present trend is one of a widening gap between social and private costs rather than the reverse.

Secondly, educational planners can cooperate with development economists to secure a closer match between educational output and manpower needs. Close correlation depends on the ability of governments to resist political demands for educational expansion and requires accurate forecasting of manpower needs, which is not easy. However, it is a goal towards which planners can and should aim.

The third strategy concerns the nature of schooling. It is widely suggested that school curricula are highly academic and contribute to unemployment by orienting pupils to urban opportunities rather than to rural ones. This subject will be discussed at greater length in Chapters 4 and 7. Here we may remark that there is little evidence that efforts to 'ruralize' or vocationalize curricula have had the benefits that their initiators anticipated. The chief determinant of pupils' aspirations is not so much the nature of curricula as the structure of the economy. Thus, so long as the existing differences in income and status of modern and traditional sector employment remain, pupils will aspire to the former, and attempts to use the curriculum to orient them towards the latter are unlikely to have much effect. Moreover, ruralization programmes have implications for social stratification, and imply that rural children will be prevented from gaining an education which will give them access to modern sector jobs while urban children will gain a different education which will give them such access. In other words, there is a danger that such programmes will increase imbalances between rural and urban areas.

What other measures should be taken to reduce unemployment?

Finally, if we are suggesting that education by itself can play only a minor role in reducing unemployment, we should briefly consider some of the more important means of doing so. They include choices of technology, official wage and income policies, relationships in international trade, and population growth rates.

The question of the most appropriate technologies hinges on the relative availability of labour and machines or other capital. It is frequently argued that developing countries have an abundance of labour, but suffer from a scarcity of capital. If this is the case, then the most appropriate technologies to make best use of scarce resources and eliminate unemployment will usually be labour intensive ones.[12]

In practice, however, labour intensive technologies have not been adopted to a large extent in the modern sector of most African countries. Partly this is because for some processes they are not the most appropriate.

Petroleum drilling and refining, for example, have to be capital intensive processes if they are to operate efficiently and obtain economies of scale. In other operations, for example in the bread industry and in road building, it would be possible to use more labour intensive processes. But employers have often avoided such processes because they fear labour disputes, and governments have not encouraged labour intensive processes because there is a common idea that capital intensive ones are more 'modern'. Yet even developed nations now suffer economic depression and high unemployment, and so even for them capital intensive processes may no longer be appropriate. Thus we should query the wisdom of introducing large-scale mechanized agriculture projects in Africa, for they might increase productivity but would also displace smaller farmers and make them unemployed. It may be added that the nature of technologies adopted also has educational implications. In general, small-scale technologies do not demand such high levels of education as do large-scale ones. Small-scale technologies also make use of more widely available craft skills.

The question of the choice of technologies is related to strategies for rural development. Small-scale, labour intensive enterprises can be located in rural areas and spread over a wide area more easily than can large-scale ones. Governments which are really concerned with rural-urban imbalances and migration promote the use of small-scale labour intensive enterprises in rural areas as one way to encourage individuals to remain in the villages.

Wage and income policies are important because they influence the differences between modern and traditional forms of employment. In the colonial period, middle and higher level government officers were expatriates, and demanded salaries comparable to those given at home. A dual economy was established which gave much higher incomes to modern sector than to traditional sector work, and this structure has been retained in the post-colonial period. Governments set salaries for their own workers at what they consider a reasonable level, and because private modern sector enterprises compete for educated labour, their wage levels are closely linked with government salary levels. While it is usual for increased competition in the informal sector to reduce individual earnings, because of the bargaining power of those within the system formal sector wage rates tend not to be affected by the number of unemployed. Instead, wages are set at a fairly fixed level, adjusted according to the cost of living, and are received only by a fortunate minority. In addition, because farmers have little bargaining power and because governments are conscious that food prices should not rise too steeply, pricing mechanisms discriminate against agricultural producers and in favour of urban dwellers.

Relationships in international trade concern local unemployment rates in so far as goods produced abroad may compete with goods produced at home. Governments may prohibit or restrict importation of foreign goods. However, it must be recognized that sometimes goods can be produced more cheaply and more qualitatively abroad than at home, and that this was one main reason for international trade in the first place. It may actually be cheaper for governments to import radios, refrigerators and cars, for example, rather than to try to make them at home.

Finally, we should mention population growth rates. Over the last three decades, death rates have declined markedly and birth rates have increased. Average life expectancy in developing countries has risen from 42 to 54 years, and African populations are now growing annually at an average of 2.8 per cent.[13] In contrast to other continents, African fertility rates show no signs of decline. Thus, both the present and future labour forces are growing rapidly, and are doing so much faster than the number of job openings. Yet official programmes to reduce population growth rates are unimpressive, especially by comparison with such countries as China and India. This is partly because some status is accorded a nation in international affairs if it has a large population. Further, in poorer families, children are seen more as producers of wealth than as consumers: parents want to have many children in order to increase the family labour force and thus provide a form of insurance against sickness and death and an economic security in their old age.

Educational policies may have some influence on population growth, and therefore on the long-term size of the labour force. Studies have indicated a correlation between higher levels of education, particularly of woman, and smaller families. This is partly because individuals become more aware of the role of contraceptive devices, and partly because families become more affluent and begin to see children more as consumers than as producers. However, research in Kenya suggests that primary education gives women better knowledge of nutrition and hygiene which reduces child deaths and raises the rate of population growth rather than reduces it. It seems that only in the case of mothers who have received some secondary education is there a tendency for family size to decline.[14]

In conclusion, we must note that open and disguised unemployment are serious problems in Africa which are likely to get worse in the foreseeable future. This is chiefly because the structure of the population is shaped like a pyramid, and the annual number of entrants to the labour force is greater than the number of modern-sector employment opportunities acceptable to them. Moreover, the rate of population growth is still increasing.

Although educational planners can play some role in reducing unemployment, we have suggested it is a relatively minor one. The educational qualifications of the unemployed show a tendency to rise, and a large number of the unemployed are school leavers, but this is more a coincidence than an indicator that education itself is causing unemployment. More important are the economic differences between the modern and traditional sectors. They contribute to unemployment by promoting aspirations among members of the traditional sector, even though only a minority are actually able to join the modern sector. In time, many people's aspirations become adjusted by necessity, and some migrants return to the villages. This is a painful process, and while.it is probably good to have a better educated rural labour force, governments should examine the ways this is being achieved and adopt more positive strategies of rural development. Greater commitment to the provision of employment in villages would reduce the rate of rural-urban migration and its attendant economic and social problems; and throughout the economy greater use of labour intensive technologies would reduce the pool of unemployed and distribute wealth more evenly.

Case study: Education and employment in Zambia and Togo

This section will examine the ways in which some of the forces discussed above operate in practice. Two countries have been chosen for case studies, one in Anglophone Central Africa and the other in Francophone West Africa. Differences in their size and economic circumstances provide useful contrasting information. However, the basic issues are strikingly similar in both countries. Economic and political circumstances are seen as the main determinants of employment, and education plays a supporting role in providing skills.

Education and employment in Zambia

Zambia is a land-locked country, which gained independence from the UK in 1964 and which has an approximate population of five and a half million. At the time of independence, the working population was engaged mainly in rural occupations. Over the next decade there occurred substantial rural-urban migration. In 1974 the urban population represented 35 per cent of the total,[15] and in 1980 it represented 43 per cent.[16] This is higher than in the majority of African countries, though as elsewhere the largest single group in the labour force works in subsistence agriculture. As in most African countries, the government is the largest employer in the modern sector of the economy. The second largest employer is the mining sector. Zambia's prosperity is heavily dependent on copper production, and the problems facing this industry in recent years have contributed to major economic difficulties.

During the late 1960s, paid modern sector employment grew at an annual rate of nearly 6 per cent, which was much more rapid than population growth. Both the public sector and manufacturing industries expanded rapidly in response to mining revenues; and also, in the case of the manufacturing industries, in response to the increase in demand for locally produced goods as a result of trade restrictions imposed after Rhodesia's Unilateral Declaration of Independence.

In the first half of the 1970s, however, growth of modern sector employment was almost negligible, and it actually fell after 1975 when declining copper revenues and transport problems in foreign trade depressed the economy. Statistics indicate that employment increased from 365,500 in late 1971 to 384,800 in late 1974. However, the latter figure included 13,000 workers on the TAZARA railway, the majority of whom were laid off upon its completion in 1976. Total employment in late

1976 stood at approximately the same level as in late 1971. Wage employment declined in commercial agriculture, construction, transport and communications; it remained virtually stationery in manufacturing; and registered only modest increases in mining and other sectors. Figure produced in 1977 suggested open unemployment of about 33 per cent of the modern sector labour force.[17] Putting these figures another way round, statistics showed that only 27 per cent of the labour force had wage-earning jobs in 1969, that the proportion fell to 21 per cent in 1979, and that it will probably be only 13 per cent in the year 2000.[18]

In 1977 an International Labour Office (ILO) report commented on the remarkable economic transformation that had taken place since independence. However, it suggested that the fruits of this progress had not been shared equally, and that a large percentage of both urban and rural population still lacked the basic necessities of life. Four major employment problems were identified, namely the low incomes of the so-called 'working poor'; the unemployed and frustrated job-seekers; the under-utilization of labour; and women's employment problems in both rural and urban areas. To tackle these problems, the report suggested, fundamental economic, social and political reforms would be required.[19] Similar points were repeated in a 1981 ILO Report.[20]

The Third National Development Plan reinforced these views. In its review of the 1970s, the plan concluded:

> The dominant factors affecting the employment situation were: the wide rural-urban gap in income caused and accentuated by a rapid increase in urban wages and movement of the terms of trade in favour of urban consumers against the rural producers; continuous migration of the people from rural to urban areas in search of employment; the overwhelming predominance of large firms, large shops, large-scale and highly mechanised agriculture, [and] capital intensive technology used in implementing . . . projects . . .[21]

The planners saw education as a potential supportive factor for improving the situation rather than as either a cause or a fundamental solver of unemployment. However, the plan should have mentioned population growth as an additional factor. The increased birth rate of the 1960s was contributing to an annual expansion of the labour force by 4 per cent, and present high birth rates will be felt in the labour market in 15 years' time.

When the National Plan turned to the place of education, it began by stressing the importance of matching the nature and size of educational output with the needs of the economy. It noted that despite very rapid educational expansion at all levels, the country still suffered a shortage of skilled manpower. Rapid Zambianization of senior positions had occurred, but 11 years after independence still 19.4 per cent of professional, technical and related workers in the public sector were non-Zambians, and proportions rose to 45.3 per cent in the private sector and 46.3 per cent in the parastatal sector. While progress in meeting demand for clerical and low skilled occupations had been good, there was a shortage of engineers, builders, medical personnel and post-primary teachers.

Clearly this indicated an unsatisfactory situation, in which training could play a major part. However, the education system was still not closely geared to manpower needs. The plan predicted, for example, that:

1   The demand for high level engineering and technical personnel would be about 250 persons at the end of the plan period, whereas only 140 persons in this sector were expected to graduate from university. At middle levels, a shortfall of 1,000 persons was predicted.
2   Projected demand for primary teachers would be met by supply. But a shortage of secondary teachers was expected, especially since a large number of trainees would not actually join the profession.
3   Some 165 doctors would graduate from the University of Zambia. However, not all would stay in the country, and some expatriate doctors would leave. Thus, there would be a shortfall of nearly 400 doctors.

In the management sphere, the plan noted the high percentage of expatriates, and that about 30 per cent of Zambians in management jobs were either partially qualified or unqualified. 'The lack of good educational background', it continued, 'has impaired the performance of Zambian managers and seriously limits their potential for further advancement.'[22] Thus, the manpower shortage at higher levels was severe, and education was expected to play a crucial role in correcting it.

At lower levels, by contrast, projected supply of educated labour was greater than demand. The manpower chapter of the National Plan provided data on junior and senior secondary school output, but omitted information on primary leavers. This largely reflected a view that primary schooling was more concerned with social objectives than with economic ones and that, in any case, most primary leavers were too young fully to enter productive work.

The idea that they were young certainly had some basis in fact. In 1981/2 only 18.5 per cent of primary 7 leavers proceeded to secondary school, and 81.5 per cent had to seek some form of employment.[23] However, if the school leavers were young to begin with they soon grew older, yet still possessed qualifications which were geared more to the wage economy than to self-employment or agriculture.

Review of both primary and secondary enrolments in the mid-1970s showed them to be higher than had been originally planned. Furthermore, the government had stated its intention to achieve universal enrolments of children aged 7 in the near future, and to reduce drop-out rates within the primary system. Among the important political objectives which universal primary education would achieve, it was argued, were a reduction in regional imbalances and provision of equal opportunity for enrolment throughout the country. It must also be noted, however, that these measures will greatly increase the number of primary school leavers, most of whom will be unable to find wage-earning jobs.

To some extent, the mere fact of increasing educational enrolments changes the outlook of school leavers. As primary education expands to include most children, school leavers become increasingly aware that they are not a minority and that it will probably be fruitless to aspire to the limited number of vacancies at their level in the wage sector. Thus, there is evidence that the expectations of primary 4 leavers have been reduced by the realities of the labour market, and they no longer present so great an unemployment problem.[24] With continued educational expansion, similar changes may be expected at higher educational levels.

Nevertheless, it remains true that primary schooling is more oriented towards the needs of the minority who continue their education than towards those of the majority for whom it is terminal. The authorities are well aware of this, and in 1976 initiated a proposal for fundamental educational reform. Few of the proposals have actually been implemented, however, and they provide a notable example of the obstacles to reform. They were widely discussed in 1976 and 1977, but chiefly because of resistance from those benefiting from the existing system and from the teaching force, little action has resulted from them. A 1977 document presented a much less radical set of proposals, and actual reforms of the type originally envisaged have been very limited.[25]

Effective tackling of employment problems in Zambia would require such a fundamental reordering of priorities and of political power that the authorities may not be prepared to embark on it. As the ILO reports commented, there has been a wide gap between what politicians have said they intend to do and what has actually been done. Zambia has been severely affected by falling copper prices, by rising energy costs and by other factors beyond its control. However, major improvements in employment and in the living standards of the majority have been and still are possible, even in this poor economic climate. For example, the position of both the rural and urban poor could be improved by a redistribution of income. In the mid-1970s, the richest 2 per cent of households owned 20 per cent of Zambia's wealth, while the poorest 50 per cent owned only another 20 per cent.[26] This could be changed by more vigorous rural development policies, by a more progressive taxation system, and by a pricing policy which gave greater incomes to producers of food and other basic items. However, such measures would inevitably be opposed by the rich, who, because they are rich, also tend to be politically powerful.

Open unemployment is both an obvious waste of resources and emotionally very destructive for those concerned. On the other hand, Zambia has no shortage of land, and is desperately in need of increased food production. These two facts suggest that the unemployed should be attracted to agriculture. The ILO stressed the danger of employment policy concentrating on the wage-earning sector, as it had until that point. Further, the report suggested:

> It would be misleading and it could be damaging to the general creation of productive employment to concentrate further on this sort of employment, which is generally high-cost, urban-based, often linked to imports, skill and capital-intensive methods of production –

and, as if this were not enough, to outflows of profits and foreign exchange as well. This sector has created some jobs in the past – but even then nothing like the number needed to achieve the employment targets of past plans, let alone absorb all the additions to the labour force. This sector has proved incapable by and of itself, of solving Zambia's employment in the past and will continue to do so even less in the future.[27]

Accordingly, the report suggested that the rhetoric of the past be turned into concrete action, and that the informal and agricultural sectors be given the attention and resources they need. Quite apart from the economic and social effects this would have, there would also be some educational implications. There would be less need to train middle and highly skilled personnel because more simple technologies can be operated with a lower level of training. Basic education, which it is planned to make universal, would therefore have more widespread productive application. And because the gaps between the wage-earning and other sectors would be narrowed, school leavers would be more attracted to the latter and open unemployment would be reduced.

While this reasoning is logical, however, it is by no means new. It may be significant that the Third National Development Plan made no specific mention of the earlier ILO report or its recommendations. Nor did it pay specific attention to the employment needs of women, who at present play a much more important economic role than is generally recognized, but for whom specific provision is generally lacking. As with the poor in general, this may reflect their current lack of bargaining power. Whether there will be fundamental changes in the future remains to be seen. But the authorities' failure radically to reform even the education sector makes it difficult to be optimistic about wider economic and political reforms in the near future.

Education and employment in Togo

Togo is a fairly small country in West Africa, covering an area of 56,000 square kilometres, with an approximate population of 2.5 million. It gained independence from France in 1960, and has an economy broadly similar to the majority of African countries, with a large agricultural sector and a small modern wage sector. As elsewhere, the government plays an important role in the modern sector, but, unlike Zambia and some other countries, there is no particularly prominent manufacturing industry.

According to official figures, the working population in 1975 was distributed as shown in Table 3.3. The labour force was growing at an annual rate of 2.4 per cent in the late 1970s, and although this was expected to increase to 2.5 per cent in the next five years, it was a much smaller growth rate than that of Zambia. The 1976–80 Development Plan recognized that unemployment was also a problem, but owing to the lack of precise information, it is not possible to guage the extent of the problem at the moment.[28] The Plan also recognized that underemployment was a problem, though was likewise unable to accurately indicate its extent. The informal sector has been documented more carefully, however, and one survey has identified 23,840 enterprises in the capital.[29]

Table 3.3   Occupations of the labour force, Togo[30]

Occupation	Number	%
Agricultural Sector	670,000	75.1
Non-Agricultural Sector		
Salaried (modern): Public & Army	32,000	3.6
Private	18,000	2.0
Non-Salaried: (traditional) Artisans	56,000	6.3
Traders	70,000	7.9
Transporters	3,000	0.3
Others	21,000	2.4
Unemployed	22,000	2.4
TOTAL	892,000	100.0

Like most African governments, the Togolese authorities are concerned to modernize agriculture and reduce economic disparities in order to limit rural-urban migration. Specific proposals for the introduction of labour-intensive processes have been announced for road construction and other projects. The government has also recognized the role of demographic factors and economic policies in employment generation, and has identified sectors in which indigenization programmes may be implemented. In the private sector, non-Togolese staff accounted for 13.5 per cent of building and public works and 13.4 per cent in banking operations in 1973. Proportions were lower in other sectors, and expatriates were concentrated at top levels, but there was clear scope for Togolese nationals to take over some jobs.

The government has also noted the links between education and employment, and has placed strong emphasis on the need to train skilled personnel. Although national planners have identified specific middle and high level training needs, a recent initiative has placed more emphasis on the political and social benefits of education than on the economic ones, and has led to considerable expansion of basic education. A major programme launched in 1975 sought to achieve universal education within ten years and to make schooling free and compulsory for all children from kindergarten age to 15 years. As a result, educational output at the bottom level is far greater than the number of modern sector opportunities.

A comparison of middle and higher level educational output with modern sector opportunities is given in Table 3.4. There was an excess output of higher level administrative and legal, and economic personnel, and middle level and specialized commercial personnel. In large measure, this reflected an inappropriate enrolment pattern in the University of Benin. In 1974–5, 20 per cent of the students were enrolled for economics and management; 17 per cent were for law; 12 per cent were for English; 10 per cent were for modern literature; and only 7 per cent for agriculture,

5 per cent for mechanics, 4 per cent for medicine and 2 per cent for physics and chemistry. Moreover, a similar pattern was to be found among Togolese students overseas, and a large proportion of University of Benin graduates left the country on completion of their courses. Thus according to one study, France attracted more Togolese doctors than it sent to Togo, and throughout the last two decades a large number of engineers, teachers and scientists have emigrated to Europe and America in search of higher salaries and better working conditions.[31]

Table 3.4   Projected balance of manpower needs and resources, Togo, 1976–80[32]

Sector		Needs	Resources*	Surplus/ deficit
Agriculture	higher level	180	108	− 72
	middle level	170	50	− 120
	specialized	350	125	− 225
Science and technology	higher level	275	109	− 166
	middle level	346	250	− 96
	specialized	1,489	960	− 529
Commerce	higher level	102	27	− 75
	middle level	175	300	+ 125
	specialized	325	500	+ 175
Economic and financial	higher level	175	268	+ 93
	middle level	80	—	− 80
	specialized	222	—	− 222
Administrative and legal	higher level	105	233	+ 128
	middle level	200	190	− 10
	specialized	534	—	− 534
Medical and social	higher level	240	224	− 16
	middle level	1,137	702	− 435
	specialized	1,722	—	− 1,722
Teachers	higher level	917	673	− 244
	middle level	769	245	− 524
	specialized	2,898	400	− 2,498
Literary and artistic	higher level	83	48	− 35
	middle level	93	—	− 93
	specialized	106	—	− 106

* i.e. graduates from the educational system with appropriate training.

Especially at higher levels, therefore, the education system was not well geared to the needs of the economy. In some professions, there was an over-production of graduates, and they faced unemployment. In others, there was an acute shortage, and the considerable expense devoted to training personnel did not benefit the Togolese people. The École Nationale d'Administration, however, does provide training for most of the country's civil servants.

The National Plan pointed out that most of the posts for which qualified staff were not available would be filled by underqualified personnel, and that this would relieve unemployment at lower levels. These posts would absorb 7,190 individuals during the plan period, it suggested, and a further 9,520 were required for low level manpower. As many as 158,980 school leavers would find no formal sector employment, however, and would have either to find informal sector work or join the unemployed.

Like most African countries, therefore, unemployment in Togo was low among the highly educated and also among the uneducated, but much greater among those with a little education. Available information on unemployment in the mid-1970s indicated that workmen and labourers were the largest groups, followed by domestics and clerks.

The rate of unemployment in Togo is much less than that of Zambia and most other countries. The authorities are clearly aware of key needs in real rural development, are now giving much greater attention to the previously neglected informal sector, and are attempting to promote a better match between high level educational output and manpower needs. It must be noted, however, that as in Zambia this will require considerable commitments from the authorities, who will have to resist pressures from the currently favoured geographical areas and social groups. It must also be recognized that at present a large number of primary leavers only enter informal sector work for negative reasons – because they have failed to find formal jobs – rather than for positive ones. Thus even if they are working, they are not necessarily content with the nature of their work. Finally, it is worth noting that like many African governments, the Togolese authorities do not at present place strong emphasis on measures to reduce the rate of population growth in order to reduce future pressure in the labour market.

Questions and project work

1 Comment on the suggestion that schools in African countries are insufficiently concerned with the creation of skills for rural or urban employment, and discuss the obstacles to making curricula more skill-oriented.

2 Find the most recent official statistics on unemployment in your country. Note the ages, the sexes, the levels of education and the skills of the unemployed. Comment on the adequacy of these statistics and their implications for educational and manpower planners.

3 What is meant by the 'informal sector'? Discuss, with examples, the types of workers in the informal sector. Comment on the attitude of the government towards it, and indicate the role of formal and nonformal education in its development.

4 Most African countries suffer from high open unemployment, and the job prospects for educated individuals have deteriorated rapidly over the last few years. In view of this fact, why do individuals and governments continue to invest so heavily in education?

Notes

1   Psacharapoulos, George *Returns to Education: An International Comparison,* Elsevier, Amsterdam 1973; Psacharopoulos, George 'Returns to Education: An Updated International Comparison'. *Comparative Education,* Vol. 17, No. 3, 1981.
2   International Labour Office *Employment, Incomes and Equality: A Strategy for Increasing Productive Employment in Kenya.* Geneva 1972, p. 6.
3   Edwards, Edgar O. (ed.) *Employment in Developing Nations.* Columbia University Press, New York 1974, pp. 10–11. See also Todaro, Michael P. *Economic Development in the Third World.* Longman, Essex 1981, pp. 207–8.
4   Jolly, Richard 'Introduction to Part I' in Jolly, Richard (ed.) *Third World Employment.* Penguin, Harmondsworth 1973, p. 6; Carnoy, Martin *Education and Employment: A Critical Appraisal.* International Institute for Educational Planning, Paris 1977, p. 13.
5   From Sabolo, Yues 'Employment and Unemployment, 1960–90'. *International Labour Review,* Vol. 112, No. 6, 1975, Table 3 and Appendix.
6   Hinchliffe, Keith 'Labour Aristocracy – A Northern Nigerian Case-Study'. *Journal of Modern African Studies,* Vol. 12, No. 1, 1974, p. 65.
7   The World Bank *Education Sector Policy Paper.* Washington 1980, p. 42.
8   The World Bank *World Development Report, 1980.* Washington 1980, p. 48.
9   Ibid., p. 48.
10 See Chapter 4.
11 See Arrow, K.J. 'Higher Education as a Filter?' *Journal of Public Economics,* July 1973.
12 See Schumacher, E.F. *Small is Beautiful.* Abacus, London 1974.
13 The World Bank *World Development Report.* op. cit., pp. 1, 99.
14 Myers, Norman 'Kenya's Baby Boom'. *New Scientist,* 18/9/80, p. 849. A more detailed review of research is contained in Cochrane, Susan *Fertility and Education: What do we Really Know?* Johns Hopkins University Press, Baltimore 1979.
15 Republic of Zambia *Third National Development Plan 1979–83.* Office of the President, 1979, p. 55. Unless otherwise indicated, statistics presented here are taken from this source.
16 Fägerlind, I. and Valdelin, J. *Education in Zambia, Past Achievements and Future Trends.* Swedish International Development Authority, Stockholm 1983, p. 61.
17 Fincham, Robin 'Employment and Unemployment' in Fincham, Robin (ed.) *Employment in Zambia.* University of Zambia, 1979, p. 14.
18 International Labour Office *Zambia: Basic Needs in an Economy Under Pressure.* Addis Ababa 1981, p. 39.
19 International Labour Office *Narrowing the Gaps: Planning for Basic Needs and Productive Employment in Zambia.* Addis Ababa 1977, p. 6.
20 International Labour Office, *Zambia: Basic Needs.* op. cit.
21 Republic of Zambia, op. cit., p. 56.
22 Ibid., p. 66.
23 Fägerlind and Valdelin, op. cit., p. 93.
24 International Labour Office, *Narrowing the Gaps,* op. cit., p. 163.
25 See Republic of Zambia *Education for Development.* Ministry of Education, Lusaka 1976; Republic of Zambia *Educational Reform.* Ministry of Education, Lusaka 1977; Garvey, Brian 'Educational Development in an Evolving Society: Zambian Education, 1964–1977' in Markakis, John and Fincham, Robin (eds.) *The Evolving Structure of Zambian Society.* Centre of African Studies,

Edinburgh 1980; Alexander, D.J., 'Problems of Educational Reform in Zambia'. *International Journal of Educational Development*, Vol. 3, No. 2, 1983.

26 International Labour Office, *Narrowing the Gaps*. op. cit., p. 26.

27 Ibid., pp. 37–8.

28 République Togolaise *Plan de Développement Economique et Social 1976–1980*. Ministère du Plan, Lomé 1976, pp. 433–4. Unless otherwise indicated, statistics in this part are taken from this source.

29 Demol, Erik 'Analyse des Résultats du Recensement du Secteur Non Structuré de Lomé'. International Labour Office, Geneva 1978, p. 20.

30 République Togolaise *Plan de Développement Economique et Social 1976–1980*, op. cit., p. 453

31 UNDP/ILO 'Togo: Résultats du Projet et Recommandations en Découlant'. Geneva 1977, p. 45.

32 République Togolaise, op. cit., p. 451.

Chapter 4

Education and social stratification

When applied to society, the term 'stratification' uses an analogy from geology. In that subject, it refers to the way layers of rock are laid on top of each other. Social stratification refers to the way society is divided into layers, and we can identify some layers, or groups of people, which are in socially superior positions to others.

Max Weber, the German sociologist, identified three separate elements of social stratification, namely class, status and power.[1] People belong to a class when they share economic interests, and in a class society some groups dominate others through their control of land, labour and capital. Marxist analysts attach particular significance to the evolution and interaction of social classes. Karl Marx himself noted that conflict between classes is not necessarily open, and that even those who are oppressed may be too busy securing the necessities of life to have time and energy to actively oppose their oppressors. However, he was strongly critical of the social ranking, and wished to reduce control and oppression through social reform and revolution. Marx's writings are thus a principal inspiration to the conflict theorists as opposed to the functionalists.[2]

The nature of classes in Africa has changed with time. Various forms of domestic slavery existed in many pre-colonial states, and groups of rulers and ruled were readily identifiable.[3] To some extent these patterns still exist, though traditional structures now compete with newer ones based on the cash economy introduced with colonialism. In a cash economy, a distinction often emerges between employers and employed, with corresponding implications of control and disparities in wealth. In general, class structures in Africa are not as developed as in most European and Latin American societies, but they are rapidly becoming more pronounced.[4] Sometimes members of the élites in the cash economy also hold superior positions in the traditional hierarchy, but generally traditional structures are ceasing to be so strong, and economic stratification is becoming more prominent.

The second element is that of status, which concerns the respect and deference given to individuals and groups. Sometimes status is achieved by and linked to occupations. University professors, for example, usually have a high status, while labourers have not. Other kinds of status are ascribed, and are beyond the control of the individual: in most African societies, old people have a higher status than young ones, and males have a higher status than females. Sometimes status coincides with class power, but it does not always do so. Religious leaders, for example, are usually accorded high status, even if they are poor and have little economic or political influence.[5]

The third element is that of political power. This refers to the ability to take decisions which will affect other people. Its most obvious application is in central and local government, though it may also exist in other forms and places. A headmaster, for example, generally has political power both inside and outside his school. He can take decisions involving the future of his teachers, his pupils and by implication, their families. He also often plays a separate political role in the community.

Often, but not always, these three elements coincide and reinforce each other. Thus, businessmen may have a high status in part because they also wield economic and political influence, and groups who acquire political power may use it to strengthen their economic position and therefore their status. In this chapter, we are mainly concerned with the first element, that is, with classes based on economic interests. However, we shall also note some links between education and the other elements of stratification.

In Chapter 2, we also noted the existence of vertical 'pillars' in society which may cut across these forms of horizontal stratification. Factors such as religion or ethnic identity may unite class groups, especially when there is a conflict with other religious or ethnic groups. However, ethnic conflicts also frequently involve class conflicts. Thus, it may be suggested that the revolution in Rwanda, in which the Hutu people rebelled against domination by the Tutsi, was as much concerned with class as it was with ethnicity. Similarly, white South Africans constitute an economic class which is also united by the vertical pillar of race. Within the black population in South Africa there are many horizontal class, status and power divisions, but all may be united when faced with a common oppressor.

Education is often said to promote mobility within society. It is easy to point to individuals who through education, have emerged from backgrounds of low class, status and power to achieve the opposite. Sekou Touré, for example, was born into a peasant family but became President of Guinea; and Alhaji Sir Abubakar Tafawa Balewa was born into a slave family but became Nigeria's first prime minister.

However, it is dangerous to generalize from the social mobility of individuals to that of whole groups. If the lower groups as a whole rise in the social scale, by implication they join or displace the groups in higher positions. This has happened in some societies, as can be seen by examining the present position of some traditional ruling groups which have been displaced by a Western educated élite. It has occured because of the links between education and class, status and power, and because education – formal, nonformal and informal – has favoured lower groups more than higher ones. But changes in the hierarchy do not happen often. Whole societies can improve their economic position, but disparities usually remain between rich and poor, between those who control and those who are controlled. In practice, education and economic structures have combined to *create* stratification which, once created, has frequently been reinforced over time.

Education and social stratification in the colonial era

In Chapter 1, we noted that formal Western-type education in most African countries was established by Christian missionaries and subsequently supplemented by colonial governments. Education was a major activity of all Christian missions since they considered schools a good medium in which to mould the attitudes of youth and a valuable source of future manpower for the spread of the Gospel. Because of geographic factors, such as the closeness of the coast or the existence of cool areas favourable to Europeans' living conditions, and because of different responses by chiefs to mission initiatives, some groups were influenced more strongly than others. Peoples who had previously existed more or less independently found themselves surrounded by colonial boundaries. With the introduction of the cash economy, those who had received the most education came to dominate the rest. Examples of educational and economic imbalances which arose in this way may be given from almost every country. To give just two examples, the Lagoon peoples of Ivory Coast were strongly influenced because they inhabited a coastal region and because the French colonial administration was anxious to forestall the influence of the British in neighbouring Gold Coast, while educational development among the Senoufo in the north was much less. Similarly, in southern Sudan, the Dinka have responded to availability of education much more than the Nuer. In both countries the groups with the greater educational development have come to dominate economic and political processes. Once these imbalances have been created they tend to persist, and successive governments have found them very difficult to eliminate.

Colonial authorities were aware of the potentially disruptive effect of the economic and social structures they and the missionaries were importing, and in both British and French colonies efforts were made to ensure the dominance of certain groups in both the old and new systems by making special provision for sons of chiefs. The idea was that by the time the sons took over from their fathers, they would have acquired the skills necessary for leadership in the new system as well as in the old. In many cases, this policy was successful, and it reinforced existing social stratification.[6] Moreover, official initiatives were sometimes supplemented by mission ones. In Uganda, for example, both Protestant and Roman Catholic missionaries established schools for the ruling groups with the idea of converting lower classes to their religion through the chiefs.[7] However, it also often happened that traditional rulers were suspicious of European activities, and when placed under pressure some sent children of slaves to school instead of their own children.[8]

During the colonial era, many governments also used education to reinforce stratification by operating racially segregated schools. The European, Asian and African schools could be ranked in order of quality, and had different curricula. The Asian schools of East Africa, for example, employed Indian languages and English as the media of instruction, and did not teach any African languages. Since in general Europeans and Asians attended school for longer periods than did Africans, the former acquired the most economically and politically powerful positions.

Education and social stratification in the post-colonial era

In the post-colonial era, obvious forms of racial segregation have been removed. However, other forms of stratification have remained and have become more developed. They are based on both the quantity and the quality of education received by different groups.

Looking initially at formal education, we must first ask which groups are most likely to enter the system and stay longest in it. Bowles has pointed out that schools tend to have 'recruiting' and 'gate-keeping' mechanisms.[9] They recruit those types of people who are most likely to fit in with the values and requirements of the school, and they keep the others out.

Where education is not universal, some groups are clearly favoured and others are disadvantaged. Those who have not attended school have neither the skills nor the certificates of the others. They are unable to compete so successfully in the labour market, and this means that, in a situation in which there are differences of income between those who are employed and those who work in subsistence agriculture or in the informal urban sector, they suffer a disadvantage from the beginning. Thus a clear distinction exists between the schooled and the non-schooled. It is also probable that those who are recruited for school are from middle and high social groups while those whom the gate keeps out occupy lower social positions.

Even where basic education is universally received, differences still exist at post-primary levels. No African country is even approaching universal secondary education, and the recruiting and gate-keeping mechanisms clearly operate at the transition point between primary and secondary education. Even if secondary education were universal, the same watershed would occur at the transition point between secondary education and university. It is therefore impossible to give equal quantities of education to every member of the population.

Quantitative differences in education are reinforced by the tendency of children to drop out at each stage. The rate of dropping out from the group of students beginning grade 1 in 1970 in a number of African countries is shown in Table 4.1. There is wide variation throughout the continent, but drop-outs are often very high and in Madagascar reached 75.4% of the 1970 primary 1 cohort. Studies have shown that drop-out rates tend to be particularly high in poorer countries, and especially to affect lower income groups, girls and those in rural areas.[10]

The chief reason why drop-out rates are relatively high among lower income groups is that pupils cannot afford to remain in school. Even if schools are nominally free, there are usually uniform costs and textbook fees. Poorer children often cannot afford to attend even free schools because they need to be working to support themselves and their families. Even if in the long run they would have higher incomes if they remained in school, in the short run they cannot afford to do so.

Table 4.1   Drop-out rates from primary Grade 1 after six years[11]

	Per cent		Per cent
Benin	39.9	Madagascar	75.4
Botswana	16.5	Mali	50.6
Burundi	55.1	Niger	40.3
Cameroon	42.5	Rwanda	66.8
Chad	71.5	Senegal	34.0
Congo	29.2	Sudan	25.0
Gabon	49.6	Swaziland	31.0
Gambia	4.9	Tanzania	14.6
Ghana	28.2	Togo	31.3
Ivory Coast	19.8	Zaire	59.4
Kenya	22.3	Zambia	21.8
Lesotho	53.0		

Girls are similarly disadvantaged because they are often required for domestic duties and because parents are often afraid that they will become pregnant at school. They also have weaker incentives to remain in school than boys because they are less likely to seek paid employment and are therefore less likely to need a school certificate.

High drop-out rates in rural areas are chiefly explained by their general neglect by education authorities. Rural areas tend to receive much poorer quality teachers, so that pupils are more likely to get bored with schooling. In addition, pupils in villages do not have the same number of out-of-school complementary learning experiences as do those in towns. The difference in drop-out rates was demonstrated by one ILO study in western Nigeria. It indicated wastage as follows: small village schools (0–700 population size) 84.9 per cent; all village schools (0–5,000 population size) 69.5 per cent; rural towns 47.2 per cent; Ibadan city 20.0 per cent.[12]

Allied to drop-out rates is the frequency of repetition of classes. Repetition is disliked by many educational planners because it causes inefficiency. Repeaters occupy places which could have been taken by other pupils, and it therefore hinders efforts to educate larger numbers of children and the resultant democratization of opportunities. As with drop-outs, the tendency to repeat classes is higher among pupils from low socio-economic backgrounds, in rural areas and among females.[13] Since the other groups proceed through the education system more rapidly, again they receive advantages, and stratification is maintained.

Informal education also affects social stratification, for the formal education system requires a set of skills and attitudes which are reinforced by types of informal learning. This is most clearly seen in the language issue. As we have noted, for practical and political reasons every African country has to use an ex-colonial language as an official language. In addition, all higher and most secondary education is conducted in a colonial language, and fluent speakers of it have a major advantage throughout the education system. In both learning and assessment, children who are good at, for example, physics, geography or even mathematics cannot get far without language fluency. Examinations tend to discriminate against pupils who are less fluent in the official languages, and these pupils are generally from lower socio-economic backgrounds. Children from high strata families are much more likely to have contact with European languages outside school, which reinforces their abilities and gives them opportunities not available to other children.

Similar factors apply to parental help. Barbara Lloyd's work among a group of southern Nigerians may be considered generally true of the continent. She showed that parents who have themselves been to school, or who understand the ways in which school works, are much more likely to encourage their children, to assist them with homework and generally provide a background which supports activities in the school.[14] Children from wealthy homes are more likely to be acquainted with television and with literature, and urban children have a wide range of education experiences not available to rural ones. It has been shown that the impact of informal education tends not to be so strong in developing countries as in developed ones,[15] but we can state that out-of-school factors usually combined with in-school ones to increase stratification rather than the reverse.

Finally, we should mention one other factor which promotes differences in the quantity of education received, namely the existence of pre-primary education. Nursery schools, which are usually attended for two or three years before a child begins primary school, tend to be patronized only by children from high social strata. Nursery schools are generally fee-paying, and the extra training children receive often gives them a head start which permits them to gain entry to better primary schools. At present, pre-primary education is not very widespread in Africa; where it does exist, however, it caters mainly for the children of the urban élite, and it is likely to become more common in the future.

Turning from quantitative to qualitative differences, we see another clear way in which stratification is maintained and increased; namely through the existence of private schools. In most African countries there is a clear distinction between government schools, which are usually highly subsidized or free, and voluntary agency ones. The latter group covers a wide range of mission schools and business enterprises, and also has a wide range of quality. Some fee-paying institutions cater mainly for children who have failed to gain entry to government schools and usually provide a second-best education. Other fee-paying institutions are for children for the élite. They charge very high fees and usually produce better results than the government schools. In both cases, attendance depends on the ability of parents or guardians to pay fees, and thus children from the poorer sections of the population are excluded.

The impact of boarding schools on stratification is also marked. Because boarding pupils remain within the environment of the school for much longer periods, than do day pupils, the schools tend to have a greater impact on students' attitudes. The values instilled tend to correspond to the high status values of society, and since the schools also usually give a high quality education with good examination results, they also facilitate entry of their students into powerful positions. Such schools as Achimota in Accra, Van Vollenhoven in Dakar, Lenana in Nairobi and King's College in Lagos have become famous for the quality of education they provide and the subsequent high status of many pupils.

Two points about the cost of education and the subsequent earnings of its recipients should also be made. The cost of a year's education increases sharply at higher levels in the system. Recent cost figures for Nigeria, which show a pattern comparable to the rest of the continent, indicate annual recurrent pupil costs as follows:[16]

Primary school	₦ 86
Junior secondary school	₦ 205
Senior secondary school (day)	₦ 405
Senior secondary school (boarding)	₦ 880
University	₦ 4,704

All levels are either free or highly subsidized. Yet although the nation is already paying a very large sum to educate university students, when they graduate they expect, and are usually given, high salaries. Thus, they benefit twice over. First, the community is paying a large amount for their education and then it is paying a large amount for their work. This mechanism operates throughout the capitalist world, and is a clear way in which education reinforces income differentials and social stratification.

At the other end of the scale, illiteracy in Africa, though being reduced in proportional terms, remains very high. Estimates for 1980 suggested that 48 per cent of adult males and 73 per cent of adult females were illiterate, which in absolute terms meant 61 million and 95 million people. The role of literacy should not be overestimated, especially in view of the increasingly widespread existence of radio, which provides an alternative way to spread information. Nor should it ever be assumed that illiterate people are stupid and have no idea what is happening around them. Yet illiterates are often exploited and subjected to disadvantages in a world where literacy is increasingly taken for granted and becoming an ever more essential skill. On the one hand, illiterates lack a skill valuable for increasing their income, and on the other hand they are frequently exploited by money lenders, tax collectors and others. Illiterates therefore lack economic and political power, and an imbalance will continue to exist until illiteracy is eradicated. Table 4.2 shows past and projected illiteracy rates for a number of countries.

Finally, we should point out one factor through which poorer groups are disadvantaged even *before* they enter school. This is through the incidence of malnutrition, which in the early years can seriously damage a child's brain and subsequent intellectual development. Malnutrition hits poorest groups hardest, and is another reason why children from those groups are unable to perform well in school.[17]

Table 4.2 Estimates and projections of illiteracy for the population aged 15 and over.[18]

| | 1970 | | 1980 | | 1990 | |
	per cent	*million*	*per cent*	*million*	*per cent*	*million*
AFRICA	71	197.0	61	257.0	49	341.3
Botswana	73	0.3	60	0.4	37	0.6
Burundi	82	1.9	77	2.4	78	3.1
Cameroon	66	3.5	45	4.2	29	5.3
Ethiopia	95	13.9	95	17.6	88	22.8
Gambia	91	0.3	85	0.3	76	0.4
Ghana	69	4.6	55	6.2	44	8.4
Kenya	69	6.1	50	8.3	31	11.6
Lesotho	38	0.7	31	0.8	19	1.0
Liberia	83	0.9	75	1.1	61	1.4
Malawi	74	2.5	67	3.1	50	4.1
Mali	93	2.9	90	3.6	84	4.6
Mauritius	25	0.5	15	0.7	10	0.8
Nigeria	76	30.4	70	39.4	57	52.6
Senegal	87	2.2	80	2.8	71	3.6
Sierra Leone	89	1.5	80	1.9	67	2.5
Sudan	85	8.6	78	11.6	67	16.1
Tanzania	63	7.3	53	9.6	37	13.1
Uganda	66	5.5	52	7.3	43	9.9
Zaire	57	12.3	42	15.8	30	20.5
Zambia	51	2.3	31	3.1	19	4.3
Zimbabwe	41	2.8	29	1.9	21	5.5

The vocational school fallacy

So far, we have looked mainly at links between stratification and the formal education system. In this section we shall examine some different educational routes and relationships between formal and nonformal education. By nonformal education we mean instruction that is organized but which is outside the school system.[19]

In 1966, Philip Foster published a very influential article entitled 'The vocational school fallacy in development planning'. In it, he discussed the relationships between academic education and technical, vocational and agricultural instruction, and examined the proposal, made many times before and since, that the school should provide the nucleus of modern agriculture and play a central role in raising rural standards of living. Present educational facilities, the argument runs, are an obstacle to rural progress because pupils are not given agricultural training, and indeed formal education makes pupils hostile to rural life. It is suggested that since schools both make students aware of opportunities existing in towns and give them the certificates with which they can obtain urban jobs, formal education is to a large extent responsible for rural-urban migration.

Foster's article began by pointing out that it was not true that no schemes for agricultural and vocational training were implemented during the colonial era, or that education was entirely academic. On the contrary, a great many missionaries and colonial officers were very keen on such programmes. He then suggested that the failure of agricultural and vocational schemes to become more prominent was mainly the result of low demand for them, and that this was largely determined by the structure of the economy.

> An examination of opportunities within . . . [the European dominated] sector throughout the colonial period reveals that *relatively* there was greater demand for clerical and commercial employees than for technically trained individuals. Opportunities certainly existed in technical fields and in agriculture, but they were inferior to the other alternatives. Access to most of the highly paid occupations was, therefore, achieved through academic institutions. Those who criticise the 'irrational' nature of African demand for 'academic' as opposed to 'vocational' education fail to recognise that the strength of academic education has lain precisely in the fact that it is pre-eminently a *vocational* education providing access to those occupations with the most prestige and, most important, the highest pay . . .[20]

This situation existed in many countries. In Kenya, Zambia, Malawi, Zimbabwe and southern Nigeria, for example, Africans deliberately rejected vocational training because they considered it a second-best education, designed to maintain the dominance of their European masters.[21] It is no coincidence that many of the early nationalist leaders, such as Awolowo, Akintola and Nkrumah, were lawyers who had received a highly formal education and through it were able to confront the colonialists in the system the latter had themselves introduced.

In the post-independence era, the obvious racial features of stratification are less prominent, but the structure of the economy and the nature of class divisions have remained. Although artisans and farmers can become quite prosperous, bureaucratic jobs usually yield an income which is higher, more dependable, and unaffected by seasonal fluctuations. Consequently, bureaucratic jobs, which are chiefly acquired through academic education, are almost invariably considered more desirable. On the other hand, where the incomes of agricultural workers and artisans are significantly higher than those of white-collar workers, Foster pointed out that there is no shortage of recruits. It is therefore a myth to suggest that formal school in itself makes it products unwilling to get their hands dirty, and the real factor of importance is the reward given to each type of training in the economy.

In many African countries, pupils who continue their education after primary school are faced with three options – they can go to a secondary grammar school, to a teacher training college, or to a vocational training school. The tendency is for prospective pupils to rank these in order of priority. They will go to grammar school as a first choice if they can, to teacher training as a second choice and to vocational school only as a third choice. Foster's paper suggests that this is principally because of economic rather than educational factors.

In the early and mid-1970s, nonformal education became a major focus of attention among educational planners. Formal schooling, it was pointed out, was usually a highly expensive and inflexible activity which catered for a small section of the population and often contributed to open unemployment and rural-urban migration. Because of these problems, attention turned to nonformal education as a complement and an alternative to formal schooling. In contrast to the failings of the formal system, some authors presented nonformal education as generally cheaper, more flexible, able to cater for larger numbers, and more closely related to work.[22]

As the decade progressed, however, the disadvantages of nonformal education became more apparent. Two major problems were that it was frequently more expensive than formal education, and that it was often difficult to organize and coordinate. A third was that it tended to promote stratification.

Particularly where nonformal programmes were developed as alternatives to formal ones, there arose the familiar question of which route was the most direct for acquiring the most rewarding jobs. Nonformal education was often a second best option which would be pursued only by those to whom formal avenues were not open. For example, the Rural Education Centres (RECs) of Burkina Faso were established to provide an alternative kind of vocationally oriented rural education for young people. The aim was to redistribute resources away from traditional primary education towards the RECs, though in the event the REC programme grew much more slowly than planned while the primary school system continued to expand as before. Once parents' hopes that the RECs could be converted into conventional primary schools were shown to be unfounded, villagers lost interest in the programme.[23] In other words, 'real' education tended still to be acquired in the formal system. Indeed the fact that unit costs in this and other nonformal schemes were lower was not insignificant, for it illustrated the way resources were being distributed and society was being stratified. Because of such problems, towards the end of the decade many of the earlier advocates of nonformal education were redirecting their attention to the formal system.

Policy alternatives

We have seen that educational provision is closely linked with the class, status and power of its recipients. Our discussion has concentrated on the first of these, and we have noted that, principally because education gives access to employment and income, it may either consolidate existing hierarchies or it may be a factor in reordering them. Where it has done the latter, which may be shown by the present lower position occupied by most traditional ruling groups in comparison with Western educated élites, the introduction of Western-type schooling coincided with the introduction of the Western-type economy. In the absence of another economic revolution, education is much more likely to consolidate stratification than to weaken or restructure it.

The policy implications of this situation depend very much on public and official attitudes. In many countries, the system and its inequalities are generally accepted. Although in-built factors tend to militate against certain groups, there is a tendency even among those disadvantaged peoples to accept 'the rules of the game', and for individuals to try to achieve as much as they can within the system rather than to attack the system itself.

For those governments which do wish to reduce social disparities, strategies are complex. Policies have to include measures both within the education system and outside it. Within the system, specific efforts can be made to promote education of poorer groups by offering scholarships. Education in rural areas and education of females can also be encouraged by specific programmes. Efforts can be made to reduce the discriminatory aspects of examinations and to spread quality as uniformly as possible.

Outside the education system, health programmes and general measures to improve the prosperity of poorer groups can reduce some stratifying factors. Efforts to reduce disparities in income can also be important. However, it must be stressed that these measures would encounter opposition from the existing élite. Strategies which promote social mobility may clash with programmes to relate education more closely to economic and social circumstances. Thus, while many nonformal education projects are, at first sight, cheap alternatives to formal schooling and are more directly related to the probable future lifestyles of their recipients, they may also clash with the concept that all groups should be able to compete within the same system. It can be argued that in some African societies where social units such as the extended family are closely knit, 'equity' may best be achieved by ensuring that the ablest members of the family – in most countries the albest males – attend secondary school and beyond, rather than guaranteeing that all persons attend a primary school.[24] However, this strategy is not widely advocated. Governments seeking equity of opportunity instead are more usually advised to reform the school system so that it incorporates some features of nonformal as well of formal education and then to cover as much of the population as possible. This implies emphasis on basic rather than higher education, and these arguments are strengthened by the high unit costs of the latter.

Case study: Education and social stratification in Kenya and Tanzania

Kenya and Tanzania have been chosen for this case study because they have similar geographic features and historical backgrounds, but have adopted very different economic, political and educational policies since the late 1960s. Kenya has a population of approximately 18 million while Tanzania's is about 19 million. Until the early 1960s, both countries were ruled by the British and both have similar colonial legacies, including a British-style education system. Mainland Tanzania received independence in 1961, and Kenya gained it two years later. Until 1967, government policies were similar, but in that year President Nyerere and the Tanzanian political party launched a programme of socialism. From that point,

Kenyan and Tanzanian paths diverged, and while the former has pursued a capitalist line which tolerates social stratification, the latter has emphasized socialism and has attempted to reduce social stratification. This section will examine each country in turn, and then make some comparative observations in conclusion.

Education and social stratification in Kenya

As in most African countries, regional economic and educational imbalances in Kenya were established very early in the colonial period, and have persisted until the present. The main route for missionary and colonial penetration was by sea, and in consequence the coastal areas were more highly influenced in the early years. With the completion of the Kenya–Uganda railway, however, missionaries advanced into the interior. Because of its altitude, the central region was cooler and was particularly favoured by Europeans. Many Europeans also moved to the west, and by 1914 the main missionary settlements were in the present Central, Nyanza and Western provinces. Although further mission settlements were founded after the First World War, and the colonial government opened a few African schools, the early pattern of concentration remained fundamentally unchanged.[25]

The African response to these activities varied. In some areas the people resisted European penetration and the economic and educational influences which came with it. But other people responded more positively. In some cases, independent African schools were established, which reinforced European educational work and increased regional imbalances.

The colonial authorities, as in many other African countries, maintained racially segregated schools. These were divided into three 'schedules', A, B and C for Africans, Asians and Europeans respectively. The schedule C schools had the best quality teachers and facilities, and were followed in order by B schools and A schools. The quality of education was reinforced by quantity. Although African schools were more numerous, the population was by far the largest. The African schools catered only for a small proportion of the population, and children tended to remain in school only a short time.

The school system promoted obvious class divisions. The schools also promoted regional ones since they were concentrated in areas in or near white settlements and in urban centres. At independence, about 30 per cent of all secondary schools were in urban areas, and although Asians and Europeans comparised only 3 per cent of the population, they represented a third of secondary school enrolments.[26]

At independence, racial segregation was abolished. However, clear qualitative differentiation of the ex-scheduled schools still remains, and attendance is based on economic criteria. While no fees were changed in ex-schedule A schools, in 1977 fees were about 800/- per annum in schedule C schools. These fees are not in themselves highly exclusive; but competition to enter the schools is now so great that attendance at a pre-primary school, where fees range from 1,200/- to well over 3,000/-, is a virtual pre-requisite.[27] Thus, only children from the richest groups can attend these schools. In addition to the three main groups, there is a fourth group which may be called schedule D schools. They are mainly private institutions run by the Catholic Church, and in 1977 charged annual fees of 1,800/- to 3,000/-.

Qualitative differences between these schools in 1972 were apparent from the nature of their teaching forces, shown in Table 4.3, and from examination results. In 1972, 32 per cent of teachers in C schools were graduates, compared with 9 per cent in D schools, a mere 1 per cent in B schools and virtually none in A schools. In 1971, passes in the Certificate in Primary Education examination were 63.6 per cent for C schools, 57.4 per cent for D schools, 55.6 per cent for B schools, and 46.7 per cent for A schools.

Table 4.3   The distribution of primary school teachers in Nairobi[28]

Teacher qualification	Category of schools				Total	No.
	A	B	C	D		
	per cent	per cent	per cent	per cent	per cent	
Graduate	0.1	1.2	32.3	9.1	3.4	(72)
Secondary teacher 1	4.1	14.4	26.0	8.4	7.6	(159)
Primary teacher 1	18.8	46.8	35.4	49.6	28.5	(593)
Primary teacher 2	28.0	19.6	3.1	10.5	22.8	(474)
Primary teacher 3	44.2	16.5	1.6	8.4	32.4	(674)
Other	4.8	1.5	1.6	14.0	5.3	(111)
Total	100.0	100.0	100.0	100.0	100.0	
	(1,343)	(327)	(127)	(286)	(2,083)	(2,083)

These inherited social imbalances are paralleled by regional ones. Because of past development patterns, a child born today in an urban area has a much greater chance of attending school than one born in a rural area. And one born in Central Province, for example, where primary enrolments approach 100 per cent,[29] has a much greater chance than one born in Northern Eastern Province, where they are nearer 20 per cent. Regional imbalances are shown in Table 4.4.

Moreover, even though primary education in ex-schedule A schools is nominally free, an economic burden is still imposed on parents. They usually have to pay for uniforms, for books and often for buildings, and they still have to do without their children's labour during school hours. Thus the poorer groups are still discriminated against. In addition, because of a policy requiring only rural communities to pay for the initial building of staff houses and classrooms, urban families again receive an advantage.[30]

Kenyan secondary schools, which do not even pretend to be free, can be categorized according to their recruitment base. Some, which recruit nationally, are called national schools. Until 1973 they were designated high-cost institutions, and some were formerly European schools. The second group includes the provincial schools. Their intake is mostly from

the provinces in which they are located, and they receive most government aid. A third category embraces private profit-oriented schools,
which operate mainly in the urban centres. The Harambee schools, which
in 1977 had more pupils than all the others added together, make up the
fourth group.

Table 4.4   Enrolment rates by province, Kenya, 1979[31]

Province	Enrolment	per cent of population aged 6–13
Central	662,985	142.5
Coast	210,328	91.3
Eastern	706,654	139.7
North Eastern	10,590	17.0
Nyanza	767,249	126.4
Rift Valley	787,898	129.4
Western	539,946	139.2
Nairobi	94,202	92.1
KENYA (total)	3,698,170	124.5

Literally, the word 'harambee' means 'let's pull together'. The schools
are organized on a self-help basis by communities which consider government provision inadequate, and the catchment area is usually very local.
They attempt to provide an education as good as that in the government
schools, but because their resources are much smaller they are usually
qualitatively inferior. Annual fees in Harambee schools are 450/- to
1,200/-, compared with 200/- to 450/- in aided schools.[32] For this reason
as well, therefore, only pupils unable to attend aided schools are willing to
enrol, and this reinforce their inferiority.

In one way, Harambee schools reduce élitist tendencies in society.
They supplement the aided institutions, and thus make education available to a much larger section of the population. From another angle,
however, because the more prosperous and enthusiastic areas organize
more schools than others, Harambee institutions may be a mechanism for
increasing imbalances. In addition, although almost all members of the
community are taxed for Harambee schools, only those families capable
of paying the fees and of doing without the labour of their youths can
afford to attend them.

Because of qualitative problems, the value of the education provided by
Harambee schools is very questionable. Even when they have achieved
comparable examination results, employers tend to prefer pupils from
government schools, and a high percentage of ex-Harambee pupils remain
unemployed for long periods. From a general viewpoint it may be suggested that the movement represents a misdirection of resources, but
individuals are caught in the system. Though the chances of success are
small, such are the potential rewards for the lucky few that for individuals
it is worth trying their luck in a Harambee school. Yet the mere existence

of these schools leads to further impoverishment of some groups. As Court of Kinyanjui have stated:

> To meet the financial pressure of fees, parents in the rural areas are under strong pressure to sell land or cattle or to divert funds from farm improvements to education. In other words, *Harambee* schools have diverted funds which would have been used for higher levels of present consumption or productive investment in agriculture to investment in education, the value of which to the individual and society is in doubt.[33]

The official response to this situation has been to attempt to give disadvantaged areas more schools, and to operate a quota system to ensure that at least some pupils from disadvantaged areas gain places at higher levels of education. Actual implementation of these policies of positive discrimination has not been wholehearted, however. Teachers prefer to work in urban areas and in better schools, and for political reasons the government has been unwilling to compel them to do otherwise. The existence of self-help schemes relieves the government of a burden it would otherwise have to shoulder, and community activities undoubtedly promote interest in schooling. Because of this, even though the Harambee movement maintains and increases imbalances, governments have felt unwilling to change the situation.

Prevailing official thinking gives a prominent place to the individual. This was clearly indicated in the 1974–8 Development Plan, which stated that:

> . . . the present plan provides opportunities for everyone to participate actively in the economy and in so doing improve his standard of living. Such improvements are bound to be achieved more quickly be some than by others. . . Equal income for everyone is therefore not the objective of this plan. Differences in skill, effort and initiative need to be recognized and rewarded.[34]

The authorities, and indeed the general public, therefore accept much of the inequality that is increased by the education system.

Yet even if it were not accepted, the results of those programmes which have attempted to reduce inequalities demonstrate the difficulties of so doing. For example, in the 1960s efforts were made to increase the educational participation of Masai living in the underdeveloped Narok District. They included provision of expensive boarding facilities and construction of extra schools. However, the boarding schools were in fact largely filled by eager immigrants and outsiders, and most of the few Masai who did attend were relatively prosperous local inhabitants. In other words, the programme broadly failed to attract the traditional pastoral Masai.[35] Particularly at the secondary level, school places were filled by outsiders and thus tended, at least in the short run, to increase imbalances rather than the reverse. The education system was seen by traditional Masai to be irrelevant to their lifestyles, which principally revolve around cattle and a pastoral existence. This posed a dilemma for the authorities, for until programmes were seen as relevant there was unlikely to be much demand for them. But at the same time, as we have pointed out, differences in educational provision do not create equality of access and opportunity. Thus, almost whatever they did, the authorities would be caught in a system whereby education facilitated the process of social stratification.

In conclusion, we may point out that because of the links between education and the economy, Kenyan society is becoming increasingly stratified. In large part this is because the government and the public have accepted that this should be the case. But even when they are actively opposed, inequalities once established are very difficult to remove. This point may be illustrated even more clearly by the Tanzanian experience.

Education and social stratification in Tanzania

During the colonial period, social and regional imbalances developed in Tanzania along very similar lines to those in Kenya. Segregated schools consolidated obvious racial and class divisions, and the highland and some southern areas became more developed than the central and western parts. Imbalances at the bottom level were accentuated at the middle level, and particularly at the higher level some areas were over-represented.

The watershed in Tanzania's economic and social policy was marked by the Arusha Declaration in 1967. In the accompanying document, *Education for self-reliance*, Julius Nyerere suggested that 'we have not until now questioned the basic system of education which we took over at the time of independence. . . It is now time that we looked again at the justification for a poor society like ours spending almost 20 per cent of its Government revenues on providing education. . .'[36] He then attacked the following four aspects of the inherited colonial system:

1 The education system was élitist and designed to meet the interests and needs of a very small proportion of those who entered the school system. 'Although only about 13 per cent of our primary school children will get a place in secondary school, the basis of our primary education is the preparation of pupils for secondary schools. Thus 87 per cent of the children who . . . will finish primary school this year . . . do so with a sense of failure, of a legitimate aspiration having been denied them. . . . On the other hand, the other 13 per cent have a feeling of having deserved a prize – and the prize they and their parents expect is high wages, comfortable employment in towns, and personal status in the society. The same process operates again at the next higher level, when entrance to university is the question at issue.'

2 Tanzania's education, Nyerere felt, was divorcing its participants from the very society it was supposed to be preparing them for. Children and their parents hoped that the schools would make it unnecessary for youths to become farmers and continue living in the village. 'The few who go to secondary schools are taken many miles away from their homes; they live in an enclave, having permission to go into the town

for recreation, but not relating the work of either town or country to their real life – which is lived in the school compound.' The lucky few who went to university lived in comfortable quarters, fed well and studied hard for a degree which, when obtained, made them expect a high salary.

3   The present system encouraged pupils in the idea that all worthwhile knowledge was acquired only from books or "educated" people. 'The knowledge and wisdom of other old people is despised. . . Government and Party themselves tend to judge people according to whether they have "passed school certificate", "have a Degree", etc.'

4   Finally, Nyerere pointed out that the system was taking out of productive work some of the strongest and healthiest young men and women. 'Not only do they fail to contribute to that increase in output which is urgent for our nation; they themselves consume the output of older and often weaker people.'[37]

These points were a powerful criticism of the education system inherited by Tanzania, and were broadly applicable to every other country in Africa. The most notable difference between Tanzania and most of the others, however, is that the former has made radical efforts to change the system.

Since 1967, Tanzania has sought to revolutionize society and, as part of it, the education system. Among the most obvious changes has been the emphasis on basic at the expense of secondary and higher education. Between 1969 and 1973, the secondary education budget was cut by 2.5 per cent in order to facilitate increased primary and adult education expenditure of 11 per cent and 57 per cent respectively.[38]

In 1970, a major adult literacy campaign was launched in Tanzania, which has succeeded in sharply reducing illiteracy and the social differentials it implies. Between 1970 and 1978, 97,700 instructors were trained, and in the latter year four million adults look a literacy test. Other major projects have concentrated on political participation, health and agriculture.

These campaigns were followed in 1977 by a Universal Primary Education scheme. Primary enrolments are now approaching 100 per cent, and the bulk of the incresed attendance has come from previously disadvantaged geographical areas and social groups.[39]

Two further ways in which efforts have been made to combat social stratification have been to alter assessment procedures inside the school and to alter the incentive structure outside it. New regulations have reduced the influence of examinations, and correspondingly increased emphasis on course work and the character of pupils. This reduces one mechanism of stratification clearly evident in Kenya, where the examination system favours urban and more affluent children. Further, Tanzania has been fortunate to have a language, Swahili, which is sufficiently widely spoken for it to become the medium of instruction throughout primary school and the principal official language. In Kenya this has not been possible, and for political and practical reasons English has had to be retained in a much more prominent place, despite its stratifying influences.

Some constraints on the Tanzanian reforms must, however, be noted. Officially, secondary pupils must have a satisfactory character record as well as academic attainment if they are to receive their school certificate. But old values are not easily abandoned, and as Court and Kinyanjui have noted, although in 1977 5 per cent of secondary Form 4 candidates fell in the lowest category of the character scale and hence were disqualified from receiving a certificate, almost all this group also failed to reach a minimum academic standard. A mere 0.1 per cent of candidates the previous year qualified on academic criteria but failed on character assessment. In other words, academic standards remained the major criteria, and only when it was 'safe' to fail pupils on character did it actually happen.[40] In the language sphere also, it has proved impossible totally to abandon English. Because of the greater availability of textbooks in English and the desire to be able to communicate with nationals of other countries, the language has been retained as the medium of instruction at post-primary levels. Thus although the stratifying effects of language have been reduced, they have not been eliminated.

The principal changes concerning incentive structures outside the school relate to a new policy which aims to allocate scarce and expensive opportunities for further training and employment according to community need for different types of expertise, and measures to reduce the financial rewards associated with formal education. To gain university admission, students must show evidence not only of academic ability but also of at least two years' work experience and a party recommendation on their character and commitment. Efforts to reduce educational imbalances have been complemented by efforts to reduce income imbalances. Whereas in 1967 the highest civil service income was twenty times the lowest, in 1977 it was only nine times the lowest.[41] Policies have also reduced differences in incomes in the non-public sector.

It should also be pointed out that in the efforts to make schools self-reliant and more closely related to their communities, policies have sought an integration of formal and nonformal educational styles. Schooling has become more oriented towards agriculture and the rural life that over 90 per cent of pupils will continue to lead, and while the remaining urban children might have a slightly different education, they too embark on self-reliant, community oriented activities. Some differences between urban and rural patterns inevitably remain. But at least at the primary level, Tanzania has generally avoided the trap of promoting nonformal education alternatives which could have become a stratifying second-best.

However, although Tanzanian policy concentrates on lower educational levels in order to spread provision widely and reduce inequalities and élitism, under the new system some differences are sharper than before. Whereas in 1967 13 per cent of pupils proceeded to post-primary training, ministry projections indicate that in the mid-1980s only 2 per cent of primary leavers will proceed to government secondary schools.[42] Thus in one sense those who do get through secondary school are even more of an élite than before. The official response has been to suggest that just because they are a minority they do not need to be exploitative, and it is hoped that the education system will shape their attitudes sufficiently for them instead to serve their communities.

While secondary education in Tanzania is more evenly spread than it is in Kenya, one clear socially stratifying mechanism remains in the shape of private schools. Enrolment in private secondary schools rose from 1,065 in 1965 to 17,196 in 1976, when there were 61 private schools in existence as compared with 81 government schools.[43] By 1981 private schools had 29,310 pupils.[44] The schools are expensive, qualitatively superior and cater principally for the more wealthy groups and more developed areas. Mainly for political reasons, however, the government has generally preferred to permit them to exist without much interference.

In conclusion, we can say that Tanzania has made major strides to fulfil its commitment to socialism and the reduction of social stratification. To this end, changes in the education system have been initiated to support wider social and economic changes. However, despite the efforts, forces tending to maintain stratification still operate. In Kenya, commitment to reduction of stratification is much less strong, and it is therefore to be expected that differences there are becoming more marked. But where efforts are made to combat stratification, the battle proves far from simple. Imbalances have arisen for historical and economic reasons, and once created, they are very difficult to remove.

Questions and project work

1 What is the meaning of 'social stratification'? Discuss, with examples, the impact of the introduction of Western education on social stratification in your country, and comment on the role of Western education today.

2 Outline the intentions of Tanzania's Arusha Declaration and Education for Self-Reliance, and comment on the implications of Tanzania's subsequent experience for educational planners in other African countries.

3 Discuss the ways in which universalization of primary education may affect social stratification in your country.

4 Obtain the most recent educational statistics for your area. From them, show the extent of (a) urban-rural inequalities; (b) male-female inequalities and (c) regional inequalities. Discuss the reasons for these inequalities and outline some ways in which they could be reduced.

Notes

1 Worsley, Peter *et al*. *Introducing Sociology*. Penguin, Harmondsworth 1978, pp. 420 ff.
2 See Chapter 2.
3 For examples of pre-colonial social structures see Suret-Canale, J. and Barry, Boubacar 'The Western Atlantic Coast to 1800' in Ajayi, J.F.A. and Crowder, Michael (eds.) *History of West Africa*. Longman, London 1976, pp. 464-6; and Smith, M.G. 'The Hausa System of Social Status'. *Africa*, Vol. 29, No. 3, 1959, passim.
4 See Sandbrook, Richard and Cohen, Robin (eds.) *The Development of an African Working Class*. Longman, London 1975; and Allen, V.L. 'The Meaning of the Working Class in Africa'. *Journal of Modern African Studies*, Vol. 10, No. 2, 1972.
5 See Yeld, E.R. 'Islam and Social Stratification in Northern Nigeria'. *British Journal of Sociology*, Vol. 11, No. 2, 1960, pp. 112-8.
6 See for example Heussler, Robert *The British in Northern Nigeria*. Oxford University Press, London 1968, p. 112 ff; and Clignet, Remi and Foster, Philip *The Fortunate Few*. Northwestern University Press, Evanston 1966, p. 34.
7 Oliver, Roland *The Missionary Factor in East Africa*. Longmans Green, London 1965, p. 212.
8 See, for example, Thomas, Roger G. 'Education in Northern Ghana, 1906-1940: A Study in Colonial Paradox'. *International Journal of African Historical Studies*, Vol. VII, No. 3, 1975; Harding, Leonhard 'Les Ecoles des Pères Blancs au Soudan Français 1895-1920. *Cahiers d'Etudes Africaines*, Vol. II, No. 41, 1971.
9 Bowles, Samuel 'Education, Class Conflict and Uneven Development' in Simmons, John (ed.) *The Education Dilemma*. Pergamon, New York 1980, p. 215.
10 The World Bank *Education Sector Policy Paper*. Washington 1980, p. 31.
11 Ibid., p. 118.
12 International Labour Office 'Interim Report on Education in a Rural Area of Western Nigeria' (mimeo). Ministry of Economic Planning and Social Development, Ibadan 1967, p. 35.
13 The World Bank, op. cit., p. 31.
14 Lloyd, Barbara B. 'Education and Family Life in the Development of Class Identification among the Yoruba' in Lloyd, P.C. (ed.) *The New Elites of Tropical Africa*. Oxford University Press, London 1966.
15 Alexander, Leigh and Simmons, John 'The Determinants of School Achievement in Developing Countries'. The World Bank, Washington 1975, pp. 51-2.
16 Federal Republic of Nigeria *Implementation Committee for the National Policy on Education: Blueprint*. Federal Ministry of Education, Lagos 1979, pp. 191, 214.
17 See Shneour, Elie A. and Shneour, Joan B. 'Malnutrition and Learning'. *Prospects*, Vol. VII, No. 1, 1977.
18 Unesco *Estimates and Projections of Illiteracy*, Paris 1978, p. 111.
19 In turn, nonformal (structured) education may be contrasted with (unstructured) informal education, such as the knowledge we gain from radios, televisions and our friends in daily conversation. See P. Coomb *et al: New Paths to Learning*. ICED, New York 1973, pp. 10-11.
20 Foster, P.J. 'The Vocational School Fallacy in Development Planning' in Anderson, C.A. and Bowman, M.J. (eds.) *Education and Economic Development*. Aldine, Chicago 1966, p. 145.

21 Ranger, Terence 'African Attempts to Control Education in East and Central Africa 1900–1939'. *Past and Present*, No. 32, 1965, pp. 57–85; Abernethy, D.B. *The Political Dilemma of Popular Education*, Stanford University Press, Stanford 1969, p. 73. For another view, however, see Echerno, Michael J.C. *Victorian Lagos*. Macmillan, London 1977, pp. 59–66.

22 See for example Sheffield, James R. and Diejomaoh, Victor P. *Non-Formal Education in African Development*. African-American Institute, New York 1972, p. 204, Farrar, Curtis 'AID's Policies for Education and Rural Development' in Niehoff, Richard O. (ed.) *Non-Formal Education and the Rural Poor*. Michigan State University, East Lansing 1977, p. 38.

23 Simkins, Tim *Non-Formal Education and Development*. Department of Adult and Higher Education, University of Manchester 1977, p. 35. See also Colclough, C. and Hallak, J. 'Some Issues in Rural Education: Equity, Efficiency and Employment'. *Prospects*, Vol. VI, No. 4, 1976.

24 The World Bank, op. cit., p. 26.

25 Court, David and Kinyanjui, Kabiru 'Development Policy and Educational Opportunity: The Experience of Kenya and Tanzania' in Carron, Gabriel and Ta Ngoc Chau (eds.) *Regional Disparities in Educational Development*. Unesco/IIEP, Paris 1980, p. 341.

26 Court and Kinyanjui, op. cit., p. 339.

27 Somerset, Anthony 'Aptitude Tests, Socio-Economic Background, and Secondary School Selection: The Possibilities and Limits of Change'. Paper Presented at the Social Science Research Council conference, Bellagio 1977, p. 4.

28 From Court and Kinyanjui, op. cit., p. 350.

29 The enrolment rates in Table 4.4 are swollen by school attendance of over-and under-aged pupils.

30 Court and Kinyanjui, op. cit., p. 348.

31 Maas, J. and Criel, G. *Distribution of Primary School Enrolments in Eastern Africa*. The World Bank, Washington 1982, p. 47.

32 Court and Kinyanjui, op. cit., p. 357.

33 Ibid., p. 357.

34 Republic of Kenya *Development Plan 1974–1978*. Government Printer, Nairobi 1974, Pt. I, p. 3.

35 King, Kenneth 'Development and Education in the Narok District of Kenya'. *African Affairs*, Vol. 71, No. 285, 1972, pp. 397–9.

36 Nyerere, Julius *Education for Self-Reliance*. Ministry of Information and Tourism, Dar es Salaam 1967, p. 1.

37 Ibid., pp. 10–15.

38 Hall, Budd L. *Adult Education and the Development of Socialism in Tanzania*. East African Literature Bureau, Dar es Salaam 1975, p. 97.

39 Carr-Hill, Roy *Primary Education in Tanzania: A Review of the Research*. Swedish International Development Authority, Stockholm 1984, pp. 19–21.

40 Court and Kinyanjui, op. cit., p. 387.

41 Nyerere, Julius *The Arusha Declaration Ten Years After*. Government Printer, Dar es Salaam 1977, p. 16.

42 Court and Kinyanjui, op. cit., p. 393.

43 Ibid., p. 391.

44 Carr-Hill, op. cit., p. 83.

Chapter 5

Islamic education: continuity and change

This chapter surveys the history of Islamic education in sub-Saharan Africa, and analyses the structure and goals of Islamic education. It discusses Islamic educational theory and school organization, the interaction between the Islamic and Western systems of education, and the role of Islamic education, as Muslims themselves understand it, in the processes of development and nation building.

The growth of Islamic education in Africa

Islam has a long history in Africa, and its education system has operated much longer than the Western one. A Muslim presence was established in North Africa in the seventh century, and in the eighth century Islam began to spread along the trade routes into the western, central and eastern Sudan, the Horn of Africa and East Africa. By the close of the ninth century Arab immigrants had established an Islamic state at Shoa in the Horn of Africa, and by thirteenth century there were several Muslim kingdoms in this region. One of these kingdoms controlled the port of Zayla on the Somali coast, and by the early fourteenth century Muslim students from Zayla were attending the Islamic University of al-Azhar in Cairo. Ibn Battuta (AD 1304–1369) was a widely travelled North African Muslim scholar who visited Somalia in AD 1331. Mogadishu, he wrote, was 'a town endless in size' which was ruled by a Muslim, Sultan Abu Bakr.[1] Ibn Battuta was given accommodation in a house for students of Islamic religious studies, and he noted the recognition and use of Islamic law.

Likewise, by the tenth and eleventh centuries AD communities of Muslim merchants and scholars had been established in several commercial centres in the Western Sahara and Sahel. By the end of the eleventh century the rulers of kingdoms such as Takrur, Ancient Ghana, Kanem-Borno and Gao had converted to Islam, and had appointed Muslims who were literate in Arabic as advisers.[2] From the fourteenth century the Timbuktu region was also a centre of Islamic learning, exerting an influence far into modern-day Mali and Mauritania.

Centres of higher Islamic education have also existed for many centuries. Even before the world-famous al-Azhar University was founded in Cairo in AD 996, the Qarawiyyin school was established in

Morocco. In addition to Timbuktu other towns in West Africa such as Shingiti, Jenne, Agades, Kano and N'gazargamu became well known and influential centres of Islamic learning during the period from the thirteenth to the seventeenth centuries.

During the present century the Islamic education system has had to compete with the Western one. In the early years of the century there were many more students in Islamic schools than in Western ones. In Guinea, for example, in 1910 there were about 6,400 Qur'anic schools with 27,000 pupils, but hardly any Western schools.[3] However the statistics for Guinea show a decline in Qur'anic schools and a growth of Western ones. This situation has been paralleled in other countries.

Nevertheless, in parts of Mauritania and Mali there are still more pupils in Qur'anic schools than in Western ones. Efforts have also been made in several countries to modernise and strengthen the Islamic system. Key institutions for this have been the Islamic University in Khartoum (Sudan) the Islamic Institute in Dakar (Senegal), the Islamic Institute of Higher Learning in Boutilimit (Mauritania), and the Islamic Education Centre in Kano (Nigeria).

Although aspects of the system have been criticized both by Muslims and non-Muslims, it offers an unique approach to learning and life. It is also held in high esteem both for what it has accomplished in the past and for what it can contribute to African societies today. Particularly notable is the contribution of Islamic education to countries which are attempting to decolonize, to industrialize and to build national unity.

Some distinctive features of the Islamic education system

The Islamic education system has several distinctive features which should be contrasted with those of the Western system. The Islamic system is in many respects far less dependent for its operation on specific administrative, institutional and organizational patterns. It also tends to be much more flexible and, as one scholar comments, has an 'admirable leisureliness'.[4] For example, whereas in the Western system people speak negatively about 'perpetual students', in the Islamic system education is seen as an unending process and an individual can remain a student till old age or death. Some Islamic teachers prefer older and more mature students 'who have already shown evidence both of piety and of responsibility'.[5]

The Islamic education system also puts less emphasis on certificates or diplomas than does the Western one. However, paper qualifications do exist in the Islamic system. The *ijaza*, for example, is a diploma given by a master to his students, and allows a student to teach with authority. Linked to it is the *isnad*. This is a list of names of those who have handed down a tradition or who have taught a given work, which validates the ijaza. A student can find out how prestigious his teacher is by looking at the names of the scholars who appear on the teacher's isnad. If these scholars have a high reputation, then the teacher will also be highly respected.

The theory of Islamic education is found in the Qur'an and in the *hadith* or traditions of the Prophet Mohammed. One hadith states that 'the quest for learning is a duty incumbent on every Muslim male and female', and another that 'wisdom is the goal of the believer and he must seek it irrespective of its source'.[6] Other hadiths describe learning and wisdom as equal to worship, and of men of learning as successors to the prophets. For example, one hadith states that 'God eases the way to paradise for him who seeks learning', and another states that 'angels spread their wings for the seeker of learning as a mark of God's approval or his purpose'.[7]

Muslims have a long tradition of travel in search of knowledge. The origin of this practice is linked to the geographical spread of Islam. In order to verify whether a hadith was authentic, it was often necessary to travel long distances to question and learn from authorities. Muslims in Africa have been travelling in search of authorities for more than twelve centuries. The Tunisian Muslim scholar Ibn Khaldun (1332–1406) wrote that a scholar's education was greatly improved by travelling in quest of knowledge because 'habits acquired through contact with a teacher are more strongly and firmly rooted' than those acquired through other study and lectures.[8] We know that Usuman dan Fodio (1754–1817), the Muslim reformer from northern Nigeria, travelled to Niger in 1774 to study under Shaikh Jibril Umar.[9] The practice of travel continues today, little changed.

Although most Muslim children attend Qur'anic schools, attendance is not usually universal, even at the basic level. Students can attend and leave as they see fit, and registration is not compulsory. Students may leave schools and join others if they want particular subject specialisms.

The time at which classes in Islamic schools begin varies, and is arranged by individual teachers. Two sessions are usually held each day, one in the morning and the other in the afternoon. Sometimes a third evening session is held for pupils unable to attend during the day, often round a bonfire. The existence of evening sessions makes it possible for children to attend both primary and Qur'anic schools. Classes are held from Saturdays to Wednesdays, with holidays on Thursdays and Fridays.

Parents can pay for their children's education by giving the teacher a gift or donation. If they cannot afford to do this they can still send their children to Qur'anic schools, and the children pay their way by working on the teacher's farm and by performing a number of other tasks such as collecting firewood. If a student from a very poor background wants to continue his education after Qur'anic school he may simply place himself in bondage to his teacher till he completes his studies and becomes a teacher himself.

Although the system we have just described is more common, some communities do charge a fixed fee for Qur'anic education. One can find a precedent for this far back in Islamic history. In the ninth century AD the Islamic specialist in law, Ibn Sahnun, wrote about the work of teachers. His writing, it has been suggested, shows that the practice of charging fees had already become well established, at least in Tunisia, by the ninth century AD.[10] Al Ghazali, however, who was a Persian (Iranian) authority and lived from AD 1058 to 1111, maintained that a Muslim teacher should not accept payment for teaching religious subjects, but could be paid for teaching such 'extra' subjects as mathematics and medicine. The teaching of religious subjects, in Al Ghazali's opinion, was a personal duty of the believer and should be done without charging fees. This does not, of course, prevent the student from working for his Qur'anic teacher or the student's parents from giving the teacher gifts in recognition for what he has done for their child.

The curriculum

There are basically two types of Islamic schools: the Qur'anic and the Ilm. These schools can be located almost anywhere, for instance under the shade of a tree, in a private house, or in a mosque. The Qur'anic school is equivalent to the Western primary school, and the Ilm School to the Western secondary school.

The age at which children begin Qur'anic school varies. Among the Dyula communities in Mali, Guinea, Burkina Faso and the Ivory Coast, the children usually begin Qur'anic school at the age of six, while among the Jakhanke in Senegal and the Gambia they may begin as early as three.[11] In some cases a formal ceremony takes place on the day a pupil is first admitted to the Qur'anic school. In Jakhanke schools the pupils' heads are shaved, and the words 'in the name of Allah' are written on the palms of their hands.[12] The pupils lick the sacred writing while the ink is still fresh. Then they stretch out their hands to receive small balls of pounded grain which are taken home and given to first their fathers and then their mothers. This seems to indicate that the child has in some sense been 'bought' by the teacher. At the later passing out ceremony the parents 'buy back' their child.

There is some variation in the curriculum of the Qur'anic school, but in most of Islamic Africa it is strikingly uniform. Al Ghazali, the Iranian scholar whom we have just mentioned, had a profound influence on the curriculum of the Islamic schools and universities throughout the world. According to his philosophy, learning contains two elements. There is human reasoning, which involves an effort of mind and body, and there is divine illumination. The latter is more important, but it does not eliminate the need for clear thinking and careful observation. Al Ghazali also insisted on the need for physical exercise. He wrote: 'After school the pupil must be allowed to play . . . To prevent play and to insist on continuous study leads to dullness in the heart, diminution in intelligence and unhappiness'.[13]

Ibn Khaldun had a similar philosophy. He recommended that knowledge should be linked to the capacity of the learner and should be imparted gradually. Ibn Khaldun felt that learning consisted in discovering and understanding the meaning of the spoken and written word, and in building up rules to show the connections between different meanings. This, Ibn Khaldun recognized, is a difficult task even for the advanced student. To the student in difficulty he offered this advice: 'Abandon all artificial means of learning and appeal to your rational innate reason . . .

Seek God's guidance which . . . illuminated the way of learners before you and taught them that which they knew not'.[14]

At the intellectual level, Qur'anic education chiefly consists of memorizing the Qur'an. For this purpose the Qur'an is usually divided into 60 parts. The method employed in memorization may vary slightly, and depends to some extent on the availability of blackboards, chalk, ink, and paper or slates. Of course it also depends on the competence, qualifications and dedication of the teacher. In Jahanke (Senegambian) schools, the teacher begins with the letters of the Arabic alphabet, the vowel sounds, and writing.[15] Then, starting with the shortest chapter (*sura*), the pupil goes on to learn the Qu'ran by heart. Some pupils take five years to complete this process, and others take longer. The process of memorizing the Qur'an is divided into five stages, and completion of each stage is marked by a ceremony.

The curriculum of the Qur'anic school has often been strongly criticized. Ibn Khaldun, for example, felt that to restrict students to learning the Qur'an by heart was fruitless. He argued that 'a person who [only] knows the Qur'an does not acquire the habit of the Arabic language. It will be his lot to be awkward in expression and to have little fluency in speaking'.[16] He seems to have preferred the method of instruction and the curriculum used in Qur'anic schools in Spain, where the emphasis was on poetry, composition, arithmetic and Arabic grammar, and where the student went on to detailed study of the Qur'an after having studied these subjects.[17] Other observers in more recent times have made similar judgements, suggesting that the instruction of Qur'anic schools has little pedagogical value, and pointing out that in many communities which do not use Arabic in everyday life the students do not even understand the meaning of the words they chant.

Some people, however, evaluate matters differently. For example Wilks' study of Islamic learning in Mali, Guinea, Burkina Faso, Ivory Coast and Ghana suggests that many of the criticisms of the Qur'anic schools are too severe. It points out that the schools do provide at least a grounding in Arabic, which can be built on by those who have the interest and ability, and maintains that 'a talented and well taught pupil will rapidly acquire a command of Arabic, and in his early teens may be studying grammar and syntax, and reading basic works of law'.[18] The schools also teach students to respect their elders and the culture of which they are a part.

After Qur'anic school some students go on to an Ilm school of higher learning. In these schools students of all ages learn a wide range of Islamic literary, theological and legal subjects. Many Ilm schools trace their origins back several hundred years. Mauritania, for example, had Ilm schools as far back as the thirteenth century.

In the Ilm schools the formal curriculum consists of tafsir, which is basically the interpretation of the Qur'an, and the study of literature, much of which has been derived from Qur'anic commentary. The study of hadith is also a central part of the Ilm school curriculm. These traditions cover subjects such as marriage, divorce, inheritance, and personal conduct. They give the student a clear idea of the behaviour expected from an orthodox Muslim, and insight into how an Islamic society should be organized, administered and governed.

Ilm students also study *fiqh*, which is the theory of Islamic sacred law (*Shari'a*). The Qur'an is believed to contain the whole of the Shari'a, and many Muslims feel all that is required from the legal experts is interpretation and advice on how to apply it. For example the Qur'an prescribes the payment of an alms-tax, but since it does not specify how much or on what possessions, legal experts are needed to provide advice. The Shari'a occupies a central position in Islamic society, for upon it depends not only people's status, duties and rights, but also their prospects of eternal reward or punishment. The Shari'a, moreover, is believed to apply not only to Muslims but to all mankind.

Ilm students also learn Arabic and about various types of literature. For example, the literature includes *madih*, which mostly consists of praises addressed to the Prophet Mohammed. There is also *sira* literature in either prose or verse, which contains stories about the life of the Prophet. Wa'z is another type of literature which describes the Islamic notions of paradise and hell. Not every Ilm school teaches all these subjects. Some schools specialize, and gain the reputation as the best ones for the study of particular subjects or for groups of subjects.

In some parts of Africa, students who graduate from the Ilm school are allowed to wear a turban and are henceforth regarded as being among the *ulama*, the men of learning. The title given to these people varies. Among the Malinke-speaking people of West Africa they are known as *Karamokos*, while among the Hausa they are called *malamai*. The Swahili word for teacher is *Mwalimu*. It no longer necessarily implies that the teacher is a Muslim, but the word has the same origin as ulama and malam.

When they complete Ilm school, some students go on to further studies in fiqh or hadith. Others become assistants to an established teacher, while others establish their own schools. Some may acquire positions as *imams* (prayer leaders in the local community) or judges.

The education of women in Islam

We have written so far as if learning and teaching were exclusively male activities in Muslim societies. Though in practice some Muslim societies have given this impression, it is certainly not the case in theory. On the right of Muslim women to receive education, Muslim scholars cite verses of the Qur'an such as Chapter 9 verse 39 and refer to several hadiths. They also point out that the Prophet Mohammed's wife Aisha was an Islamic scholar. Usuman dan Fodio, the Muslim reformer from Hausaland, spoke out against the neglect of women's education, and in Egypt in the nineteenth century there were at least two strong protagonists of women's education. One was Rifa'ah al Tahtawi who called for the provision of the same educational facilities for women as for men, and the other was the lawyer Quasim Amin. In more recent times in Nigeria, Usman Nagogo,

Isa Wali and Aminu Kano, among others, have emphasised the right and even the duty of women to be educated.

Women also have the right to teach. Usuman dan Fodio wrote of Muslim widows in Nigeria being employed by the wealthy to teach their families and added that they also had 'a collection of children mainly girls to teach in their homes in addition to teaching the grown-ups'.[19] Usuman dan Fodio's own daughter Khadija gave lessons on Islamic law and the Qur'an, and wrote poetry. His other daughter Asama'u Nana also wrote poetry and taught Islamic religious knowledge. In this century there have been several well-known Muslim women teachers in Nigeria. Among them were Malama Dada in Kano, who taught both men and women, and Malama Atika from Zaria. In 1977 a Women's Arabic Teachers' College was opened in Kano specifically to train female teachers of Islamic religious knowledge.[20] Many Muslims accept, however, that in general there has either been serious neglect or at the very least insufficient attention given to the subject of women's education.[21]

Teacher-student relations in the Islamic education system

Although many Qur'anic teachers are understanding and gentle with their pupils, the majority are commonly said to be harsh taskmasters who punish students severely. Recalling his own education, for example, Sanneh refers to one time he incurred his teacher's displeasure:

> He called me one morning and asked whether I had finished reciting the portion of the Koran he had copied out on my slate the previous day. I said I had memorised it, and when he asked me to recite it in front of him I did so, whereupon he directed me to wash off the old material so that my slate was clean and ready for the new material. During our midday recitations he asked if I had washed my slate. When I answered 'Yes', he asked me to bring it to him. I brought the wooden slate to him, but the Arabic characters were still faintly visible on it. That was not really my fault because the ink we used for writing was manufactured by ourselves, and we obtained it by scraping the undersides of cooking pots. There was not always a plentiful supply of the substance, so that we often ended by scraping off more than just the soft black soot on the surface. The harder material was difficult to remove once it had dried on the wooden slates, and this is what had happened in my case. I had scrubbed the stubborn surface with all my strength but had not realised that the wet surface concealed the faint characters which, I must admit, were clearly visible after I had dried the slate.
>
> Teacher was furious. . . . He pulled both my ears and I crawled on the ground towards him. . . . With my two ears firmly in his hand he could balance me on either side of him as he pleased. He swayed me to the right at arm's length, and when I tried to recover my balance, he closed in with a powerful left-hand swipe. Then he grabbed me by the ears again, pinched me tightly and shook me firmly as if to test his grasp on the substance of power.[22]

Sanneh also records that this type of treatment was supported by his father, who felt that one of the chief purposes of the Qur'anic school was to instil discipline and respect. Such an attitude, one might add, is not uncommon.

Nevertheless, harsh aspects of discipline have not always been approved. Al Ghazali, who was one of the greatest of all Islamic educational theorists, stated that the Islamic teacher was the spiritual father of his students and should give advice rather than reproof, correcting moral lapses 'through hinting rather than direct prohibition'.[23] Likewise Ibn Khaldun felt that: 'Severe punishment in the course of instruction does harm to the student, especially to little children. . . . It makes them oppressed and causes them to lose energy. It makes them lazy and induces them to lie and be insincere.'[24] Ibn Khaldun did not rule out corporal punishment entirely, but recommended that 'if children must be beaten, their educator must not strike them more than three times'.[25] Many present-day educators agree with this view, and would like the atmosphere of Qur'anic schools to be based much more on confidence than fear.

The status and public role of the Islamic teacher

Teachers are obviously indispensable in Islamic societies, because the transmission of knowledge of the Qur'an, hadith, Shari'a and Arabic is essential to the Islamic religion and way of life. Islamic teachers generally hold a high social status because of their learning and their ability to make charms and to divine. At the same time, however, Islamic tradition expects them to live simply and without ostentation. Of course the situation could hardly be otherwise, given that that Islamic teachers have a duty to teach religious knowledge without being paid for it.

In the past, and still in many parts of Africa today, very few books existed. This meant that the Islamic teacher was effectively the only library available to students. Even where there are books today, the teacher is widely seen as the only one capable of guiding students to and through them. Knowledge, it is widely believed, requires a mediator who has thought about it and internalized it in his memory. Among Muslims there exists a belief that 'an independent approach to the written word is fraught with mystical dangers'.[26] The teacher is therefore needed to interpret and transmit the knowledge.

The status of Islamic teachers may be illustrated by comments made by some young men in Northern Nigeria. These youths stated that when their teacher was present, they never drank alcohol, smoked, roamed about with women, or wore European or tight clothes. Tight clothes, they explained, were unacceptable because 'by wearing them you show your body'. They said that if their teacher found them out, he would scold them, tell their parents, and inform the whole village of their bad behaviour.[27]

This situation is changing, however, and the status of the Islamic teacher is generally deteriorating. The decline is being slowed by the work of a few institutions. The Islamic Institute in Dakar, for example, was opened in 1974 and has greatly improved the qualifications and skills of teachers in the Islamic schools of Senegal. However, many youth are affected by Western culture and technology, and in general they do not give Islamic teachers as much respect as their counterparts did in former times.

The goals and relevance of Islamic education

Although we have already said a great deal about the goals and relevance of Islamic education, it is useful to enlarge on some issues and to pull threads together. First, we should distinguish between three types of goals in the system: instrumental, expressive and normative.

Goals are instrumental when they are merely the means, or instrument, for achieving something else. For example, pupils may see education just as a way to get certificates, which in turn they can use to get jobs. Education becomes simply a means to a particular end for the individual concerned. Thus instrumental goals generally encourage students to be individualistic and competitive rather than to cooperate and work in groups.

In contrast, expressive goals seek to create unity, cohesion, equality and common identity among students. They are expressive because they express some ideal. And normative goals are concerned with the development of standard beliefs and patterns of behaviour through learning.

We have already mentioned that the Islamic system places less emphasis on examinations and diplomas than does the Western system. In general, therefore, it places less emphasis on instrumental goals and more on expressive and normative ones than does the Western system. Ibn Khaldun stressed the importance of normative goals when he stated: 'The basis of all the traditional sciences is the legal material of the Qur'an and the Sunna, which is the law given us by God and his messenger.'[28]

Secondly, we should ask what relevance, if any, the Islamic education system has for modern African states striving to overcome the problems of underdevelopment. Several authors have argued that Islam hinders development, and we should consider whether their views are reasonable or not.

Max Weber was one critic of Islam. His arguments were partly based on the low priority that Islam places on instrumental goals.[29] He suggested that the religion was dominated by a warlike morality, and felt that its emphasis on conflict and its rigid hold over its members restricted the growth of capitalist attitudes and business activities. He contrasted this with the outlook of Protestant Christianity which, he said, was likely to be much more competitive and individualistic. Weber also felt that Islam encouraged conservative economic and political systems to remain so and that many of the systems suffered from contradictions which were only occasionally challenged by radical forces.

This view was largely shared by Marx and Engels, who described Islam as 'anti-developmental' and 'anti-modernizing'. Engels maintained that the French conquest of Algeria was 'an important and fortunate fact for the progress of civilisation', and he claimed that the French brought 'industry, order and at least relative enlightenment', to a 'barbarous' society.[30] Marx and Engels described capitalism as a dynamic force which introduced necessary changes into stagnant societies in danger of extinction. They viewed Islamic administrative structures as rigid and inflexible, in contrast to what they considered the progressive and civilised structures of the colonising powers.

More recently, Claude Lévi-Strauss has criticised the legal and inflexible philosophy of Islam. He has argued that Islam is set in contemplation of a society which only existed many centuries ago, and that it attempts to solve the problems of the modern world with arguments, logic and solutions which are no longer relevant.[31]

These views should not necessarily be accepted, however. Weber's idea that Islam is dominated by a warrior class whose life-style and interests determine its philosophical and religious outlook is certainly a misinterpretation. As Ali Mazrui has pointed out, the reason why Islam did not encourage attitudes similar to the Christian capitalists was not because it was dominated by a warrior ethic but because it was dominated by the expressive goals of communal loyalty to members of the family and to members of the same religious group. Mazrui also points out that the Islamic laws of inheritance prevented accumulation of capital and the growth of large estates in a way that did not occur among the Christians.[32]

Moreover, these factors do not necessarily make Islam an 'anti-modernizing' force. Certainly the religion discourages individualism and accumulation of wealth and property. However, if 'modernity' is considered to include socialism and communalism, Islam is very progressive.

Further, not all historians and sociologists agree with Marx and Engels. Two Nigerian historians, for example, claim that Islam, albeit unintentionally, 'brought to Nigeria the concept of a nation state transcending the personal bounds of loyalty to clan, a traditional ruler, or particular locality'.[33] The aim of the nineteenth-century Muslim reformers in West Africa – Usuman dan Fodio in Northern Nigeria, and Al-Hajj Umar and Ma Ba Diakhou in the Senegambia to name but three – was 'ecumenical'. Their objective was to re-create the Muslim community of the time of the first four Caliphs, which was an era known as the 'Golden Age of Islam'. One consequence of their work was the emergence of 'larger political systems with new economic opportunities and the establishment of new religious obligations and social values'.[34] From this perspective, Islam in West Africa was a more significant revolutionary force than was the attempt inspired by Christian ideals to substitute legitimate commerce for the slave trade.[35]

In the Senegambia there has also existed a strong alliance between the Islamic brotherhoods and the government, which has helped develop the groundnut economy, the transport network and the system of cooperatives. The leader of the Mouride brotherhood, Ahmadu Bamba, transformed senegambian Islam in the early years of the present century by his teaching about the 'sanctification of labour'.[36] According to Bamba, work was more important than prayer. This philosophy also influenced the Tijaniyya brotherhood, who comprised over a million people.

Finally, it is worth summarizing the way Muslims expect the Islamic education system to encourage community and national development in Africa. First, they suggest that the real problems of nation building and underdevelopment have an important moral dimension. As one Nigerian Muslim expressed it when commenting on the proposals for a new constitution in his country: 'The bitter truth is that our nation is in dire need of complete mobilization more than anything else. . . . I bet even if "Operation Feed the Nation" results in plenty of food in the country, the nation at large will never benefit from it unless and until attitudes change. And it is only through moral and spiritual training that the people can change for good.'[37] Many Muslims thus believe that Islam can make a major contribution to development by strengthening the morals of the nation.

Secondly, many Muslims argue that Islam can provide community, society, dignity and personal identity in the chaos created by industrialization. The education system, they suggest, is an essential instrument for achieving this. Thirdly, many people claim that Islamic law is an effective weapon against such crimes as murder, theft and rape, which are becoming more common with industrialization. They also claim that Islam's commercial, financial and economic code of practices would, if implemented, rid Africa of the worst abuses of the capitalist system. Finally, emphasizing that Islam is independent of both Marxism and Western capitalism, some Muslims claim that the divinely inspired Islamic socialist system is the most appropriate one for the developing nations of Africa. This, they say, is because people will only accept a socialist ideology that contains a supernatural dimension. These arguments may not be universally applicable, but they are important and should be noted.

We can now turn to a detailed consideration of the development of Islamic education in Nigeria, which has a very large and diverse Muslim population. It is instructive to see how Islamic education has responded to the challenges posed by Western education and modernization.

Case study: Islamic education in Nigeria

The Islamic education system has a long history in Nigeria, especially in the north. For example it has existed for many centuries in the northern districts of Borno, Kano and Katsina, and was only seriously challenged in recent times. N'gazargamu, the former capital of the Borno Kingdom, had four central mosques in the seventeenth century, all of which ran Qur'anic schools. The rulers possessed excellent libraries, and gave Muslim scholars considerable privileges, including exemption from tax and military service. Islamic teachers had considerable moral and religious authority in the towns and villages.

The Islamic reform movement, also known as the Sokoto jihad (holy war), began in the eighteenth century and contributed a great deal to Islamic education in northern Nigeria. Literacy in Arabic was spread over a wide area, and this made it possible for many more people to read the Qur'an. The reform movement also led to greater concern over the education of women, to the establishment of Islamic schools, and to the training of Islamic teachers.

In northern Nigeria a sound Islamic education became one of the principal vehicles of upward social mobility, through which many people became clerks, scribes and judges. This has to be taken into consideration when assessing the Muslim response to Western education. So also does the fact that for Muslims an Islamic education system was not simply an option that could be replaced with another system, even if the latter appeared to be more relevant and effective. The establishment and maintenance of Islamic schools was a divine obligation. Moreover the institutions were considered an integral part of Muslim society and the most important means of sustaining Islamic faith and culture. For these reasons a very large proportion of Nigerian Muslims, especially in the north, continue to put great emphasis on Islamic education.[38]

In the mid-1960s there were 27,600 Qur'anic schools in northern Nigeria, and 2,800 Ilm schools.[39] Some of them were long established, dating back to the time of Shaikh Usuman dan Fodio (1754–1817), and many, like the Gwarrio Fara Ilm school in Zaria city, had gained a reputation for excellence that drew pupils from all parts of northern Nigeria.

Attempts at reform and modernization

Usuman dan Fodio's reform movement was primarily concerned with improving the religious and intellectual climate in Hausaland, which required the reform and modernization of the education system.[40] This objective was taken up again in the colonial era, and has received considerable attention since then. Reform and modernization, of course, have meant different things to different people in different historical circumstances.

One approach to modernization and reform adopted by the government during the colonial era was to integrate the Islamic and Western systems of education. The principal idea was to introduce into the Islamic curriculum a limited number of new subjects, particularly arithmetic and literacy in the Roman script. This approach, adopted in both northern and southern Nigeria, was considered to have two main advantages. First it avoided the expense of operating the Islamic and Western education systems separately, and second the system remained recognizably Islamic and it was therefore much easier for at least some Muslims to adapt to Western education.[41] The government also felt that the strategy was a good way to introduce new teaching methods into the Islamic education system.

In southern Nigeria, the government at the end of the last century attempted to avoid the close association of Western education with the work of Christian missionaries by sponsoring several schools for Muslims in which Western subjects were taught alongside the Islamic sciences. Schools were opened in Lagos in 1896, at Badagry in 1898, and at Epe in 1899. Before this date no Epe Muslim had ever attended a school in which Western subjects formed part of the syllabus, but 150 enrolled when the government Muslim school was opened.[42] The system was not given adequate financial backing, however, and collapsed within a few years.

More important efforts at integration have also been made by several Islamic societies. In some respects, Muslims have found themselves in a dilemma. If their children attend Western, Christian schools they might abandon Islam. On the other hand if they attend Muslim schools which teach only Islamic subjects, their children would not have the skills demanded in a society undergoing rapid modernization. To resolve this dilemma the Ansar-ud-Deen society was established in 1923. By 1960 it had a membership of 50,000 and had opened over 200 primary schools plus several secondary schools and teachers' colleges.[43]

The Ahmadiyya movement, which emerged in India in the 1880s and made its first contacts with Nigeria in 1911, has similar educational objectives to the Ansar-ud-Deen society and has also had a major impact.[44] The movement has inspired its followers to repond positively to the challenge of Western education by establishing Islamic schools which include Western subjects in the curriculum and use Western styles of teaching. Ahmadiyya schools have been opened in Lagos, Ibadan, Ijebu-Ode, Jos, Kano and other Nigerian cities, and the movement's influence in education has spread to Sierra Leone, Liberia, Ghana, the Gambia and Mali.[45]

However, the Ahmadiyya movement is regarded by Sunni Muslims as heretical, because it teaches that its founder, Ghulam Ahmad, was the promised Messiah and Mahdi. This belief is unacceptable to orthodox Muslims, who believe that Mohammed was the last of the prophets. The rejection of the Ahmadiyya beliefs has been one reason why some orthodox Muslims have also rejected attempts to integrate Western and Islamic education, for they associate one with the other. Other leaders have focused on the curriculum, and have criticized what they consider to be the neglect of Arabic and Islamic education. Ādam 'Ab Allah al-Ilūri from southern Nigeria, and Ibrahim Niass, who was himself Senegalese but who led the 'reformed' Tijaniyya movement which has many followers in northern Nigeria, were among the critics.[46]

It was, moreover, especially clear in the case of the unorthodox Ahmadiyya movement that the reform and modernization of the Islamic education system was not simply a matter of educational method and the introduction into the curriculum of Western subjects. It also involved doctrinal issues and questions concerning the correct practice of the faith. In other cases, as we shall see, it would involve political matters.

We can now turn again to northern Nigeria, where the government at first decided to leave the Islamic education system intact and to build up alongside a separate government-controlled Western education system. Then in the 1920s the attempt at integration got under way. Arabic became part of the curriculum in most government middle schools in the early 1930s, and at the same time provision was made for Qur'anic instruction in all schools in northern Nigeria. Integration at a higher level of the education system began with the establishment of the Shahuci judicial school in Kano in 1928. This institution aimed to broaden the education of malams from Kano and elsewhere, many of whom were employed in the Shari'a courts. Instruction was in Hausa and Arabic, and arithmetic and a small amount of English were taught alongside the traditional Islamic subjects. Then in 1934 the government opened the Kano Law School, which in 1947 became the Kano School for Arabic Studies. At the outset the Kano Law School taught all the Islamic sciences and arithmetic, and drew its students from all over northern Nigeria.

It was after the Second World War that some of the most interesting and significant efforts were made to reform and modernize the Islamic education system in the north. Once again it was Muslims themselves who led the way. Aminu Kano, for example, was a qualified teacher in both the Islamic and Western education systems, and for many years until his death in 1983 was a prominent politician. Aminu opened a school in Kano in 1950. Persuaded that 'modern' teaching methods could achieve better results in much less time, he provided his pupils with lessons in the Qur'an and Abrabic in the first year, and in the second year alongside these subjects he introduced arithmetic and literacy in the Roman script. This made it unnecessary for children to transfer from the Qur'anic school to an elementary or primary school.

These schools proved popular at first, and in the 1950s around 60 were established throughout northern Nigeria. However political opponents came to see them as a challenge, and through hostile campaigning forced the majority to close down.[47] The situation improved when Sir Ahmadu Bello, premier of Northern Nigeria (1960–1966) set about the reform of the Qur'anic school system. A special ministerial committee, set up to consider the reform, recommended that Qur'anic schools be organized into classes according to age, year of entry and ability of the pupils, and that arithmetic and literacy in the Roman script should be included in the syllabus alongside the study of the Qur'an and Arabic. Schools which complied with these recommendations were given financial incentives to improve their buildings and equipment, and an honorarium for the teachers (malams). Very little further development took place after the assassination of Ahmadu Bello in 1966, however, and in practice only a few schools benefitted from the financial assistance.

Reforms were also attempted at the level of the Ilm schools. These reforms were in many respects simply an extension to the secondary level of the educational model developed by Aminu Kano. They formed part of what has come to be known as the Islamiyya school system, a system proposed by the Northern Muslim Congress (NMC) which was established in Kano in 1950.[48] Later in the 1960s Ahmadu Bello's reforms included a provision for the payment of grants to Ilm schools that included English and Hausa in the curriculum. Small grants were also made available for the building of classrooms and the partial payment of salaries of qualified teachers.[49]

By the late 1970s some 65 Islamiyya schools had been established in northern Nigeria, a majority of them in Kano, by individuals, societies and whole communities concerned for the education and general welfare of the young. They adopted a five day week from Saturday to Wednesday. Some Islamiyya schools offered four year courses while others made provision for courses lasting six or even seven years. In this way they replicated the middle school and the secondary school systems. The schools tended to attract a relatively large number of female students, for they offered an acceptable alternative to many parents anxious about the values of the other school systems.

In some instances the problems encountered in educating girls were overcome by the establishment of single sex schools such as the Girls' Grammar School in Ibadan founded in the 1950s by Alhaja Humana Alaga, leader of the Isabatudeen (Band of Religious Enthusiasts) society. Included in the curriculum alongside Islamic knowledge were Arabic, English language and literature, history, geography and domestic science. Elaborating on the reasons for establishing this school, Alhaja Humana spoke of the difficulties she encountered in getting her own daughters into mission-run schools, of the need to give Muslims greater confidence in themselves, and of her desire to raise the status of Muslim women.[50]

In both the north and the south, however, attempts at modernizing the Qur'anic and other tiers of the Islamic education system did not meet with the approval of all Muslims. Ibrahim Niass, the Senegalese Muslim leader with a large following among members of the 'reformed' Tijaniyya brotherhood, saw no need for Western education and insisted that Arabic literacy and religious education alone were indispensible for achieving the aims of the brotherhood.[51] Niass and his representatives in Nigeria did much from the 1950s onwards to encourage Islamic education, the education of Muslim women, and the spread of literacy in Arabic and Hausa.

An institution which played a central role in this spread of literacy in Arabic and Hausa in northern Nigeria was the Zawiya system developed by both the Tijaniyya and Qaderiyya brotherhoods. The Zawiya serves a number of functions and is to be found in both urban and rural areas. It is in essence a centre where members of a brotherhood travelling from one town or village to another can obtain accommodation. It also functions as a school. In the urban areas like Kano city the Zawiya may provide advanced classes in Islamic studies, and in rural areas a basic training in the fundamentals of Islamic faith and practice. Moreover in both cases the Zawiya may also function as a library and an extremely important channel of communication. To take as an example the 'reformed' Tijaniyya led by Ibrahim Niass, an extensive Zawiya network was established across northern Nigeria and indeed throughout West Africa, making possible the spread of literacy in Arabic, and Hausa in the Nigerian context, on a very wide scale.[52]

The response to UPE

One of the strongest recent challenges to the Islamic system of education has come from a campaign for Universal Primary Education (UPE), which was launched in 1976. Here we will concentrate on the Muslim reaction in northern Nigeria, particularly in Bauchi, Gongola, Sokoto and Kano States. While discussing this reaction it is worth bearing in mind some of the observations already made about the long and respected tradition of

Islamic education in these areas. The section is chiefly based on research by Clarke and by Bray during the 1970s.[53]

In all northern states, there had been considerable educational expansion in the decade before the launching of UPE. In the North Eastern State 200,000 children were attending primary school in 1975, which was a 42 per cent increase on the 1968 figure. The number of secondary school pupils increased by an even greater percentage, for in 1975 11,000 pupils attended 48 secondary schools, compared with 3,400 pupils in 19 secondary schools in 1968. The same upward trend was observed in the teacher training sector. Both Bauchi and Gongola States, therefore, which formed part of North Eastern State until 1976, had experienced rapid educational development and expansion. The picture was duplicated in the other states.

When UPE was launched in 1976, even more people entered primary schools, secondary schools and teacher training colleges. In Bauchi State, for example, 300,000 primary school pupils enrolled in September 1976 compared with 132,000 in September 1975. In Sokoto State about 40 per cent, i.e. about 80,000 of the state's six-year-old children signed on for UPE. In Kano State Grade 1 enrolment in 1976 was nearly five times as big as it had been in 1975. In these states and throughout the federation, huge sums of money were spent on the scheme. This fact reflected the high priority attached to it for national development.

Many Muslims interviewed felt that the effects of the scheme on Islamic society would be deep and widespread. They maintained, for example, that the Qur'anic education system, the Islamic ethical and religious system, male and female roles, the nature of parenthood, and models of marriage and authority would be changed. It was argued that different types of knowledge, of work ethic and of educational psychology would be introduced. In turn, this could threaten the role and livelihood of malams.

The common practice among many Muslims in northern Nigeria, especially in the rural areas, is for a father to give his daughter in marriage when she is about twelve years of age. A girl, ideally, should experience her first menstruation in her husband's home and should be married before her sexual potential is fully developed. Underlying this attitude is the fear of a possible conception outside wedlock. Lost virginity and illegitimacy are considered to be more the result of parental irresponsibility than the outcome of 'uncontrolled' sex. Thus the implication for a father of such developments can be serious. He may, for example, be prevented from acquiring a position of authority in the community, for a man is often chosen for such a position on the basis of his ability to control, manage and rear his family correctly. To send a daughter to school – the Western-type school – increases in the minds of many Muslim parents the risk, if she stays at school beyond Primary 4, of losing her virginity. Loss of virginity makes it more difficult, many argue, to find a husband for a girl. A venerable malam in Bauchi State stated that to send a girl to school beyond Class 4 of primary school was 'not a safe practice'. His three daughters would not, he affirmed, continue on at school beyond this stage.

'Western' education would not only lead to a higher incidence of loss of virginity and its attendant consequences, but also, it was argued, undermine the system purdah, which is a fairly widespread practice in northern Nigeria. Muslim girls who went to schools attended by pupils of a variety of different religions, it was argued, would want to imitate the ways of non-Muslims and thus would refuse to accept early marriage and seclusion. Muslims in other parts of Nigeria have no such fears on this score, for they have never accepted seclusion as an integral part of the Prophet's teaching or the tradition of Islam. In the north also, some of the educated Muslim élite argue against the practice of purdah, stating that it has no basis in 'pure' Islam. What the 'purists' contend is that women should not be confined to the home or prevented from engaging in occupations such as teaching and nursing outside the home. This does not mean, however, that there should be unrestricted intercourse between men and women or the indiscriminate adoption by the latter of 'masculine roles and functions to which they are not naturally suited'. The idea of a person being fashioned by nature was widespread among the Muslims interviewed.

Many rural and urban Muslims did not accept the opinion of some of the educated élite with regard to purdah. For the former, sending girls to school would destroy a valuable tradition. Secluded women play a very significant role in rural communities with the aid of their children. These women carry on house trade in food stuffs such as groundnut oil, boiled cassava, hard-boiled eggs and other snacks. Some engage in the retail trade in such items as pepper, salt and vegetables. In both types of trade children act as 'go-betweens', playing a crucial role in linking the secluded women with their customers and suppliers. Placing the children in school meant depriving women in purdah of their 'go-betweens' for a considerable part of every day. The family could thus suffer a considerable decline in income, and the village community could be deprived of important 'social services'. The bicycle mechanics, the blacksmiths, the cobblers, butchers and tailors in many village communities have come to rely on such 'house trade' for their breakfast, lunch and supper.

Western education can lead to certain other unacceptable 'innovations'. It is already altering the accepted view held by the male members of society of the 'ideal' wife and bringing about a change in the prescribed roles of women which have been rigidly defined by religion and custom. Educated male members of society, for example, frequently say that they cannot marry an illiterate: they require a 'social wife'. As some students expressed it: 'a wife must be able to entertain friends, speak to them, talk about current affairs, talk sensibly at parties, purchase the books one needs, etc.' Thus women must be educated – though not to the same level as the men – and must appear in public. Some parents, fathers in particular, and malams view all these changes with alarm. Women, they claimed, would begin to behave like men, to determine their role in society, to regulate the dispensing of their services, to act independently. Thus, they felt UPE would radically alter the male-held conscious model of the ideal woman and wife. Muslim men, particularly in the rural areas as has been indicated, saw the ideal woman as submissive, obedient and content to enjoy reflected status from her husband. It is the men not the women who have the right to participate in public life and who monopolize public affairs. Women are almost entirely excluded from public ritual, worship and politics. According to some Muslim men, however, an educated woman would want to enter public life, thus usurping male roles and functions, and undermining the social order.

Islam is considered to be a blueprint of the social order. As one Muslim graduate stated, 'the Islamic religion totally organizes society'. He suggested that it sets out the criteria for the correct relationships between ruler and ruled, between parents and children: 'Islam maintains order and unity and lays down strict guidelines for what is considered to be good and bad. Changes brought by the introduction of a Western system of education will lead to alterations in the entire life style of Muslims.'

Though they are not opposed to education *per se*, and indeed they highly value the Qur'anic system of education, many Muslims interviewed found it difficult to see what beneficial effects Western education might have on their society. The Muslim chief of Luishi village near Bauchi town thought that his daughter might have an easier and better life as a result of her Western education. However, he was an exception. Some malams still regarded the Western-type school as an instrument of Christian evangelization. This, it would appear, is not simply on account of the sometimes real and sometimes apparent alliance between missionaries and colonialism, but also a consequence of the different theory of knowledge, educational psychology and pedagogical approach held by Muslims.

With some exceptions,[54] UPE also threatened the specific livelihood of the malams. As we have noted, malams have had strong control over Muslim children to the extent of being able to take them from place to place without the permission of parents. Traditionally, children have also worked on their malams' farms, and to replace this with paid labourers would be very costly. With the full implementation of UPE, which would eventually become enforceable by law, many malams believed that the number of pupils attending Qur'anic school would drop considerably, thus depriving them of their responsibility, weakening their authority, and leading indirectly to a decline in their standard of living.

In 1977 indeed, when the UPE scheme was barely a year old, some malams stated that they had already experienced some of these effects. Malam Dahiru had only three pupils that year. They were supposed to attend his Qur'anic school after primary school classes, but the malam reported that they were too tired either to learn anything or to work on his farm. Malam Ahmadu, a colleague of Malam Dahiru, had only 12 pupils in his Qur'anic school in 1977, whereas he used to have 40. He explained that with the introduction of Western education and the other social and economic changes taking place in society, Qur'anic education was now seen as non-functional and irrelevant in relation to job opportunities and the new expectations of the young.

Malams reacted to these threats in different ways. Some launched a mini-jihad against the UPE scheme, while others offered to participate in the scheme after the adoption by the authorities of an 'appeasement strategy'. Provisions were made for malams to give instruction in Islam and Arabic Studies in the primary schools. However, the teaching in primary schools posed problems for the malams. Few of them were trained in the educational methods and techniques used by other teachers, and they suffered problems of status with the other staff. Though the policy both ensured that Islamic religious knowledge was taught in schools and helped provide teachers for UPE, therefore, it encountered problems.

Finally, we should consider the extent to which the widespread resistance to the UPE scheme, which the national and state government politicians considered to be a key instrument in nation building, can be viewed as reactionary and a hindrance to national development. There would appear to be an inverse relationship between the response of many Muslims to UPE and the process of nation building. Many older Muslims appear to be convinced that traditional Islamic education can produce better Muslims than the Western system, and that it ought to be a part of whatever future educational system is imposed.

This view is supported, though not without qualifications, by third generation Muslims who have been educated along Western lines. They acknowledge that the Islamic system of education produces a good Hausa Muslim, but they believe that the education system should also produce full Nigerian citizens and that the traditional system cannot do this on its own. Likewise, second generation Muslims educated along Western lines do not want to be Hausa Muslims only but also to be Nigerian citizens. Both of these groups add that some of the protests against UPE are unfounded. Many Muslims who have been educated in Western schools are, they say, leading exemplary lives, teaching in rural areas and spreading Islam by example and learning. Muslim girls who have attended primary and secondary school, they maintain, are no more lax or promiscuous than those who have not. They also point out that the belief that a girl who is married off at twelve accepts her role in life and is faithful to it without protest is misleading.

Second and third generation Muslims and others educated in Western schools hold the view that if the nation, and Islam too, is to develop, the skills and techniques required for organizing and administering a modern state must be acquired. In the past Muslims possessed these assets, but now things have changed and the historical process cannot be reversed. They argue, with force, that the Islamic and Western systems of education must be integrated.

Questions and project work

1 Why in your view have Muslims placed so much emphasis on Islamic education?

2 What are the distinguishing features and goals of the Islamic education system?

3   Discuss the Muslim response to Western education in Nigeria.

4   Suggest ways in which the Islamic and Western education systems
    might be more fully integrated. Where possible discuss this matter with
    teachers, parents and educational planners in your area. As well as
    putting forward proposals, discuss the obstacles to integration.

Notes

1   Hamdun, S. and King, N. *Ibn Battuta in Black Africa*. Rex Collings, London
    1975, p. 12.
2   Clarke, P.B. *West Africa and Islam. A History of Religious Development
    from the 8th to the 20th Century*. Edward Arnold, London 1982, Chaps. 1
    and 2.
3   Johnson, R.W. 'Educational Progress and Retrogression in Guinea
    (1900–1943)' in Brown, G.N. and Hiskett, M. (eds.) *Conflict and Harmony in
    Education in Tropical Africa*. George, Allen and Unwin, London 1975,
    p. 223.
4   Hodgkin, T. 'Scholars and the Revolutionary Tradition: Vietnam and West
    Africa'. *Oxford Review of Education*, Vol. 2, No. 1, 1972, p. 122.
5   Tibawi, A.L. *Islamic Education*. Luzac, London (2nd edition) 1979, p. 38.
6   Ibid., p. 24.
7   Ibid.
8   Ibn Khaldun *The Muqaddimah: An Introduction to History*. Translated from
    the Arabic by Rosenthal, F., edited and abridged by Dawood, N.J., Routledge
    and Kegan Paul, London 1967, p. 426.
9   Hiskett, M. *The Sword of Truth. The Life and Times of Shehu Usuman dan
    Fodio*. Oxford University Press, New York and London 1973, p. 23.
10 Tibawi, op. cit., p. 40.
11 Wilks, I. 'Islamic Learning in the Western Sudan' in Goody, J. (ed.) *Literacy in
    Traditional Societies*. Cambridge University Press, Cambridge 1968,
    pp. 162–79.
12 Sanneh, L. *The Jahanke*. International African Institute, London 1979, Ch. 7
    and passim.
13 Tibawi, op. cit., p. 41.
14 Ibid., p. 43.
15 Sanneh, op. cit., p. 154. See also Sanneh, L. 'The Islamic Education of an
    African Child: Stresses and Tensions' in Brown, G.N. and Hiskett, M. (eds.)
    Conflict and Harmony in Education in Tropical Africa. George, Allen and
    Unwin. London 1975, p. 170.
16 Ibn Khaldun, op. cit., p. 423.
17 Ibid., pp. 423–4.
18 Wilks, op. cit., p. 166.
19 Quoted in Hodgkin, T. (ed.) *Nigerian Perspectives*. Oxford University Press,
    Oxford 1975, pp. 254–5.
20 Bray, M. *Universal Primary Education in Nigeria. A Study of Kano State*.
    Routledge and Kegan Paul, London 1981, p. 120.
21 e.g. Tibawi, op. cit., pp. 79–80 and passim; Adamu, Haroun Al-Rashid *The
    North and Nigerian Unity*. Daily Times Press, Lagos 1973, p. 36.
22 Sanneh, 'The Islamic Education of an African Child', op. cit., pp. 179–80.
23 Tibawi, op. cit., p. 40.

24 Ibn Khaldun, op. cit., p. 425.
25 Ibid.
26 Goody, op. cit., p. 13.
27 Clarke, P.B., Research notes. Bauchi, Nigeria, 1974–75 and 1981.
28 Ibn Khaldun, op. cit., p. 344.
29 Turner, B.R. *Weber and Islam*, Routledge and Kegan Paul, London 1974.
30 Engels, F. 'Defence of Progressive Imperialism in Algeria' in Fever, L.S. (ed.) *Marx and Engels: Basic Writings on Politics and Philosophy*. Fontana Collins, London 1969, pp. 488–9.
31 Lévi-Strauss, C. *Tristes Tropiques*. Plon, Paris 1958, p. 438.
32 Mazrui, A.A. *Political Values and the Educated Class in Africa*. Heinemann, London 1978, pp. 139–42.
33 Ade Ajayi, J.F. and Oloruntimehin, B.O. 'West Africa in the Anti-Slave Trade Era' in Flint, J.E. (ed.) *Cambridge History of Africa*, Vol. 5. Cambridge University Press, Cambridge 1976.
34 Ibid.
35 Ibid.
36 Cruise O'Brien, D. *The Mourides of Senegal*. Oxford University Press, Oxford 1971.
37 *New Nigerian*, 11/5/1976.
38 Bishop, V.S. 'Language Acquisition and Value Change in Kano Urban Area' in Paden, J.N. (ed.) *Values, Identities and National Integration: Empirical Research in Africa*. Northwestern University Press, Evanston 1980, pp. 191ff.
39 Paden, J.N. *Religion and Political Culture in Kano*. University of California Press, Berkeley 1973, p. 58. See also Bray, op. cit., pp. 56ff; and Stephens, D.G. 'A Study of Teacher Education and Attitudes over Two Generations in the Kano Metropolitan Area of Northern Nigeria'. Ph.D. thesis, University of Exeter 1982, pp. 55–66.
40 Usman, Y.B. (ed.) *Studies in the History of the Sokoto Caliphate*. Dept. of History, Ahmadu Bello University, Zaria/Sokoto State History Bureau, Sokoto, n.d.
41 Bray, op. cit., p. 58.
42 Gbademosi, T.O. *The Growth of Islam among the Yoruba*. Longman, London 1978, pp. 102ff.
43 Clarke, op. cit., p. 225.
44 Fisher, H.J. 'The Modernization of Islamic Education in Sierra Leone, Gambia and Liberia: Religion and Language' in Brown, G.N. and Hiskett, M. (eds.) *Conflict and Harmony in Education in Tropical Africa*. George, Allen and Unwin, London 1975, p. 187.
45 Ibid., pp. 188ff.
46 See Ryan, P.J. *Imale: Yoruba Participation in the Muslim Tradition*. Scholars Press, Missoula, Montana 1978, pp. 201ff. for reactions to modernizing trends in western Nigeria. See Paden *Religion and Political Culture in Kano* op. cit. pp. 140ff. for reaction in the north.
47 Bray, op. cit., p. 60.
48 Paden, *Religion and Political Culture in Kano*, op. cit., p. 141.
49 Bray, op. cit., p. 62.
50 Clarke, op. cit., p. 225.
51 Paden, *Religion and Political Culture in Kano*, op. cit., p. 140.
52 Ibid., pp. 141–2.
53 The research by Clarke was carried out over a number of years, beginning in

Bauchi State in 1974. It has been partially reported in Clarke, P.B. 'Islam, Education and the Development Process in Nigeria'. *Comparative Education,* Vol. 14, No. 2, 1978. The research by Bray was carried out over a number of years, beginning in Kano State in 1976, and has been mostly reported in Bray, op. cit.

54   See Bray, op. cit., pp. 147–8.

Chapter 6

Indigenous forms of education: the individual and society

There is no one, single indigenous form of education in Africa. Societies, differing from each other as they do, have developed different systems of education to transmit their own particular knowledge and skills. The differences are not necessarily great, but it is quite clear that, for example, the indigenous system of education among the Yoruba of South-Western Nigeria and that of the Akan in Ghana, differ in method and content.[1] Again, practices such as child weaning which form part of the 'curriculum' in the indigenous education systems of many African societies vary widely in method and perspective.[2]

On the other hand indigenous forms of education are sometimes remarkably similar, and one form can be seen to have influenced another. Part of the reason for this is that certain educational specialists, as is the case in the Western-type and Islamic systems, are extremely mobile. The impression has often been given of pre-colonial Africa as consisting of static cultural units dwelling in isolation. However, cultural and economic interaction between different societies has at times been very fluid and intense. An example of this is the way the peoples of different ethnic origin in parts of what are now Ghana and the Ivory Coast came to share some of the same artistic traditions. The mobility of specialists such as the Dyula dyers and Numu blacksmiths in the Ivory Coast and Ghana was in large measure responsible for this.[3]

African perspectives on freedom and the individual

Although there has always been and still is exchange of ideas between societies, one cannot examine indigenous education in just one society and then draw sweeping and unqualified general conclusions about it in Africa as a whole. There is, for example, a considerable difference between the indigenous educational systems of the urbanized Yoruba and those of the pastoral Fulani. One can, however, generalize about the philosophical and sociological foundations of indigenous forms of education in Africa. For instance, African philosophy tends to define people in terms of the social context to which they belong, and this has important implications for the nature and goals of indigenous forms of education. African thought also recognizes the uniqueness of the individual with his uniqueness of the individual with his or her own personality, talents and 'destiny'. Thus in a sense individuals are thought of as transcending the socio–cultural context. There is, however, a strong tendency to situate a person's individuality and freedom within the overall social, cultural and historical context of the community or society.

Among the Dogon of Mali, for example, an individual's actions are regarded as being closely interlinked with the way society in general and the world operate. The individual is not thought of as a being having one 'self' or 'soul', but rather as a multiple entity made up of several 'selves' or 'souls', each one of which reflects a concrete relationship between that individual and the wider world. Among the Dogon a person at birth is only potentially a human being and it is the society into which that person is born that provides the individual with a spiritual, sexual, social and intellectual identity. This process happens only gradually. The community, for instance, during one of numerous naming ceremonies which the newborn person must undergo, confers upon the child both an 'intelligent' soul, which provides the individual with the capacity for acquiring knowledge, and the 'grains' which connect the person with the laws of the universe.[4]

One finds a similar set of ideas among the Yoruba for whom, though an individual has freedom and responsibility, life is divinely pre-ordained and sociologically conditioned.[5] The Tallensi of Ghana, like the Dogon and the Yoruba, recognize that each individual is unique and free but also see the thoughts and actions of that individual as being inextricably related to his external, social world.[6] To some, these views may appear to imply conflict between individual freedom and dependence upon society. However, the Tallensi definition of freedom requires social responsibility and maturity, so that the individual adapts his thoughts and actions to the needs and requirements of the world within which he lives. This idea of freedom is compatible with the notion these peoples have of the ideal social and moral order.

Among the Dinka of the southern Sudan the concept *cieng* means both 'morality' and 'living in harmony', and the product of cieng is well being. As one authority expresses it, 'a Dinka strives to maintain unity and harmony between himself and the world outside', and this is best achieved by adapting the individual's desires and requests to those of the rest of society.[7] Some knowledge of indigenous ideas concerning the relationship between individual freedom and society, and of how people acquire social identities is essential for an understanding of the goals of indigenous education.

The goals of indigenous education

Although indigenous education systems can vary from one society to another, the goals of these systems are often strikingly similar. The emphasis, it seems to us, is placed on what we have described in Chapter 5 as normative and expressive goals. To recapitulate, normative goals are concerned with instilling the accepted standards and beliefs governing correct behaviour, and expressive goals with creating unity and consensus. In singling out normative and expressive goals as the principal objectives of indigenous education we do not mean to suggest that there is no competitive element within the system, giving rise to what are termed instrumental goals. Indigenous education does encourage competitiveness in intellectual and practical matters, but this competitiveness is controlled and subordinated to normative and expressive aims.

There is, or ought to be, a direct link between the goals and content of education. A great deal of the content of indigenous education consists of what sociologists like Durkheim refer to as moral education. According to Durkheim, morality is 'a system of rules and actions that predetermine conduct'.[8] An essential element of morality, Durkheim maintained, was a spirit of discipline, which assumed the existence of organization and authority. With regard to the content of morality in general he stated that: 'To act morally is to act in the light of a collective interest'; and he added: 'the domain of the moral begins where the domain of the social begins'.[9] According to Durkheim, it was society in the sense of a supra-individual element in social life consisting of collective sentiments and beliefs, which gave moral rules and ideals their authority. In Durkheim's view a child needed to be taught morality, and this meant among other things teaching him or her about the nature of family life and in general 'about the nature of the social contexts in which he will be called to live'.[10]

Durkheim's ideas on moral education help us to understand the content and goals of indigenous forms of education. Though indigenous education in its various forms has a many-sided character, it is intimately intertwined with social life. What is taught is related to the social context in which people are called to live. Among the Chagga of Tanzania, for example, there is a 'course' for children in what is called 'imitative play'. It consists of representations of scenes from adult life by means of which the young are made familiar with the norms and ideals expected from full, responsible members of society.[11]

Indigenous education, however, is not only concerned with the systematic socialization of the younger generation into the norms, religious and moral beliefs, and collective opinions of the wider society. It also lays a very strong emphasis on learning practical skills. It is not that the idea of art for art's sake, or the notion that the acquisition of knowledge and wisdom and the improvement of an individual's intellectual capacities, have no place in indigenous education. They do, as we shall see; but there is greater emphasis on the acquisition of knowledge which is useful to the individual and society as a whole.

The educators and the curriculum in the indigenous education process

As we mentioned at the beginning of this chapter, what people learn varies from one African society to another. It depends greatly on the level of stratification and the mode of political and economic organization of the society itself and in many African countries the whole community is the principal educative and socialising agent. However, some specific organizations and individuals have the task of educating the young. Some people specialise in teaching particular disciplines.

On the question of the whole community as the educative agent, one scholar has described how among the Akan of Ghana education is a joint enterprise of both the old and the young. Children have complete freedom to attend many adult activities. At birth they are given a symbolic introduction to adult language, a few weeks later they begin to eat adult food, and from the age of six they commence adult work. The main purpose of this early introduction to adult life is 'to free the infant as quickly as possible from dependence upon the parent'.[12] Akan indigenous education is then adult rather than child centred. It is based on the assumption that an individual can participate in community life and benefit from the education the community has to offer at what is, relatively speaking, a very early age.

Among the Chamba of north-eastern Nigeria, the situation is somewhat different. Educating the individual to be independent is a much longer process, and in one sense the Chamba do not regard the child or even the adolescent as a person or individual. As one informant expressed it: 'the child is not a person; he is his father's property . . . a young man, moreover, cannot own what he kills in a hunt without being given it by his father. The father and his brothers have complete control over the children.'[13]

In African societies, including the Akan where there is strong emphasis on the community as educator, parents also play a very important role in the education of their children. There is very often a clearly marked division of labour. The mother educates all children in the early years, but later the father takes over the education of the male children while the mother remains in control of the females. After learning to walk, speak and count, the male child goes to his father and male elders and begins his training for manhood. The female child continues to be taught by her mother, assisted by the other women in the community, and begins to learn how to live and work as a women in that society.

Among the Chamba and in other African societies there exists a conscious model of the ideal man and the ideal woman, and it is with this ideal in mind that the children are educated in the second stage of the educational process. The ideal man preserves and strengthens the cultural, social and moral features of the society. The ideal woman is a wife and mother who, through the bearing of children and in her role as educator, assists her husband in the task of preserving and strengthening the customs and traditions of the group.

This is the ideal that is aspired to; meanwhile both parents attempt to provide their children with a very practical type of education and one based on sound principles of common sense. The nature and content of this practical education, as far as the male child is concerned, is often be determined by his father's occupation. If for example the father is a farmer, then the male children are trained as farmers. Likewise the practical education provided for the female child will be determined by her mother's role as wife and mother and her occupation which might well include cooking, and possibly dyeing or trading. It should be mentioned that though children are instructed and guided by their parents, there is strong emphasis in the learning process on participant observation.

Apart from the parents, institutions such as age-groups participate in the education process. The age-group is important as a means of moulding the personality of its members and defining their attitude to tasks and problems which they will face in adult life.[14] The age-group encourages and teaches respect for elders, solidarity and cooperation. In many African societies age-groups are also part of a division of labour, for (economic, social, cultural and political functions) are allocated on the basis of age.

In addition to the age-group system there are other institutions such as the craft guilds, the secret societies, of which examples from Sierra Leone are given in the case study at the end of this chapter, and the 'convents' where specialists are trained. Many of the crafts are hereditary occupations where the family hands down, usually to the oldest male child, the techniques and secrets of the trade. This seems to have been the case, for example, with beadmaking and blacksmithing. Membership of certain families or clans appear to have been a necessary qualification for entry into the *lantana* beadmaking industry and trade in Ilorin, western Nigeria. One can, however, exaggerate the extent to which certain crafts remained the preserve of certain families and closely knit groups, or the extent to which participation in these crafts was rigidly determined by sex. With regard to the lantana beadmaking craft there is evidence that though the emphasis was on the teaching of family members, anyone could learn the craft. Women also assisted the men in the beadmaking, and even made a special type of bead themselves. Their role, however, was a minor one; but this was not necessarily on account of the fact that they were women, for as one scholar points out it might simply reflect 'the difficulty of assigning primary occupations to women who followed a number of activities part-time.'[15]

In other parts of Africa many of the craft guilds were caste based and seem to have been less open than the lantana beadmaking guilds of western Nigeria. This was the case, for example, in parts of Senegal such as Futa Toro where the caste system of Mandinka origin was very rigidly observed. These blacksmiths, jewellers, tanners, tailors and *griots* (praise singers) were all members of different, exclusive castes.

In some parts of Africa, centres also exist for training religions specialists. In the People's Republic of Benin, priests and mediums are taken out of society for a time and trained in 'seminaries' and/or 'convents'. In these isolated institutions the recruits are transformed into new personalities. This transformation is symbolized in a number of ways. For example, the recruit's hair is shaven off several times during the course of his training, which lasts about nine months. Learning a new language dialect forms part of the training, and the recruit is also given a new name and trained in a new occupation. The whole process aims to create a 'new' personality, who will engage in a new kind of life. Recruits learn both about the spirit world and about more practical matters. For instance they are taught how to make the priestly garments and necklaces, and also such things as mats and baskets which are then sold to ordinary people.[16]

The priests are also the traditional doctors and have to learn a great deal about plants, roots and herbs. Treatment, however, is rarely seen in purely material or physical terms. In his treatment of the patient the doctor must use his knowledge not only of plants, herbs and roots and their healing properties, but also his knowledge of the spiritual universe which enables him, among other things, to release the hidden powers of the medicine.[17] We will return later to the question of the scientific character of medical training and practice in the indigenous education system, while simply mentioning here that the introduction of Western medicine has by no means put an end to traditional medicine. A recent study shows that in many parts of Africa all groups in the population use both traditional and Western medicine constantly.[18]

The training of a diviner can be a long, highly specialized and complicated process. Not all diviners, are trained for the same role in society. Among the Ndembu of north-western Zambia, for example, the diviner is, in addition to being a doctor, concerned with analyzing the past. The Yoruba diviner (*babalawo*) of south-western Nigeria, by contrast, is concerned with forecasting the future. This does not mean, that their functions are essentially dissimilar, however, for both provide their clients with authoritative models for the purpose of decision making. The Ndembu diviner's task is not to reveal the unknown but to give coherence, unity and meaning to all the known facts in a particular case. On this basis he works towards a specific, moral judgement concerning the matter, and having achieved this he prescribes a resolution for the problem. The Yoruba diviner (babalawo) on the other hand seeks to reveal his clients' destiny, and by so doing indicates how the client may improve upon it in this life.

Among both the Ndembu and the Yoruba the diviner is 'chosen', though in different ways, for his profession. Among the Ndembu a man becomes a diviner after experiencing the afflictions and sufferings of the spirit Kayongu. A person becomes a babalawo by inheriting the ability from his father or grandfather, or by being specially 'chosen' by Orumila, the god of diviners. The training for the babalawo is long and intensive, beginning some time between the ages of seven and twelve. The trainee lives with a master babalawo for about ten years, and must learn a great deal of technical and oral knowledge. By the time he is ready to practise as a diviner for the first time the babalawo will have learnt over one thousand 'poems' relating to the problems, anxieties, hopes and aspirations common in Yoruba society. These include illness, bad medicine, evil spirits, money, and family disputes and questions of status, authority and power. An experienced babalawo normally knows twice as many 'poems' as the beginner.

We do not intend here to concentrate on how the Yoruba divination system works. There is already plenty of literature available on that subject.[19] What we do want to point to is the feat of memory involved, which is very remarkable. We have indicated that in the indigenous education system one of the main ways of acquiring knowledge and skills is participant observation. This method is also used in the training of the babalawo. However the indigenous education system also places considerable emphasis on the 'art of memory', and the training of the babalawo is an excellent example of this. The art of memory was valued by the Greeks and Romans, but it is downplayed and rather despised by Western educationists today.

The trainee babalawo not only learns to memorize a vast amount of poetry, but also a wide range of medical knowledge. As we have seen the diviner is also priest and doctor. The trainee, therefore, has to learn to recognize and to distinguish between various kinds of mental and physical illness. He must know the course a particular illness will take and how to make up the medicine necessary to treat it.

Learning about medicine is a complex process, involving an in–depth study of ritual. For example, the Ndembu doctor treating pregnant women has among other things to cut bark chips from numerous species of the same tree, the Kapwipi tree.[20] This tree is used because its wood is hard, and hardness represents the health and strength desired for the patient. In addition, all these trees share the same ritually important property, namely that bark string cannot be taken from them: 'for this would "tie up" the fertility of the patient'. In this sense they may be said to counter Mwengi's medicines. Mwengi is a masked being who wears a costume made of many strings from bark cloth. The bark strings are believed to be deadly to women's procreation.[21]

Indigenous education and Western education: points of contact

The policy of replacing the indigenous, and we may add the Islamic, education systems in Africa by the Western education system has sometimes been attacked.[22] Opponents of the full-scale Westernization of education in Africa have advanced numerous criticism against this trend. If it is one of the main purposes of schools to transmit the attitudes, values, skills, social understanding and customs of the society which they serve, then is it not the case, some educationalists point out, that the so-called informal system of education (often referred to as traditional or indigenous education) does precisely this? Indeed perhaps it does it in a more effective way than the Western-type school. It would appear that indigenous forms of education in Africa place far greater emphasis on participant observation, and that they appreciate fully – and this is a point of fundamental importance – the vital link between knowledge and experience. In operating according to the principle that these are inextricably linked, the indigenous system of education can claim the support of Western educationists and philosophers such as Kant, who held that all our knowledge begins with experience.

Of course we are not suggesting that indigenous forms of education in Africa are perfect and therefore in no need of change or improvement. As societies change, education systems also have to change if they are to continue to cater for people's needs. For example, when a country seeks to transform itself from a non-industrial to an industrialized nation the education system has to play a different role from the one designed for a non–industrialized society. Instead of pursuing as one of its main objectives the goals of social stability and continuity, it will increasingly have to assist in the process of advancing controlled change. Further, where a complex, multi-cultural society is attempting to integrate itself and become one nation, the education system will need to be reshaped in order effectively to transmit different attitudes and skills.

Throughout Africa prior to the period of large-scale nationalism and industrialization, the indigenous education systems performed the role of socializing individuals into particular societies where beliefs and values were widely held in common. The education system equipped the same individuals with the skills to perform the tasks assigned by the family and the wider society. In a culturally and religiously diverse society which is undergoing industrialization and in which the extended family system is breaking down, an education system can only be relevant if it provides individuals with the intellectual equipment, moral values and skills needed to cope with the changing situation. It is clear from what we have already said that indigenous forms of education need to undergo major reforms in goals and methods if they are to perform this role effectively.

It is not only relatively recent developments such as nationalism and industrialization which have constituted a challenge to and rendered indigenous forms of education somewhat irrelevant. In West Africa, for example, the eleventh century saw the development of large-scale political entities such as the empire of Ancient Ghana, followed by the Mali and Songhay empires which reached their peaks in the fourteenth and fifteenth century respectively. But indigenous forms of education failed in some respects to meet the requirements of these much larger political units. Consequently the rulers of these empires tended increasingly to look to the Islamic education system for the personnel necessary for the organization, administration, and integration of their empires. The Islamic education system trained people in Arabic, a widely spoken language useful for such purposes as international diplomacy and trade, in which these empires were involved. The Islamic education system also trained accountants, lawyers, historians and clerks, and communicated values and attitudes relevant to the functioning of these larger political organizations. In some respects the Western-type school has been regarded as the most appropriate vehicle for performing the same or similar functions in modern times, and consequently the Islamic and more so the indigenous education systems have come to be regarded, in some African countries at least, as peripheral and irrelevant to the tasks of nation building and industrialization.

It is also worth mentioning a debate which has recently been a live issue among academics, and which is relevant to the whole question of education and the development process. The issue concerns the nature of African traditional thinking. Does it constitute a barrier to the development of a truly scientific approach necessary for modernization? Levy Bruhl advanced the view, which he modified in later writing, that the pre-logical and mystical religious character of 'primitive' thought and the rational procedures of modern thought were incompatible. As Evans-Pritchard has pointed out, however, the main theme in Levy Bruhl's treatise cannot be sustained.[23] Horton, though he has his critics, maintains that in substance there is no essential difference between traditional African ways of thinking and Western scientific thinking. Differences do exist, but these are largely differences of idiom, and do not in any way render traditional African thinking any less rational *per se* than Western scientific thinking.[24] Apparent differences in thinking are in fact often differences in language, which is used primarily as a means of representing reality. A people's reality, that is their shared experience, will be represented in the language devised by that people.[25]

Indigenous and Western forms of education therefore should not be seen as opposites; the two approaches can supplement each other in a number of ways. As we have seen indigenous forms of education tend to reflect the values, wisdom and expectations of the community or wider society as a whole. Western forms of education, on the other hand, tend to stress the 'intellectual' development of the individual while paying rather less attention to the needs, goals and expectations of the wider society. The solution does not lie in abandoning one form of education for another. A formal education system can play an important role in Africa, but such a system, if it is to meet the cultural, social, moral and intellectual, as well as political and economic needs of Africa, needs to be domesticated and indigenized. And it is here that the study of indigenous forms of education becomes crucially important. The philosophy, methodology and content of schooling in Africa needs to be shaped and moulded, not exclusively, but to a far greater extent, by indigenous perspectives. We do not simply mean those that operated before the arrival of the Western and Islamic education systems. We are also referring to the considerations, views, opinions and assessments of past and contemporary African educationists who, through research and experience, have become aware of the needs and goals of African societies. No serious educational planning can be undertaken without identification of the specific needs and goals of particular African societies.

Indigenous, Western, and Islamic forms of education can usefully be integrated. There are, however, pitfalls which need to be avoided, and which can be avoided if needs and goals are formulated and if a sound, African-inspired philosophy of education is developed. One pitfall is that of establishing an education system in which the different forms – the indigenous, Islamic and Western, where they exist in the same society – are linked rather than integrated or blended together. Integration, of course, requires a considerable amount of comparative research in the field of the philosophy of education, methodology and curriculum. Indigenous educational theory overlaps to some extent with Western and Islamic educational theory, though there are differences of emphasis and perspective, and even substantive methodological differences. However, having formulated the needs and goals of a society, the educationists can develop, on the basis of the theoretical perspectives of the different systems, a coherent, integrated education system, and not simply a haphazard mixture which will be of little benefit to the individual or society.

Conclusions

Indigenous forms of education thus tend, more than the Western form, to serve the needs and aspirations of the community as a whole. The emphasis is on normative and expressive goals. Competition between individuals is encouraged, but not to the extent that individualism and introverted élitism are held in higher esteem than education for life in the community. Indigenous educational theory holds that each of the individual's relationships affects and is affected by all the others. Though, as we have pointed out, the notion of art for art's sake exists, indigenous forms of education regard education in terms of its effects upon or consequences for society and in terms of its effects on individuals.

By comparison, Western education tends to be 'bookish', and somewhat divorced from the life and culture of the wider community. It is, therefore, less able in some respects to provide an education that will fit an individual for life in the community. Furthermore it tends to encourage competition at the expense of cooperation. On the other hand it positively seeks to promote originality of thought and outlook which can be valuable assets to any society. There is, therefore, a need to harmonize and integrate the best elements of both indigenous and Western forms of education to create a more viable system of education in Africa.

Case study: Indigenous education in Sierra Leone

Although the differences between them have become less pronounced over time, one can distinguish between two types of indigenous education in Sierra Leone. On the one hand there are the education systems of the Temnes, Mendes, Limba, Lokkos, Konas and other peoples who mostly live in the interior. On the other hand there is the education system of the Creole population, which comprises descendents of the freed slaves and other settlers who began to arrive in the country in the late eighteenth century and who inhabit what is now called the Western Area.[26]

The clearest examples of indigenous educational institutions, on which this case study will concentrate, are operated by the Poro and Bundu secret societies. These societies exist among several ethnic groups, including the Mendes, Temnes, Konos and Sherbros. The form they take varies from one ethnic group to another, and even within the same group, though one can make some generalizations.[27] The Creoles also have secret societies, which include the Hunting (Ojeh) associations. Like the Poro and Bundu societies, Creole societies have traditional rites and symbols, and members are sworn to secrecy. But while the Poro and Bundu societies play an important role in the all-round education and training of the young, the Creole societies tend to be more ritualistic and ceremonial.

The Poro society among the Temne has a history of at least four and a half centuries.[28] Many Westerners who encountered the Poro society were hostile towards it, and few considered it from an educational viewpoint. They were not alone in this, as we shall see. In the past, the Poro society performed an important political and economic role, serving sometimes as a check on government and as a mutual aid organization for its members. This role has changed, but even in recent times the society has been used to mobilize support for political purposes.[29]

The Poro society initiates and trains boys who are admitted at the onset of puberty and may remain in training for one or more years. It operates in the forest or bush on sacred ground. There are different types of sacred ground, but most have entrances resembling arches, and clearings that may contain shelters. Usually the Poro organizer, a man, arranges for the recruiting of boys, the collection of the initiation fees, the provision of food for the sacrifices, and the payment of the priests and diviners.

During the period of initiation the boys are cut off from all contact with non-members, and sleep alone in separate houses. Most of the day is spent on the farm. Discipline and cooperation are among the main parts of the curriculum. The boys are also taught the signs, symbols, structure and language of the society. In some cases, training is also given in first aid, farming, craftsmanship and construction work. The boys are taught to endure physical pain, and to be self-reliant within their communities.

Some aspects of Poro society organization and work have been strongly criticized. For example, the recruitment methods of some societies have involved seizure of boys for initiation against their own and their parents' wishes. Some Poro societies have also administered severe physical punishment to anyone who criticized them or who failed to show respect to the Poro officials. Today, however, Poro recruitment and discipline have been modified under the influence of Christianity, Islam and government legislation. Poro secrecy is no longer as impenetrable as it used to be, partly because of the development of Western education. The Poro society, nevertheless, continues to function, especially in rural areas. Fewer people undergo initiation and many people are only nominal members, but Poro healing and ritual techniques are still actively sought.

The Poro has its female counterpart in the Bundu society, to which girls are admitted from around the age of nine.[30] Again, although the disciplinary rules and regulations are not as strict as they used to be, girls still undergo an intensive training which equips them with the skills and techniques deemed necessary in a wife and mother. The Bundu society functions as a pre-marital training institution where girls are taught domestic science, child rearing, basic agricultural skills, craft work, basic medicine, and leisure activities such as music and dance. In addition to being trained for motherhood, they are socialized into the adult female way of life.

These examples indicate the way that education systems in traditional societies train the younger generations. By means of such institutions as we have been describing, the attitudes, beliefs, rituals, work ethics, skills, and communal attitudes are transmitted from one generation to the next.

The education system thus serves as a force for social integration and cohesion.

However it should not be concluded that traditional societies experience no competition, tension or conflict. While considerable common sentiment and group solidarity are characteristic of such societies, inequality, discrimination and violations of the legal and moral codes are also common. Moreover, education itself has not always served the interests of the whole society, for it may be used by some people to acquire power and authority over others for their own narrow ends. Finally, we must observe that societies and their education systems are constantly changing. The Poro and Bundu societies are forced to change and adapt to new circumstances.

Questions and project work

1   Assess the similarities and differences of indigenous forms of education in your country or in any African country of your choice.

2   What, in your view, are the most valuable philosophical and sociological insights provided by indigenous forms of education?

3   Are there, in your view, any valuable and relevant philosophical and sociological insights to be gained from a study of the indigenous educational systems of the Dogon, the Yoruba and the Tallensi? (You may widen the scope here to cover other indigenous education systems, for example those found in your own country.)

4   Suggest ways in which indigenous and Western forms of education might complement each other. To answer this question you should, where possible, compare and contrast the two systems of education as they exist in your own area.

5   What are the principal cultural and economic problems of your country and what role, if any, might indigenous education play in solving them?

Notes

1   See Callaway, H. 'Indigenous Education in Yoruba Society' and Bartels, F.L. 'Akan Indigenous Education' in Brown, G.N. and Hiskett, M. (eds.) *Conflict and Harmony in Education in Tropical Africa*. George Allen and Unwin, London 1975, pp. 26–39 and pp. 39–65 respectively.
2   Hake, C. *Child-Rearing Practices in Northern Nigeria*. Ibadan University Press, Ibadan 1972, and T.O. Pearce, Behavioural Science and Medicine, unpublished paper.
3   Bravmann, R.A. *Islam and Tribal Art in West Africa*. Cambridge University Press, Cambridge 1974.
4   Griaule, M. 'Remarques sur le mécanisme du sacrifice dogon'. *Journal de la Société des Africanistes*, 10, 1940.

5 Horton, R. 'Destiny and the Unconscious'. *Africa* Vol. 31, No. 2, 1961; and Bascom, W. 'Yoruba Concepts of the Soul' in Wallace, A. (ed.) *Men and Cultures*. University of Pennsylvania Press, Philadelphia 1960.
6 Fortes, M. *Oedipus and Job in West African Religion*. Cambridge University Press, Cambridge 1959.
7 Deng, F.M. *The Dinka of the Sudan*. Holt, Rinehart and Winston, New York 1972, p. 26.
8 Durkheim, E. *Moral Education*. Free Press, New York 1961.
9 Ibid.
10 Ibid.
11 Fafunwa, A. Babs *History of Education in Nigeria*. George Allen and Unwin, London 1974, p. 21.
12 Bartels, op. cit., p. 60.
13 Clarke, P.B. Research notes. Bauchi, Nigeria, 1974.
14 See on this subject Bartels, op. cit.; and Mead, M. *Culture and Commitment: A Study of the Generation Gap*. Panther, St. Albans 1977.
15 O'Hare, Anne 'The Lantana Beadmaking Industry and Trade in Ilorin, Western Nigeria'. (Unpublished paper.) Ilorin University, 1981.
16 Parrinder, G. *West African Religion*. Epworth Press, London (third edition) 1969, pp. 86ff.
17 Ibid., p. 158.
18 Pearce, T. 'The Sociology of Traditional Medicine'. (Unpublished paper.)
19 See for example Abimbola, W. *Ifá, an Exposition of Ifá Literary Corpus*. Oxford University Press, Ibadan 1976; Bascom, W. *Ifá Divination, Communication between Gods and Men in West Africa*. University of Indiana Press, Indiana 1969; and McClelland, E. *The Cult of Ifá Among the Yoruba*. Ethnographica Ltd., London 1982.
20 Turner, V.W. *The Ritual Process*. Penguin, Harmondsworth 1969, p. 24.
21 Ibid., p. 25.
22 Thompson, A.R. *Education and Development in Africa*. Macmillan, London 1981, p. 25.
23 Evans-Pritchard, E.E. *'Theories of Primitive Religion'*. Oxford University Press, Oxford 1965, p. 87.
24 Horton, R. 'African Thought and Western Science'. *Africa*, Vol. 37, No. 2, 1967.
25 Cole, M. et al. *The Cultural Context of Learning and Thinking: An Exploration in Experimental Anthropology*. Methuen, London 1971.
26 See Fyfe, C. *A Short History of Sierra Leone*. Longman, London 1979.
27 Dorjahn, V.R. 'The Initiation and Training of Temne Poro Members' in Ottenberg, S. (ed.) *African Religious Groups and Beliefs*. Folklore Institute, Berkeley, California n.d., Chap. 2.
28 Ibid., p. 36.
29 Little, K. 'The Political Functions of the Poro: Part 1'. *Africa*, Vol. 35, 1965; Little, K. 'The Political Functions of the Poro: Part 2'. *Africa*, Vol. 36, 1966.
30 Forde, T.J.L. 'Indigenous Education in Sierra Leone' in Brown, G.N. and Hiskett, M. (eds.) *Conflict and Harmony in Education in Tropical Africa*. George, Allen and Unwin, London 1975, pp. 70-1.

Chapter 7

Education and the community

Despite the hopes and labours of planners, politicians, parents and pupils, education systems frequently fail to produce either the economic or the social fruits that are wanted from them. We pointed out in Chapter 3 that most African countries suffer high unemployment among school leavers, and instead of helping to build communities, education systems sometimes seem to stratify and destroy them.

Education at the community level may be viewed from two sides. On the one hand one can examine issues from the viewpoint of schools and look at how communities can help them. The answer to this is usually through physical construction of buildings, maintenance of school compounds, fund-raising through Parent-Teacher Associations, and so on. On the other hand one can examine issues from the viewpoint of communities. Here the focus is on the relevance of curricula and on the school as an instrument of rural and urban development.

Perceived irrelevance of curricula is a major problem throughout the continent. As one Nigerian report has stated, 'For at least 60 years educationists in Nigeria have been saying that education is too school-oriented and not sufficiently life-oriented. It is time something was done about it.'[1] This chapter will comment on some of the reasons for this irrelevance, and on the obstacles to effective remedy. Our book does have a separate chapter on the curriculum, and we will try to avoid repetition. Since many of the issues come under the heading of community relevance, we will begin our discussion here and continue it in Chapter 9.

For many decades educationists have also complained that school systems are too exclusive. From a philosophical viewpoint, one might argue that schools exist for whole communities, and that education is a basic human right for adults as well as children. This implies that anyone who wants to learn how to read and write, or who would like to know more about politics, religion, health and agriculture, should be able to attend a local school. In practice, however, the vast majority of schools seem only to cater for children and youths. There seems to be an unwritten rule that people who are married are not allowed to attend school, and very rare are the schools which welcome people over the age of 20 to learn alongside children and teenagers. Although some villagers have to look after school compounds, they are not usually welcome to visit the schools during lesson times. Indeed some headteachers actually chase adults away from school compounds instead of welcoming them in. We shall discuss the reason for this, and also comment on the experience of the community education centres which have been created in two countries to cater for both children and adults.

The case study at the end of the chapter comments on the experience of the brigades in Botswana. The brigades have attempted to involve communities in their governing councils and to provide training in manual skills supposed to be of direct use in villages. They therefore exemplify both sides of the issue we are discussing. The difficulties the brigades have faced provide lessons for educators throughout the continent as well as in Botswana.

What is a community?

One problem which faces our discussion is that the word 'community' is vague, and has different meanings in different contexts. To begin with, therefore, we shall distinguish between four different types of community.[2]

The first type may be called the traditional community. It refers to a medium sized rural village with a close-knit group of inhabitants, largely self-contained and with everybody knowing, and standing in an accepted relationship with, everybody else. Such a community would live in the same place, have broadly common values, and be bound by multiple economic, social, religious and kinship ties. Many communities of this type exist in Africa, strongly conscious of their common history and future.

The second type is of an 'adopted' community which exists, for example, as a result of the emergence of new towns and cities in Africa. Like the traditional community it is based on residence in a particular area, and members still share some common interests. However, membership of adopted communities is determined by convenience and choice as much as birth, and a high proportion of members may have joined comparatively recently. Ties are much looser, and relationships are less multidimensional than in a traditional community. In an adopted community it is less likely, for example, that the local carpenter will also be your cousin and attend the same church. Many new cities have grown by absorbing older villages, and within urban areas one may find adopted communities existing side by side with traditional ones.

Thirdly, one may refer to 'radial' or 'dispersed' communities of people who are not neighbours but who share ethnic, cultural or religious ties. Moemeka has documented how the sons and daughters of Obamkpa in Bendel State of Nigeria, for example, have a strong sense of communal identity even when they are scattered throughout the country.[3] One educational result of their affiliation is the payment of money to finance a school in their home area. In this instance, the school becomes a way of expressing and maintaining the community identity.

Finally, the word community is also commonly used in a general sense when one refers to 'service to the community'. All citizens of a country form the national community in this sense, and the creation of a consciousness of community at this level is one of the major concerns of African governments. The present chapter is less concerned with communities in this sense, however, for they were the focus of Chapter 2.

Perhaps dangerously, the word community tends to imply agreement and harmony among its members. One should beware of this idea, for in practice even traditional communities often suffer serious division. This means that in effect one can have several communities within a small area.

School-community links: a recurring theme

Consider the following statement:

> Education should be adapted to the mentality, aptitudes, occupations and traditions of the various peoples [of Africa], conserving as far as possible all sound and healthy elements in the fabric of their social life; adapting them where necessary to changed circumstances and progressive ideas, as an agent of natural growth and evolution. Its aim should be to render the individual more efficient in his or her condition of life, whatever it may be, and to promote the advancement of the community as a whole through the improvement of agriculture, the development of [indigenous] industries, the improvement of health, the training of the people in the management, of their own affairs, and the inculcation of true ideals of citizenship and service.

Do you agree that this type of statement can be found in the policy documents of almost every government in Africa, and in the reports of such organizations as Unesco and the World Bank? In fact it comes from a publication of the British colonial office, and was issued in 1925.[4] It is just one example of the wide range of documents, both older and younger, which have raised the same issues over the years. Half a century later, the first recommendation of the African Ministers of Education who met in Lagos in 1976, was 'that a start be made, in all African States, on an all-round and complete reform of educational systems, with the effective participation of the masses, in order to adapt those systems to the real problems and preoccupations of the community'.[5]

In many respects, the solutions proposed by these documents were also similar. The 1925 paper continued: 'History shows that devotion to some spiritual ideal is the deepest source of inspiration in the discharge of public duty. Such inflences should permeate the whole life of the school. One such influence is the discipline of work.'[6] The 1976 paper continued: 'Work is an essential component of development, and the African of the future must be a worker, a producer. . . . The incorporation of manual work into education therefore has an educational significance, as it is by producing that a pupil learns to be a producer within a community itself committed to the effort of production.'[7]

The first Western-type schools in Northern Nigeria provide an example of the ways some educationists have tried to link schools with their communities. Hanns Vischer opened the first school in Kano in 1909, and the curriculum included both academic and practical work centred around a hospital, market and farm. Pupils were allowed to bring their own wives and attendants, and lived in separate compounds. To fit in with the religious needs of both Muslims and Christians, there was no school either on Fridays or Sundays, or on any of the religious feast-days.[8]

The Jeanes schools of East and Central Africa, which also sought to link schools and communities, have been mentioned already (see Chapter 1). These institutions were created as a result of the Phelps-Stokes reports in the 1920s, and trained visiting teachers who travelled around the country. After two years of study and practice teaching, the Jeanes teachers returned to the missions who had sponsored them and undertook school supervision and community work for particular mission stations. In the Kenyan context community work included 'latrines with tops, sick cases dealt with, approaches to school and houses, wells, latrines dug, improved houses, rats killed, rat traps, clean-up days, health propaganda meetings, dukas [stores], cooperative societies and banks, trees planted, improved grain stores, ploughs, separators, mills, rubbish and manure pits, ox carts in use, sewing machines, school libraries, schools with night classes, etc.'.[9]

Another prominent alternative model in the same period was the Malangali school in Tanganyika. The school was modelled on 'tribal' organizations, and 'tribal' elders accompanied the boys to instruct them in their traditions. A board of resident councillors was formed 'to guide the head master and help him base his work on native institutions and native ideas'.[10] Clothing, buildings and furniture were of modified local design, and the curriculum focused on both academic and manual matters. Twice a week, the boys practised spear-throwing and dancing in place of the football of other schools.

In the event the Malangali school was shortlived, mainly because its initiator left the country shortly after its foundation,[11] but some of the general principles on which it was founded were reiterated in later years. The 1952 provisional syllabus for Tanganyikan middle schools, for example, included 'practical activites reflecting the life and needs of the locality'.[12] After independence the Tanzanian government opened a number of community education centres to cater for both children and adults, and the whole system has been reformed to reflect the policy of Education for Self Reliance.[13] The Kwamsisi project, which was in many ways an early model preceeding the broader organization of *ujamaa*, viewed the village as a whole and the school as one part contributing to the process of development. A village development committee was concerned with overall issues, and one sub-committee was responsible for education and social welfare.[14]

During the last two decades a large number of projects in other countries have had similar objectives. For example the rural education centres of Upper Volta (now called Burkina Faso) aimed to combine basic training in literacy and numeracy with an agriculturally based education.[15] The Bunumbu Project in Sierra Leone designed community education centres similar to those in Tanzania to serve both children and adults in a single institution.[16] The Namutamba project in Uganda sought to improve school-community links by including brick-making projects and young farmers' clubs. During the afternoons, school buildings were used for a variety of adult education and community purposes, and teachers undertook community work outside their schools.[17] The IPAR project in Cameroon sought to reform the primary school curriculum to reflect village needs more closely.[18] The Asra Hawariat school in Ethiopia built on the concept of familyhood to provide both resources and orientation in the curriculum.[19]

In summary, therefore, we emphasise that concern about links between schools and communities are neither new nor isolated. Projects to improve links were initiated in many places during the colonial period, and they remain a prominent point of focus for post-Independence governments.

How can the community help the school?

One of the most obvious ways in which communities help their schools is by providing labour and materials for building. In most countries rural primary schools are built and maintained by parents, who organise themselves once a week or once a month to work on the compound. Those who cannot contribute labour send cash. Usually the work is organised by Parent-Teacher Associations (PTAs), whose membership covers communities as a whole rather than just parents and teachers. Sometimes members of dispersed communities sponsor specific projects like school libraries.

Secondly, communities may help with the curriculum. Villagers who are skilled in craftwork may help children to learn crafts; priests may help children learn about religion; health workers may help children learn about hygiene; agriculturalists may help children learn about crops and animals; and store owners may help children to learn about commerce. These activities may be achieved either through the community members coming to the school compounds or though school children going out on excursions. Community members may also help with social studies projects. As an example, Hawes has presented this 'true story from Ife' in Nigeria:

> Tunde, aged 10, in the Yoruba medium class, had been asked in his Social Studies class to find out details from his father about a local festival. At first the father was unwilling . . . it had nothing to do with the school, he said. But Tunde persisted, father told him, and Tunde made his contribution in class – with great success. He went back and told his father. A few days later the father told a project worker, 'You know that was the first time I felt I had something to offer the school'.[20]

Thirdly, communities may help recruit children for the school and help ensure their attendance. When the Nigerian government launched a Universal Primary Education campaign in 1976, the authorities in one state used the emirate hierarchy, which stretched right down to the local level, to recruit children.[21] PTAs can also be used to help promote daily attendance and to reduce drop-out rates.

Fourthly, communities can help the teachers by providing housing, either on the school compound or in the village. By making their teachers feel welcome, they may also encourage them to work hard and to stay in the schools rather than to seek transfers. In turn this encourages the teachers to work efficiently and effectively.

Finally, individual family members can help their own children by making sure that they do their homework, that they go to school on time, and that they have something to eat during the lunch break. By helping their own children, they are also helping the school.

How can the school help the community?

Obviously the school can help the community by giving its children skills in literacy, numeracy and other subjects. At the secondary level, the schools provide access to income-generating employment. Even if young people have to go to other places to take up jobs, they may help their communities by sending back money.

Schools may also sustain and uphold communities through their socialization function, i.e. through spreading common values. This becomes particularly relevant in communities which have had schools for several generations. The school gives the young members of the community a pattern of experiences similar to those received by their elders.

Thirdly, schools may help strengthen bonds in adopted communities. Anyone who has been a newcomer to a strange place will know that parental contacts and ties may be developed through friendships between children at school. The institutions act as a focus of community life, and parents are brought together by the friendships and common needs of their children.

Fourthly, schools also bring small communities into contact with wider societies. This occurs through the official curriculum, which usually has both a national and an international content, and through the existence of a national education system, with its common standards and national salary scales.

In addition, as we have mentioned, schools sometimes undertake specific community projects. These might include building schemes, agricultural work, and so on.

Finally, in some cases schools cater for adults as well as children. The Tanzanian and Sierra Leone community education centres have already been mentioned and provide examples of this. The Ugandan Namutamba project provides another example.

Some problems

Up to this point we have been stressing positive links between schools and communities. However it must also be noted that there can be negative links. For example, competition between communities can lead to inefficiency if communities refuse to work together and demand separate schools. Dondo has given a Kenyan example of this. In the Kanyamkago Location of Nyanza Province there are really three communities rather than one: the original Luo inhabitants, a group of Luo immigrants, and a group of Maragoli immigrants. Traditionally, the original Luo immigrants have been more interested in cattle than schooling, and inequalities have grown up in part because the other groups have had longer contact with education in their original homes, and have put more resources into their schools. The communities are further divided by religion, for some are Roman Catholics, some are Seventh-day Adventists, and some are members of the Salvation Army. Because they wanted specific attention to be paid to their religion, the Salvation Army members insisted in maintaining their own primary school even though it had only a dozen and a half pupils and was blatently uneconomic.[22]

Like the Nigerian dispersed communities mentioned above whose members contribute funds for their village school even when they live far away, the people of Kanyamkago also have a union for sons and daughters in distant places. However the divisions at home also make their existence felt within this association. The original Luo members feel that through historical accident the immigrant groups have become more educated and get better jobs, and they are unwilling to support the association. On their side, the immigrants feel that the original Luo are obstructing development, and the result is that the association is divided and ineffective.

Kenya has become well known for its self-help or 'Harambee' secondary schools and Institutes of Technology. The Harambee experience has not been entirely positive, however. Although Harambee efforts can liberate resources for education, they can also lead to wasteful competition between communities and to institutions which provide poor quality education.[23] The Harambee philosophy has also led to an increase in regional inequalities, for some groups have been more interested in building schools than have others.

Similarly, in some parts of Africa specific racial and religious groups set up their own schools separately from the rest. On the one hand this may be considered a beneficial way to generate resources, and to help schools to meet the needs of specific communities. On the other hand it might be considered socially divisive. Separate schools for Europeans, or Asians, or Africans belonging to particular ethnic or religious groups are not necessarily desirable.

In addition, projects to involve villagers in the curriculum require a great deal of time, organization and effort from the teachers. Considerable skills in public relations and management are required, and the question of payment may arise when community members are brought in on a regular basis. Because of these factors, teachers are often less enthusiastic about community involvement projects than are curriculum developers in Ministries of Education.

Indeed, despite the story of Tunde and his father narrated above, many parents feel that the job of the school is to teach things that are *different* from everyday life in the village. They may say to themselves that they do not send their children to school to learn how to farm, for these are things that parents can teach their children by themselves. As President Nyerere pointed out, parents often encourage their educated children to be different, and may even refuse to allow them to farm or do other 'menial' tasks.[24] In Chapter 4 we discussed the 'vocational school fallacy' and resistance by communities to attempts to introduce large portions of non-academic subjects into the curriculum. Parents may be particularly opposed to curricula with strong community activity if they think that their children will suffer when they sit the examinations.

The background of teachers may be another obstacle to school-community integration. In Ghana, for example, large numbers of Ewe teachers from the Volta Region have been posted to the Western Region, Brong Ahafo and the north. The stranger teachers may well be respected, but are likely to be regarded as outsiders and are handicapped when they try to build close links between their schools and communities.[25]

Further, teachers are usually encouraged to think of themselves as part of a national body, with professional interests that may need to be protected from local politics. Local control of schools is not popular with teachers' organizations, and teachers in such countries as Kenya, Nigeria and Botswana have been keen for central governments to take over primary schools from community, private and religious groups.

Finally, the failure of many projects to encourage adults as well as children in community learning centres arises in large part because adults do not consider themselves to have the same sorts of needs as their children. They are less interested in certification to get jobs, mainly because the labour market is not geared to older entrants and the adults consider it too late. Other reasons for the failure of many of these projects are that the teachers do not have materials developed for older learners rather than younger ones, and that many are primary school teachers who tend to treat adults like children. Adult education projects are keenly supported by revolutionary governments which want to change the attitudes of their peoples, but at the community level it is rare for them to be supported so enthusiastically as are schools for children.

For all these reasons, schools tend to be regarded as institutions which are separate from the ordinary lives of communities. The separateness is symbolised by schools standing in fenced compounds with buildings made of materials which are different from those of ordinary houses and in which pupils wear special uniforms. It is not easy to change these attitudes and link schools more effectively with their communities. However, it is to be hoped that educators will continue to try.

Case study: The Botswana brigades

Botswana's brigades are post-primary training institutions organised by local communities to train youths in practical skills. Their history has been complicated, but we can learn a lot from it.

The brigade concept

The 'founding father' of the brigades was Patrick van Rensburg. He was born in South Africa, but later became a citizen of Botswana. His work in Botswana began in 1962 when he founded the Swaneng Hill secondary school in Serowe. The account here is mostly drawn from two books which he wrote about his experiences.[26]

Soon after van Rensburg arrived at Swaneng Hill, he became aware of three major social problems. The first affected school leavers, many of whom were unable to find paid employment, and most of whom lacked the skills to become self-employed. The second concerned resources, for classrooms and other facilities had to be built but there was little money to pay for them. Van Rensburg's answer was to ask local people and the youths at the school to build them. The third issue was how to change the attitudes of the students who were privileged enough to attend school. He wanted, as he put it, to discourage 'the notion that education is just a ladder on which ambition climbs to privilege'.

Van Rensburg became convinced that the solution to these problems could be found if classes in basic subjects like mathematics and English were combined with instruction in skills which could be used to produce goods. The goods could then be sold to pay instructors and buy materials for further production. For this he set up separate institutions called brigades, which were intended to be self-financing and to have a strong community base. By 1974 van Rensburg had resigned from the head-mastership of Swaneng Hill and had switched his attention to the brigades.

The name for the brigades was borrowed from Ghana, where Builders' Brigades already existed to train young people on the job. Although he was unaware of it at the time, the name also had a meaning in Botswana. Traditionally, young men had been organized into 'regiments' for military purposes in time of war and for community purposes in time of peace. Van Rensburg chose the name in order to emphasize the difference between his institutions and ordinary secondary schools.

The first brigade was set up in 1965 to train young people to become builders. Eventually it was joined by brigades for farmers, carpenters, potters, dam builders, leatherworkers, garage mechanics and welders. In a typical working week, trainees spent 80 per cent of their time on production activities. At least four days a week were spent on manual work, and five hours a week were spent on mathematics, English and development studies. The brigades were usually grouped into Centres, each of which had between 3 and 30 students. Their immediate aims were:

1   To establish an alternative to the existing formal system of education for young people unable to find places in secondary or trade schools.
2   To combine education and training with production activities which would help to cover costs and make brigades cheap to run.
3   To provide young people with the skills they needed to employ themselves, or find employment, in their own rural communities, and to

encourage them in the attitudes which would enable them to take positive steps towards the development of those communities.

Van Rensburg and his colleagues rapidly came to recognize that the implications of what they were trying to do were far wider than they had first imagined. The following pages look at some of the ways in which these wider implications became clear.

Three sets of questions can be used to organize the following discussion. The first set of questions concerns the effectiveness with which the brigades have 'democratized' the educational process. How responsive are they to the needs of local communities? Do they encourage local control of education? Secondly, how cheap are the brigades? Have they succeeded in reducing the costs of education in Botswana? What issues are raised by their attempt to find alternative methods of securing resources? Thirdly, how relevant is the education and training whch the brigades offer? How can we begin to assess the quality of the education offered?

Democratizing the educational process

The brigades were intended to 'democratize' the educational process in at least two ways. First, they were designed to respond to the limited opportunities for employment in rural areas and to the changing needs of local communities. Second, their management structure incorporated representatives from the local community. During the 1970s van Rensburg became increasingly aware of the need to ensure effective local control and commitment to the scheme he had pioneered. He claimed that the brigade concept 'responds closely to the rapidly changing needs of a community and society in the process of development'.[27] This was one of the strongest arguments in favour of the concept.

Being small and independent of the bureaucratic structures of administration which tend to dominate school systems, brigades were far more flexible than the schools. In Serowe by 1978 there were no less than 17 different centres, and more if one counts the different centres grouped under the heading of the Mechanical Brigades. Being small and flexible, they are able to cooperate with each other over the provision of such common facilities as academic classrooms and the library. They could also adapt to the changing needs of their trainees. It had been quickly realized that skill training was not enough to create the conditions necessary for employment when the trainees finished their courses. An attempt was made to set up a cooperative to employ these ex-brigade trainees, but it was not successful for reasons which will become clear later. Instead, production groups were set up beside some brigade centres. These were intended to be separate organizations, though they were able to call on the advice of brigade staff and to use brigade equipment. The production groups appear to have been more successful than the cooperative experiment.

However we cannot accept without question van Rensburg's assertion that the brigades responded closely to rapidly changing needs. Clearly young people in Serowe needed employment, which was scarce in the outlying rural areas. To that extent, van Rensburg was justified in claiming that the brigades responded to local needs. But some of the brigade centres, particularly the Farmers' Brigade, ran into trouble over the very question of what the needs of the trainees actually were. The trainees demanded to be given certificates when the course ended. Van Rensburg refused: 'We felt that this would encourage the belief that paid jobs would be available and undermine our efforts to face them with the reality that few paid jobs were available.'[28]

In some centres, it appears that the brigade concept quickly caught on and the students became enthusiastic. In others the trainees were said to be low in motivation. 'The trainees felt like unpaid labour, they had lost all confidence in their teachers, and they had very little idea of what the brigade was all about.'[29]

These facts suggest that in some important ways the brigades did not meet the expectations of many of their trainees. The brigades were attempting to offer more relevant education as an alternative to that which was available in schools. But relevant to whom and to what? We shall look at some issues connected with the idea of relevance below (p. 126). For the moment we will concern ourselves with some other important questions about the ways educational innovations are carried out. Who defines the needs of a society or a community? How do such needs come to be defined? How should the needs of a society be reconciled with demands by local communities which appear to contradict those needs? What should be the relationship between educators and the local community? Is it their job to persuade local people to do as they are told? Where should the line be drawn between education and indoctrination? The answers to these questions lie partly in the development of more efficient ways of involving local communities in the direction of their own affairs.

By 1978 van Rensburg was insisting that: 'the demand for an alternative development has to be made . . . by a small group of highly committed, local people'.[30] In the Serowe brigades there was local representation in the overall management body – the Serowe Brigades Development Trust. Each brigade had a manager who was responsible for the day-to-day running of the centre. Each manager had a seat on the trust, along with ten representatives from the local community. The trust was a small, flexible organization which performed the duties which the more bureaucratic structures of central government carry out in relation to schools. It raised funds for new centres, and recruited teachers and instructors. It ensured cooperation between the different centres wherever this was possible and valuable.

Yet although the structures for local involvement in the brigades existed, the scheme did not secure the commitment of local people. In 1978, for example, eight of the seventeen managers in the Serowe brigades were foreigners, and of the twenty-five instructors, over half were foreign. For the brigades to strike real roots in the local community far more was necessary than the simple representation of the local community in the management body. In exploring the reasons for this failure we can usefully turn to the problems of resources and unemployment which the brigades faced. We might also consider whether the problems were unique to Botswana or whether they would have been faced by any country attempting such an experiment.

Problems of costs and resources

One of the main concerns underlying the interest in localized forms of education and training has been the need to find solutions to the problems of rapidly increasing educational costs. This was a fundamental problem for van Rensburg.

His solution was to combine education with productive work. this meant that brigade trainees had to spend a major part of each week producing goods which could be sold in order to secure an income. By the end of the 1970s, income from production activities amounted to around P500,000 a year. This figure covered nearly 70 per cent of all the costs of training and education, including production costs and overheads. However, two comments need to be made.

In the first place, these figures do not give any impression of the different kinds of difficulties which individual brigades faced in their attempts to cover their own costs. Equipment for the Mechanical Brigade, for example, cost nearly nine times as much as that for the Carpenters' Brigade, and the Farmers' Brigade needed even more. Secondly, despite the money from productive activities, the brigades were heavily subsidised by the government and foreign agencies, which provided both financial and human resources – that is, managers, instructors and academic teachers.

By the end of the 1970s the Serowe brigades were running into severe problems. Van Rensburg wrote: 'It was clear we had developed our model as far as it could be taken in the prevailing socio-economic conditions of Botswana'.[31] Inflation was rapidly increasing, and the brigades were unable to secure enough money from the Botswana government or from abroad to meet their rising costs. In 1980 many brigades collapsed, and large numbers of staff and trainees had to be dismissed.

Moreover, underlying the problems of finance were other issues of a more fundamental nature — issues of social stratification and of structural unemployment. Skill training of the sort the brigades provided could never by itself compensate for the broader problems of rural underdevelopment. Unless such skills were in demand, and unless the goods which such skills might help to produce could find markets, skill training could not begin to create the conditions necessary for local employment.

Many aspects of rural unemployment have already been discussed in Chapter 3. Here again we must stress the direct nature of the link between wider social and economic problems and the immediate difficulties faced by van Rensburg and his colleagues in attempting to develop more relevant forms of education and training. By the end of the 1970s it was clear that while the brigades had had some success in developing alternative forms of skill training, they were making little impact on the serious problems of rural unemployment.

More important for our immediate purposes is to see what was heppening to the relationship between the brigades and the formal institutions of education and training. It had been hoped that these formal and non-formal institutions would be able to work side by side, in what van Rensburg called a 'harmonized, dual policy' of educational development. However, this did not happen. Brigade trainees were soon in competition with graduates from the formal institutions for the few lower paid jobs available in Botswana (mostly in the modern sector of the economy).

What had happened, as he himself put it, was that 'the brigades were no longer an alternative but [were] just another formal sector institution'.[32] They were no longer able to keep their costs down and they were meeting the same problems as other formal institutions. In view of these facts it is not surprising that the government failed to increase its support to the brigades and that many of them were therefore forced to close.

Problems in the curriculum

In at least three important ways the brigades were intended to offer more relevant kinds of education than those kinds available in Botswana in either secondary schools or formal trade schools. As we have mentioned, they aimed to be more relevant, by linking skill training closely with the employment opportunities available in the locality. Secondly, they were intended to provide less academic, more practical kinds of knowledge which would be more appropriate to the lives of students and their communities. Thirdly, the organization of teaching was intended to be closely related to the learning of practical skills and knowledge. Thus the process as well as the content of learning was to be changed.

The structure of employment in Botswana, as in other developing countries, was such that qualifications obtained in the formal sector of education were pre-requisites for employment in the modern sector of the economy. The brigades were an attempt to begin to create the basis for wider opportunities for employment in rural areas. They failed to do so. The fault, according to van Rensburg, lay with a government that had not channelled sufficient resources into rural areas to create the demand for the skilled manpower which the brigades provided.

The irony is that if the brigades had succeeded they would very likely have quickened the process of social division in Botswana, rather than creating the basis for a less élitist society. There was in fact a real danger that, given the strength of the links between the formal institutions of education and the modern sector of the economy, Botswana might have developed a dual education system. On the one hand there was the formal system of education – academic, school-based, centrally controlled, and expensive – which provided access to a social élite. On the other, there was the nonformal system provided by the Brigade centres – predominantly practical, heavily oriented towards production, and dependent on support from abroad. The fruits of relevance might well have been not a greater degree of social justice, as Van Rensburg hoped, but an entrenchment of social inequality.

For van Rensburg, at the heart of his attempts to develop more relevant forms of education lay the introduction of productive work into the learning process. The combination of education with production was not just to enable the brigades to cover their costs. Production was, from the beginning, seen as a vehicle for skill training. A particular skill was taught, and then practised and applied. Production was organized so that the trainees were only set to work on those tasks which they had learned. For example, on a building site, first year trainees were taught to lay bricks using mud and they then built the straight walls which were required. Second and third year trainees made the corners, which were more difficult than the straight walls. Such 'learning by doing' was considered superior to the theoretical, classroom instruction which trade schools offered. It was also considered vital in encouraging appropriate attitudes towards manual work and the 'real' conditions of a working life. Van Rensburg believed that: 'productive work in schools seen in these terms can improve the learning process. Schooling as we know it almost everywhere today, is preoccupied with mental activity.'[33]

As we have seen, however, the brigades aimed to do more than merely provide the basic skills which were needed to perform particular jobs. They were also designed to give trainees some basic general education. The foundation of this general education consisted of elementary classes in English and mathematics. Development studies combined a range of different disciplines – history, sociology, politics, economics and geography.

Productive work was, for van Rensburg, the basis for a concept of education very different from that on which the schools operated. The brigades were based on a belief in the need for education to teach practical skills, on the need to be relevant to immediate, local conditions. For him the schools in Botswana and elsewhere were 'too preoccupied with mental activity', too 'academic' and therefore 'irrelevant'. However, the non-formal alternative which he pioneered existed uneasily between the need to provide a basic education designed to develop the mental capacities and social awareness of the trainees, and the need to provide a training in practical skills. The conditions and purposes of the training in functional skills were in many ways quite different from the conditions and purposes involved in developing social awareness.

To illustrate what is meant let us take up once again the notion of relevance. While it is perfectly justifiable to argue, as van Rensburg did, that people can best be trained in a practical, 'on-the-job' setting to perform certain skills necessary for a production process, this notion of what is relevant does not necessarily apply to the concept of 'education', which is much less limited than that of 'training'. Indeed it might well be argued that the primary task of education: 'is not to be relevant, but to help form a society in which its ideals of free enquiry and rationality shall themselves have become chief touchstones of relevance'.[34]

Relevance for van Rensburg was also connected with the relationship between an educational institution and its environment. His main criticism of school education was that it had been dissociated from its local environment. Yet he himself realized that it was not an awareness of the immediate local environment which the young brigade trainees desperately needed: far more necessary was the provision of opportunities to learn about the national and international significance of the problems which the people of Botswana faced. This indeed was the purpose of the development studies course.

Despite the energy with which the brigades have attempted to confront the pressing problems of limited rural opportunities for paid employment, they have encountered problems. A 1980 report comments that brigades had had a strong *impact* on rural communities.[35] For example, the Serowe Brigade Development Trust was the largest employer in the whole of Central District, and 80 per cent of the basic technical training in Botswana took place in brigades. Looking at the *involvement* of rural communities, however, the picture was less favourable:

1 Too many Brigade Secretaries used their Boards of Trustees to rubber-stamp their decisions instead of securing direct involvement.
2 Rapid expansion alienated some Centres from the communities they were supposed to be serving.
3 In one case where the Brigade Secretary did involve the community, he did not coordinate activities with the brigade staff.
4 Many trustees did not attend Board meetings because they did not feel able to contribute.
5 The inputs of foreign aid had reduced the emphasis on local financing. This had worsened both the general lack of interest and a financial crisis which arose when the aid money ceased to be available.

Van Rensburg and his colleagues found that it was much harder to operate a community-based system than they had anticipated, and other observers should learn from their experience. Nevertheless, most of their ideals were good ones, and it is important for educators to continue to try to relate education to the needs of the community it is supposed to serve.

Questions and project work

1 We began this chapter with a quotation from Nigeria's Udoji Report, which said that 'for at least 60 years educationists . . . have been saying that education is too school-oriented and not sufficiently life-oriented'. Comment, with reference to your own country, on the obstacles to reform of education systems to make them more life-oriented.

2 With reference to your own country, make a list of the financial and non-financial ways that communities help schools at the primary and secondary levels. Discuss the advantages and disadvantages of these forms of assistance, and comment on what you think would be an appropriate government policy towards the issue.

3 This chapter has focussed on links between communities and schools of the Western type. Turn back to Chapter 5 and decide whether you think the links between communities and Qur'anic schools are stronger or weaker than links with Western-type schools.

4 The case-study commented on the need for brigade-type organizations in Botswana and on the problems they have faced. Do you think that the needs and the problems are unique to Botswana? Discuss the experience in your own country in the light of the issues raised in the case-study.

Notes

1 Nigeria, Federal Republic *Public Service Review Commission Main Report (Udoji Report)*. Federal Ministry of Education, Lagos 1974, p. 137.
2 Banda, K.R. *et al.* 'The Practice of Community Education in Africa' in King, Kenneth (ed.) *Education and the Community in Africa*. Centre of African Studies, University of Edinburgh 1976, pp. 97-8.
3 Bray, T.M., Moemeka, A.A. and Dondo, J.M.C. 'Education and the Community in Africa: Two Case Studies from Nigeria and Kenya' in King, ibid., pp. 219-27.
4 Great Britain, Colonial Office *Education Policy in British Tropical Africa*. His Majesty's Stationery Office, 1925, p. 4.
5 Unesco *Final Report: Conference of Ministers of Education of African Member States, Lagos, January 27th – February 4th 1976*. Paris 1976, p. 35.
6 Great Britain, op. cit., p. 5.
7 Unesco, op. cit., p. 22.
8 Graham, Sonia *Government and Mission Education in Northern Nigeria 1900-1919*. Ibadan University Press, Ibadan 1966, pp. 79-97; Bray, Mark *Universal Primary Education in Nigeria: A Study of Kano State*. Routledge and Kegan Paul, London 1981, pp. 36-8.
9 Sinclair, M.E. 'Education, Relevance and the Community: A First Look at the History of Attempts to Introduce Productive Work into the Primary School Curriculum' in King, op. cit., p. 72.
10 Bryant Mumford, W. 'Malangali School'. *Africa*, Vol. III, No. 3, 1930, p. 271.
11 Sinclair, op. cit., p. 74.
12 Cameron, J. and Dodd, W.A. *'Education for Self-Reliance' in Tanzania: A Study of its Vocational Aspects*. Teachers College, Columbia University, New York 1969.
13 Nimpuno, Krisno 'Design for Community Education: General Proposition and Case Study Material on Community Education Centres in Tanzania' in King, op. cit.; Kinunda, M.J. and Tosh, Alex 'The School and Community Interact: Community-centred Education in the United Republic of Tanzania' in Unesco/UNICEF, *Basic Services for Children: A Continuing Search for Learning Priorities*. International Bureau of Education, Geneva 1978; Nyerere, Julius *Education for Self-Reliance*. Ministry of Information and Tourism, Dar es Salaam 1967.
14 Hawes, Hugh *Curriculum and Reality in African Primary Schools*. Longman, London 1979, p. 168.
15 Grabe, Sven *et al.* 'Upper Volta: A Rural Alternative to Primary Schools' in

Ahmed, M. and Coombs, P.H. (eds.) *Education for Rural Development.* Praeger, New York 1975.
16 Ngegba, F.B.S. 'The Bunumbu Experience in Sierra Leone' in Unesco/UNICEF *Basic Services for Children: A Continuing Search for Learning Priorities.* International Bureau of Education, Geneva 1978.
17 Hawes, op. cit., p. 60.
18 Lallez, Raymond *An Experiment in the Ruralization of Education: IPAR and the Cameroonian Reform.* International Bureau of Education, Geneva 1974.
19 Kinahan, Timothy 'Education and the Community in Ethiopia: The Experience of the Asra Hawariat School' in King, op. cit.
20 Hawes, op. cit., p. 62.
21 Bray, op. cit., p. 71.
22 Bray, Dondo and Moemeka, op. cit., pp. 227–35.
23 Wellings, P.A. 'Unaided Education in Kenya: Blessing or Blight?'. *Research in Education*, No. 29, May 1983.
24 Nyerere, op. cit., p. 15.
25 Banda *et al.*, p. 101.
26 Van Rensburg, P. *Report from Swaneng Hill.* Dag Hammarskjöld Foundation, Uppsala 1974; Van Rensburg, P. *The Serowe Brigades.* Macmillan, London 1978.
27 Van Rensburg, 1978, op. cit., p. 21.
28 Van Rensburg, 1974, op. cit., p. 35.
29 Ibid., Appendix.
30 Van Rensburg, 1978, op. cit., p. 68.
31 Van Rensburg, P. The *Guardian*, Third World Review, 25/3/81.
32 Ibid.
33 Ibid.
34 Scheffler, I. *Reason and Teaching.* London 1973, quoted by Ashcroft, R. *The School as a Base for Community Development.* CERI OECD, 1975.
35 Kukler, R. 'Vocational Training within the Brigade System' in Bude, U. (ed.) *Education for Kagisano.* German Foundation for International Development, Bonn, 1980, pp. 219–20.

Chapter 8

The school as a society

So far, this book has been looking at three 'levels' of social organization. Various chapters have in turn focused on worldwide, national and local communities. Now we should note that schools themselves are societies. Once a child, a teacher or a parent enters a school compound, specific types of behaviour and social relationships are expected.

Relationships between the children and teachers are influenced by the ways they perceive their obligations and rights, and by existing traditions. Children entering school for the first time soon learn that teachers and other pupils hold firm expectations about the way pupils should behave, and some requirements of behaviour are even written down as school rules. Pupils also learn that teachers themselves are subject to the higher authority of their headteacher or principal. Thus they learn that both teachers and pupils have certain obligations to accept the authority of others. They also learn that they have certain rights – for example that the teachers are supposed to teach them, and that the headteacher is supposed to organize the school in an effective way.

On their side, teachers also know that they have obligations and rights. They are aware of their place in the hierarchy, and know that their main responsibility is to teach the children. They usually insist on being addressed as Madam or Sir rather than by their names. Within conventional classrooms the teachers' desks have special status, with the official recognition of the teachers' privacy. The teachers may inspect pupils' desks whenever they want to, but children are not allowed to inspect the teachers'. Likewise, the staff room is usually exclusive to teachers, and is not a place to which pupils are commonly invited.

Parents are the third main group of people interested in the school. Usually, they enter the compound only in circumstances which clearly define their roles. If they are helping to maintain the compound, they attend on specific days at specific times to cut the grass or repair the buildings. If they come for another purpose, they usually go first to the office of the headteacher or another senior person, in recognition that these people are in charge of the school. Parents know that they should respect the professional judgements of the headteacher and staff, but also that they have the right to be informed about the progress of their children.

Also in this chapter, we shall examine a society even smaller than the individual school, namely a classroom within a school. We shall look at the ways teachers treat their pupils and the ways pupils treat each other. Again, relationships in this society are governed by both explicit and hidden rules. Even the physical layout and seating arrangements of classrooms may be significant.

The school as an organization

Like other organizations, schools are carefully structured and hierarchical. At the top of each school is the headteacher, followed by the deputy. Then comes a hierarchy of departmental heads and more junior teachers. Cleaners, cooks and messengers are not usually directly accountable to the ordinary teachers, but they are generally considered to be at the bottom of the pyramid of employees. A hierarchy also exists among the pupils. At the top are the prefects and pupils in higher grades, and at the bottom are the children who have just joined the lowest grade. In addition, there may be overlapping hierarchies among pupils based on sports, and academic achievement. There may also be sub-divisions within the school based on houses.

Apart from these explicit strands of organization, there may also be implicit ones. Both teachers and pupils group themselves according to friendship patterns and other social ties. To gain a full picture of a school's organization one must look at sexual, ethnic and religious groupings. In many schools, for example, the female teachers have loyalties to each other. The female pupils may have loyalties to each other, and there may be additional ties between the female teachers and the female pupils. In the playground children may tend to stick to their own ethnic groups and speak their own languages, and in schools containing both Muslims and Christians there may be strands of allegiance based on religion.

These sub-groupings within the overall organization sometimes threaten the unity of the whole. There may be tension between pupils and teachers, for example, which can lead to a strike. Or there may be bullying of pupils from minority ethnic groups and religions, which causes further division. One of the headteacher's jobs is to ensure that diversity is a positive force rather than a negative one, and to devise ways to make sure that the sub-groups work in harmony. The unity of the school is stressed when all children meet together at assembly time. It is also displayed in such symbols as the school crest and uniform, and during sporting competitions with other schools.

Leadership styles

Because of the overall responsibilities of the headteachers, it is useful to look at alternative leadership styles. Leaders can be defined as people who direct and push their organizations towards explicit and implicit goals. They should also monitor and evaluate progress. Thirdly, they should be responsible for the success or failure of their organizations, though sometimes the goals of institutions are over-ambitious and it is unreasonable to blame the institutional heads if they are not achieved.

There are three basic styles of leadership: autocratic, democratic, and laissez-faire.[1] Good leaders usually combine all three styles, though some give strong emphasis to particular ones.

We have probably all met autocratic leaders: more commanders than democrats, dictators rather than delegators. Such leaders may work towards very high goals, yet in the process they often establish and reinforce opposing implicit aims of education. For example many autocratic leaders discourage discussion and create a climate of fear, which in turn causes the learning environment to be poor.

Democratic leaders, by contrast, provide much more leadership and, unlike the autocrats, derive their authority and power from the group they lead. They represent their groups and are accountable to them. Words like 'consultation', 'discussion' and 'participation' come to mind when we think of a democratic style of leadership. It is not always easy for democratic leaders to introduce changes, for they must first secure the agreement of at least the majority of people who will be affected. If they do this, however, there is usually a greater chance of the changes being successful.

The word *laissez-faire* (pronounced 'lessay-fair') has been adopted in the English language from the French. It refers to a policy of non-interference, in which people are left to behave as they like. This can be a good policy, for it may allow people to exercise their initiative and develop their own projects without obstruction. However it can also be a bad one which reflects laziness and lack of interest. Schools with laissez-faire heads are often chaotic and unhappy places, lacking in guidance and control.

As well as combining these three styles, good leaders also balance the needs of those involved in the organization with the aims to be achieved. On the subject of school discipline, for example, good headteachers have some ideas themselves, consult their Boards of Governors, teachers and pupils, and take care to delegate authority where necessary. However, teachers might feel that imposition of strong discipline requires them to do too much work, and pupils might prefer to be free to behave as they like. In this case, good institutional heads also remember the overall aims of their schools, and do not allow the views of sub-groups within the system to control everything.

Decision-making

We have all at one time or another been faced with the task of decision-making. Usually a decision rests on awareness of several alternatives, and on awareness of the consequences of each alternative (of which one, of course, is simply 'doing nothing'). Sometimes the decision is made easier by the existence of rule books, but at other times the complexity of the situation calls for courage and wisdom based on as many objective criteria as possible.

Some headteachers decide to delegate responsibility. When they do this, they have already made one decision, namely to allow other people to decide. Delegation may improve job satisfaction for junior teachers because it allows them to feel that they can influence the operation of their schools.

Of course it is not possible for leaders to be totally objective when they make decisions. Cultural factors such as home background, ethnicity and work experience influence decision-makers because they affect the choices that they feel are legitimate and worth considering. They may also justify the decisions taken. People never like to feel that they have made wrong decisions, particularly if the decisions seem to have been made more to suit their own personal goals than the more explicit goals of their schools or colleges. In such situations, teachers may lose confidence in the integrity of their leaders.

Musaazi's model of shared decision-making (Table 8.1) helps show what happens in education systems with explicitly stated goals, well defined decision-making procedures, and clearly identifiable personnel to act as leaders. It is a useful explanation of the ideal situation towards which administrators might aim. The boxes at the top show the main thought processes and actions of the administrator, and the parallel boxes below show the same processes and actions among the staff. The dotted lines show that there may be a link between the administrator and staff at each stage. The notes at the bottom of the table provide some critical questions which decision-makers must answer.

The real world, however, is more complicated than is suggested by this diagram. Instead of school administrators being left alone to run their institutions as they see fit, they are required to respond to the demands of their communities, to senior education officers, and to politicians. The system is not therefore quite so self-contained as Musaazi's chart suggests. Also, in the real world some administrators and staff are poorly motivated. They refuse to recognise problems until they become urgent, and they take sudden decisions without either consultation or research into the issues. Finally, in the real world many systems are shaped by the forces of tradition, tribalism and corruption.

Factors in social grouping

Within a school, as we have already mentioned, pupils voluntarily form themselves into friendship groups. These may be based on common academic or leisure interests, and may also be influenced by such factors as sex, ethnicity and religion. The ways these groups form and operate deserves further discussion.

The views of different cultures on the ways girls and boys should treat each other vary quite widely. Some cultures encourage quite free interaction, while others, especially during the teenage years, restrict contact between girls and boys. Single-sex schools can be found all over the continent, in both Christian and Islamic communities, especially in the case of girls. Where the sexes are educated separately, clearly the nature of the schools are societies is different from institutions where boys and girls learn together.

Table 8.1 Diagram of the shared decision-making process[2]

Administrator row:
Administrator recognizes problem. → Administrator defines and analyses problem. → Administrator establishes criteria for acceptable solution. → Administrator collects data. → Administrator identifies and evaluates alternatives and consequences. → Administrator seeks advice. → Administrator selects alternative.

Problem exists.

Decision is implemented.

Staff row:
Staff recognizes problem. → Staff defines and analyses problem. → Staff establishes criteria for acceptable solution. → Staff collects data. → Staff identifies and evaluates alternatives and consequences. → Staff seeks advice. → Staff selects alternative.

Questions to be asked

1 Does a problem really exist?
2 Is the problem recognized by both administrator and staff?
3 Is the problem within our jurisdiction? Are we willing to accept responsibility for the decision? If we are contemplating passing the buck, do we have justifiable reasons for doing so? What do we wish to accomplish through this decision? In what stages of the decision-making process should others be involved? Which others?
4 What are the criteria for the acceptability of a decision?
5 Are all the necessary facts at hand, and can they be checked?
6 Have all the possible alternatives and consequences been identified and evaluated sufficiently?
7 Is the organization ready for a decision? Who should select the alternatives?
8 Has the decision been clearly communicated to all essential persons? Has provision been made for implementation and control of the implementation? Has provision been made for feedback, review and evaluation of the decision? Have we established a process, policy, set of criteria etc. that can serve in making other decisions? What have we learned from this decision-making?

Although quite a lot of research has been conducted on sexual group-ings in mixed-sex schools in Western countries,[3] less work has been done in Africa. Nevertheless, Durojaiye's research in Uganda and Nigeria has shown that in at least some cases similar patterns apply. Durojaiye pointed out that in the pre-adolescent period, boys and girls in mixed-sex schools tend to gravitate to separate sexual groups. With the arrival of adolescence, however, the two sexes become more interested in each other.[4]

> In early adolescence boys and girls remain in separate groups, but the group of girls will talk and walk with the boys if the opportuni-ties permit. Later, at the age of 15 onwards, pairing of boys and girls in common; 81% of the mixed-sex day secondary schools' pupils in Ibadan and Kampala, who were aged between 15 and 19, had regular friends of the opposite sex. Only 27% of the 13–14-year-olds had regular friends of the opposite sex.

Pupils may also group themselves by ethnicity. For example, in Nigeria's Federal Government Colleges, which recruit pupils by quota from all states in the federation, students have tended strongly to socialise with other students from the same ethnic group.[5] This need not be seen negatively, for it is natural for students to seek colleagues who share their linguistic and cultural backgrounds. In one problematic example, how-ever, Elliot describes a school which ran into serious administrative problems and in which the students began to organize their own affairs independently of the official hierarchy. They set up their own systems of authority, and each leader had his own group of juniors who washed for him, copied up his notes and received his protection. Elliot records that such systems were built up within each ethnic group, and unhappy were those outside it or those who had none of their own group to protect them. [6]

Thirdly, students may socialise in religious groups. As with other pat-terns of social behaviour, this tendency has not yet been extensively researched in Africa. However, it has been observed in the Nigerian Federal Government Colleges we have just mentioned,[7] and one would expect it to happen in other parts of the continent.

The classroom as an organization

Of course the style of administration of the headteacher or principal is only one factor influencing what happens inside a school, and the main business of the institution goes on in its classrooms. Just as we can describe the school as a society, we can also describe the classroom as a society. It has its own rules which influence relationships both between the teacher and the pupils and between the pupils themselves. As we know from memories of our own schooling, the quality and personal philosophy of a teacher can have a strong influence on examination performance and the pupils' attitudes. All children are also influenced by their peers (equals).

Pupil seating patterns and teaching styles

The way in which desks are arranged says a lot about the nature of the society inside a classroom. In most classrooms in Africa, the pupils sit in neat rows facing the teacher. The seating arrangement is designed to allow the children to interact with the teacher but not with each other. The pupils are made to sit in ways that allow them to see only the backs of the heads of the children in front of them. When one stops to think about how much people can learn from each other, this might seem surprising. However the seating arrangement strengthens the authority of the teacher, and enables her to control the class more tightly.

In many classrooms, children may choose to sit where they like. Indeed, in some secondary schools the children move to different rooms for each lesson, and change their places even when they return to their original rooms. However in other classrooms the teachers decide where children may sit. For example they may put troublesome children at the front, where they can be controlled more easily, or they may send two children who play and distract each other when they sit together to opposite sides of the room.

Some schools rank pupils according to their academic achievement and then seat them accordingly. The child who scores the highest marks is seated at the back in a corner, and is followed by the child with the next highest mark. This ranking and seating arrangement continues all the way through the classroom, until the front row is of pupils who have scored the lowest marks. Some teachers go even further, and display a list of names of the four children who have performed best and the four who have performed worst in the grading.

Some psychologists are very critical of this practice. Siann and Ugwuegbu, for example, point out that in this system the success of each child depends on the failure of the others.[8] The praise for and resulting pleasure of the top children is one side of the coin, but the opposite side is disgrace and emotional strain for the bottom children. Indeed, they add, only the child at the top of the whole class can experience a feeling of total success, and the others will all experience varying degrees of failure. While some teachers claim that the ranking encourages better overall performances, Siann and Ugwuegbu argue that it only reinforces the unhealthy aspects of an extremely competitive approach, and is not necessarily constructive. They recommend that such seating arrangements should be abandoned.

Whether one would go further and also recommend that pupils should cease to sit in straight rows would partly depend on one's recommendations for the style of teaching. Here it is appropriate to contrast what is often called the 'discovery' method of teaching with the 'chalk and talk' method. Discovery methods are popular in industrialised countries, where many educationists argue that children learn more thoroughly and more effectively when they discover things for themselves instead of just being told facts. Children are usually organized into smaller groups and work at their own speeds, and the teachers aim to be guides and supporters more than suppliers of knowledge.

For several reasons, however, discovery methods are not widely used in Africa. One factor is the relatively low skill and self-confidence of the teachers, for it is easier to use chalk and talk methods than to guide discovery learning. A second factor is a widespread shortage of materials, for it is hard to encourage discovery learning if the children have nothing to discover *with*. A third factor is philosophical: many teachers and parents favour an organized environment, and distrust what they consider to be the potential chaos of children learning in their own ways and at their own speeds, often with considerable noise. Many teachers also feel that discovery methods threaten their status, for the teachers may seem to have higher prestige when they are the sources of knowledge and when they direct children to do exactly as they are told. Also, child-centred approaches may be hard to operate in situations of rapid staff turn-over, for effective teaching through discovery methods requires the teachers to know their pupils quite well. Finally, the examination system in many countries discourages the pupils from demanding discovery learning. If the examinations require recall of facts or manipulation of mathematical processes, the fastest way to learn, many students feel, is by gaining the information straight from the teachers. Because of these factors, neither teaching styles nor seating patterns are likely to change much in the near future.

Nevertheless even when the approach is teacher-centred, there can be wide variations in the extent to which the teachers involve their pupils. Datta researched the amount of teacher-pupil interaction in a Zambian school, and commented on the different styles of individual staff.[9] He pointed out that some teachers encourage pupils to ask a lot of questions, while others prefer to lecture. The lessons in which the teacher asks a lot of questions generally have much more activity, and probably the students learn more. Teachers who only lecture find it harder both to know whether their pupils are really following them and to keep the pupils' attention. Datta also referred to the fact that the teachers in the school he visited devoted 'an inordinate proportion of time . . . to note-taking and reading'.[10] Long periods of note-taking may be desirable when pupils do not have their own textbooks, but frequently the activity reflects inappropriate training or a lack of imagination on the part of the teacher.

Pupil achievement and self-fulfilling prophecies

Teachers often make assumptions about their pupils' potential, predicting that some pupils will perform well in school and that others will perform poorly. These assumptions are not always initially justified, but research has shown that the teachers' subsequent behaviour may encourage the pupils who have been identified as potentially successful and discourage the ones that have been identified as poor performers. In this way, the initial predictions become self-fulfilling prophecies. Most of the research on this subject has been conducted in industrialised countries, but one would expect the same factors to operate in Africa.

One of the most famous studies on this topic was conducted in the

United States by Rosenthal and Jacobsen.[11] They randomly tested the intelligence of a group of pupils. Then they deliberately gave the teachers misleading information on the results of their tests, telling them that a few children were exceptionally bright. A year later, they tested the performance of the pupils again, and found that most of the ones that they had said were bright had in fact performed significantly better than average – even though in reality their original tests had not shown them to be particularly bright. The researchers concluded that the test children had begun to perform better because the teachers had treated them differently. It is not uncommon for teachers to ask more questions of some pupils than of others, and through their use of praise or sarcasm to give other forms of encouragement or discouragement. This may be done consciously or unconsciously. The point is that teachers often label children as good or bad performers, and through their subsequent actions actually lead the children to be good or bad performers – quite independently of the children's actual intelligence and aptitudes.

As well as occurring within individual classrooms, a similar process may apply to whole groups of children. Rist carried out a study which complemented that by Rosenthal and Jacobsen. His work was also in the United States, and over a period of three years he followed the progress of pupils. He found:[12]

> that after only eight days of kindergarten, the teacher made permanent seating arrangements based on what she assumed were variations in academic capability. But no formal evaluation of the children had taken place. Instead, the assignments to the three tables were based on a number of socio-economic criteria as well as on early interaction patterns in the classroom. Thus, the placement of the children came to reflect the social class distinctions in the room – the poor children . . . all sat at one table', the working class children sat at another and the middle class children at a third. I demonstrated how the teacher operationalized her expectations of these different groups of children in terms of her differentials of·teaching time, her use of praise and control, and the extent of autonomy within the classroom. By following the same children through first and second grade as well, I was able to show that the initial patterns established by the kindergarten teacher came to be perpetuated year after year. By second grade, labels given by another teacher clearly reflected the reality each of the groups experienced in the school. The top group was called the "Tigers", the middle group the "Cardinals", and the lowest group the "Clowns". What had begun as a subjective evaluation and labelling by the teacher took on objective dimensions as the school proceeded to process the children on the basis of the distinctions made when they first began.

This type of research highlights the dangers of streaming, i.e. of putting allegedly bright children in one particular grade into one class (e.g. Form 2A), the allegedly average children into another class (e.g. Form 2B), and the allegedly weak children into a third class (e.g. Form 2C). This practice, it is suggested, can be self-fulfilling, for the teachers may make the class of allegedly bright pupils work harder, and the children will have positive self-images. Conversely, the teachers may not push the allegedly dull students so hard, and the children will have negative self-images. Thus, even when the initial classification of children is invalid, the results could seem to bear it out.[13]

The research also highlights the need for teachers to check their own behaviour in the classroom. Whom do they speak to most? Whom do they look at when they are speaking? Whom do they encourage, and whom do they discourage? In their language and actions, do they imply that girls should be submissive to boys and not score such high marks? Do they seem to expect more from children of particular ethnic groups or social backgrounds? They should be aware of this danger so that they can try their best to avoid discrimination and be fair.

Charting social groups

Within a school, as we have already mentioned, pupils voluntarily group themselves into friendship patterns. One may chart social interaction by producing tables and drawing what are called sociograms.[14] As we know from our own experiences, the friendship and respect of a child's peers (equals) is very important. It can therefore be useful to examine relationships within individual classes. If study shows that certain children are rejected or isolated, the teacher may take appropriate action.

To collect date for a sociogram, the teacher must have the confidence of her pupils. She must also make it quite clear that the information she is requesting from them will be treated in strict confidence and will in no way damage their school careers. She then asks each of the children about whom they would like most (or least) to join them in specific situations. For example, she could ask them whom they would most like to play games with, or whom they would most like to receive homework help from (which might be different people), or whom they would most like to sit next to in class (which might be different again). Alternatively, she could ask them whom they would *least* like to pay games with, receive homework help from, or six next to in class. The questioning is probably best done in private, though it may be done in class if the children can give responses without the others knowing their feelings.

The responses can then be put on a table and in a sociogram. The example shown here is a simple one. The eleven children in a class were each asked to name the two children who they would like to sit next to them. The results were then put on a chart (Table 8.2). An *x* shows that the child named on the left hand side would like the child named at the top to six next to her/him. The 'total' row at the bottom gives an idea of the popularity of each child. In our example, Agnes is the most popular, for five children would like her to sit next to them.

The situation can then be put on a sociogram as in Table 8.3. The arrows show who each child has chosen, and the sociogram can tell you how the informal groups in the class are distributed. In our sociogram,

Table 8.2   Chart of responses of children requested to list the two classmates that they would most like to sit next to them

	Agnes	Bello	Audu	Rachel	Njere	Musa	Mark	Chima	Ahmed	Ora	Kate
Agnes				x							x
Bello	x										x
Audu		x			x						
Rachel	x		x								
Njere	x									x	
Musa											
Mark								x		x	
Chima	x									x	
Ahmad		x									x
Ora						x	x				
Kate	x							x			
Total	5	2	1	1	2	0	1	2	0	3	3

Table 8.3   Diagram to show the popularity of each of the eleven pupils of a class among classmates, regarding sitting preferences.

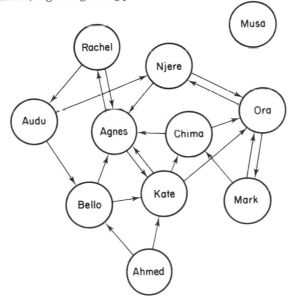

Agnes, Ora and Kate are the most popular people in the class. They are called 'stars', and would probably be class leaders. Arrows between Agnes and Kate show that their friendship is reciprocated, but there is no arrow between Ora and Kate, and they seem to operate independently. Ahmed would like other people to sit next to him, but nobody particularly wants him to six next to them. Since nobody has chosen Ahmed, he would be called an isolate. Musa is also an isolate, and in his case he also refused to indicate that he wanted anyone to sit next to him. He would therefore be called a 'true' isolate. The teacher would probably be rather worried about Ahmed, and even more about Musa.

If the teacher wanted to get a more detailed picture, she would ask different questions and build up a more complicated sociogram. She could add dotted lines to indicate negative attitudes, and colours to indicate different strengths of responses. She would also compare the pupils' statements with information gained from general observation and from the comments of other teachers.

Some dangers of sociograms must also be noted. First, it is difficult to draw a sociogram for a large group, or even to show a large number of choices for a small group. Secondly, the sociogram emphasises the number of favourable choices received by an individual rather than the person who makes the choice. In practice, a choice by someone who is generally neglected should not be given the same weight as a choice by a star. Thirdly, the sociogram shows only the feelings of the children at one moment in time, and unless it is repeated, it cannot allow for changes in attitudes. Nevertheless if used carefully, sociograms can help the observer to learn a great deal about the sociology of the classroom.

Questions and project work

1 Distinguish, with examples, between headteachers' leadership styles that are autocratic, democratic and laissez-faire. Indicate the advantages and disadvantages of each type of approach.

2 This chapter has pointed out that schools are themselves societies, with conventions that determine the ways pupils and staff interact with each other and with their peers. Go through the points that have been raised, and comment on whether they also apply to universities.

3 Discuss the view that teaching styles in African secondary schools should focus much more on discovery learning and that there should be reduced emphasis on 'chalk and talk'.

4 What did we mean in this chapter when we referred to pupil achievement and self-fulfilling prophecies? The research data that we have cited originated in the United States. Do you think that the findings could be applied to your own society? Give reasons for your answer, and provide examples where possible.

Notes

1 Musaazi, J.C.S. *The Theory and Practice of Educational Administration.* Macmillan, London 1982.
2 Ibid., p. 89.

3 See for example Schofield, M. *The Sexual Behaviour of Young People*. Longman Green, London 1965; Furlong, V.J. 'Interaction in the Classroom', in Stubbs, M. and Delamont, S. (eds.) *Explorations in Classroom Observation*. Wiley, Chichester 1976; Deem, Rosemary *Women and Schooling*. Routledge and Kegan Paul, London 1978; Delamont, Sara *Sex Roles and the School*. Methuen, London 1980.

4 Durojaiye, M.O.A. *A New Introduction to Educational Psychology*. Evans, London 1976, p. 213.

5 See, for example, Bray, T.M. and Cooper, G.R. 'Education and Nation Building in Nigeria since the Civil War'. *Comparative Education*, Vol. 15, No. 1, 1979, p. 37.

6 Elliot, K. *An African School: A Record of Experience*. Cambridge University Press, Cambridge 1970, p. 98.

7 Bray and Cooper, op. cit., p. 37.

8 Siann, Gerda and Ugwuegbu, Denis *Educational Psychology in a Changing World*. George, Allen and Unwin, London 1980, p. 185.

9 Datta, Ansu *Education and Society: A Sociology of African Education*. Macmillan, London 1984, pp. 99–107.

10 Ibid., p. 106.

11 Rosenthal, R. and Jacobson, L. *Pygmalion in the Classroom*. Holt, Rinehart and Winston, New York 1968.

12 Rist, Ray C. 'On Understanding the Processes of Schooling: The Contributions of Labeling Theory' in Karabel, Jerome and Halsey, A.H. (eds.) *Power and Ideology in Education*. Oxford University Press, New York 1977, p. 298.

13 See also Hargreaves, D.H. *Interpersonal Relations and Education*. Routledge and Kegan Paul, London 1975.

14 Siann and Ugwuegbu, op. cit., pp. 191–3; Datta, op. cit., pp. 108–11.

Chapter 9

The curriculum and society

The nature of the learning that occurs in schools obviously strongly affects the skills and attitudes of young people and, as they grow older, society as a whole. It is therefore necessary to devote a separate chapter to the curriculum.

The word curriculum covers a wide area and is often used rather loosely. To begin with, we should distinguish between the official and the hidden curriculum. When most people refer to the official curriculum, they are thinking about syllabus documents and timetables. Broader definitions, however, include official statements of goals, the structure of education systems, and the content and style of examinations.

The hidden curriculum, in contrast, covers the type of learning that takes place in schools but is not planned by the education authorities. All of us learned a great deal at school which our teachers did not specifically plan to teach us. Some of the learning was valuable, and some of it was not. As Ozigi and Canham have pointed out:

> From some of our teachers (the best) we learned to appreciate the importance of proper values and to admire the great achievements of the human spirit. These things were not planned for in the same way as our studies in the Arts and Sciences, or as extra-curricular or co-curricular activities, and to that extent they were "hidden", though school authorities no doubt planned in a general sort of way that the atmosphere of the school would be such as to encourage this type of learning.[1]

We also learned a great deal from our fellow students at school. Not all of it was useful, and in some cases it may not have been desirable. However we learned it all the same, without any planning or intervention from the teachers. The simple point is that one cannot stop human beings learning; we learn all the time, even when we are not guided to do so.

Although it is important to identify the hidden curriculum, it has already been partly discussed in Chapter 8. Also, several parts of this book have already commented on aspects of the official curriculum. This chapter therefore concentrates on official statements of goals, the structure of school systems, school timetables, language in the curriculum, gender in the curriculum, and examinations.

Official statements of goals

Government statements of goals are a logical place to begin discussion of the official curriculum, since they are supposed to set the overall structure and method of operation of the system. Among the documents which we have in mind are the Nigerian *National Policy on Education*, which was first issued in 1977 and then revised in 1981,[2] and the similar document in Botswana which was issued in 1977.[3] Separate sections in these statements indicate the official purposes of each part of the education system.

In addition to these documents are a large number of others. For example the main predecessor to Nigeria's 1977 *National Policy* was a 1973 report,[4] and all governments have education acts, policy statements and official syllabuses. Thus all countries have official papers which indicate goals, even if they are not collected into a single place and given a title like *National Policy on Education*.

However, it must also be noted that what actually happens in classrooms depends chiefly on the teachers. A large number of teachers are unaware that many of the official policy documents exist. They are too busy operating the system to have much time to think about what its objectives are and whether they are suitable. Sometimes the goals are too general, and are not translated into specific policy instructions. Yet even when they are translated into instructions, teachers and administrators do not always follow them. For example many governments have official policies of automatic promotion and forbid children to repeat grades. In practice, however, these policies are widely ignored.[5]

The structure of school systems

The length of each unit within the system can also be described as part of the official curriculum, and may be changed from time to time. The Ghanaian government, for example, decided to reduce the length of the basic education course from ten to eight years in the early 1960s and then to change it again to a 6 + 3 system.[6] Similarly, in the early 1980s Nigeria replaced a 6 + 5 + 2 + 3 system with a 6 + 3 + 3 + 4 one (i.e. six years of primary school, three of junior secondary, three of senior secondary and four of university); and in 1985 Kenya replaced a 7 + 4 + 2 + 3 system with a 8 + 4 + 4 one.

One good argument for reducing the length of the first stage is that resources can then be spread more widely. It is also possible that some families unwilling to spare children for a full seven or eight year course would be able to release them for a shorter one, for which a specific syllabus could be designed. On the other hand it is important for the first unit to be long enough for basic skills to be properly learned. It is commonly accepted that at least four years of schooling are necessary for a child to become permanently literate,[7] and an argument in favour of a longer unit is that it may encourage a child to stay in the system for a longer period.

In the Nigerian system, the chief advantage of secondary school being split into junior and senior sections is that young people who might not stay in secondary schools for five years can stay for three but still reach a recognised end point. If the government makes junior secondary schooling free, the fact that it is only for three years also limits the extent of official commitments.

Alterations in the structure can therefore be ways to meet new priorities and adapt to changes in resource availability. However, frequent alterations in the structure are undesirable because they cause confusion and require syllabuses to be rewritten.

School timetables and syllabuses

Table 9.1 compares official time allocations to different subjects in Grades 2 and 7 in the primary schools of four countries. Some diversity should be noted, both in the total time allocations (shown by the sizes of the circles) and in the allocations to different subjects. Lesotho and Swaziland pupils did not learn social studies as a separate subject, nor did Grade 2 children in Uganda. All countries taught more science in the upper grade than in the lower one, but there was a wide difference in the amount of science taught to Swaziland Grade 2 children compared to their Ugandan counterparts. At the same time, however, these differences are minor and the period allocations had a great deal in common. They all covered the same sorts of subject matter and it was taught in more or less the same styles. Even in schools in French- and Portuguese-speaking Africa the patterns would be largely the same.

Table 9.2 provides more detail on primary school timetables in Tanzania. It divides the years into four categories. The first covers the initial decade of independence, the second covers the years in which the policies of the Arusha Declaration began to be implemented, the third covers the period following the 1974 Musoma Resolution, which reaffirmed the principles of Education for Self-Reliance and took policies further, and the fourth is what has been called the period of consolidation of formal education.

Carr-Hill notes that at independence in Tanzania only two significant changes were made from the colonial syllabus which had been designed for European children and an élite minority.[8] The first followed the designation of Swahili as the national language in 1964, when it became the medium of instruction in primary schools, and the second was the Africanization of the syllabuses, for example in history. The major change after the Arusha Declaration appeared to be an overall reduction in the number of classroom periods per week to allow for self-reliance activities in the afternoons. Swahili, arithmetic and English retained roughly the same number of periods per week in each grade, but 'less important' subjects, such as geography, history, music and physical education, were reduced.

Immediately after the Musoma Resolution, Carr-Hill points out, the balances in Grades 1, 2, 6 and 7 were roughly changed back to their

Table 9.1   Official time allocations by subject, Grades 2 and 7, in four countries[9]

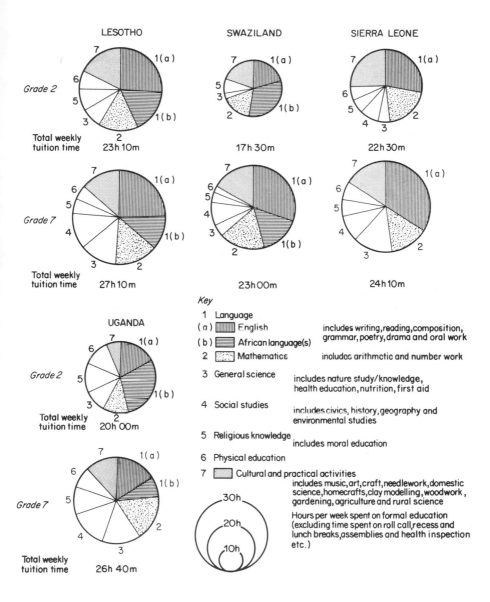

Key

1 Language
(a) ▓ English   includes writing, reading, composition,
(b) ▤ African language(s)   grammar, poetry, drama and oral work
2 ░ Mathematics   includes arithmetic and number work

3 General science
       includes nature study/knowledge,
       health education, nutrition, first aid

4 Social studies
       includes civics, history, geography and
       environmental studies

5 Religious knowledge
       includes moral education

6 Physical education

7 □ Cultural and practical activities
       includes music, art, craft, needlework, domestic
       science, homecrafts, clay modelling, woodwork,
       gardening, agriculture and rural science

       Hours per week spent on formal education
       (excluding time spent on roll call, recess and
       lunch breaks, assemblies and health inspection
       etc.)

Notes: 1 Figures shown were collected in the mid-1970s. Some systems
           may have changed since then.
        2 Some governments organise double shifts in some areas. This may
           modify the times shown.
        3 School and community involvement is occasionally permitted to
           modify time allocations shown.

Table 9.2   Official allocation of subject periods in each grade following different reforms in Tanzania[10]

Subject	1961–70 (post Independence)							1971–74 (post-Arusha)							1974–80 (post-Musoma)							1981–83 (consolidation phase)						
	1	2	3	4	5	6	7	1	2	3	4	5	6	7	1	2	3	4	5	6	7	1	2	3	4	5	6	7
Swahili	9	9	9	7	6	5	5	9	9	9	7	6	6	5	9	9	7	6	6	6	5	12	12	8	8	7	7	6
Arithmetic	5	5	7	7	7	8	8	5	5	6	6	6	7	8	5	5	6	6	7	7	7	9	9	7	7	7	7	8
English	5	5	6	6	6	6	6	5	5	5	5	5	6	6	5	5	5	5	6	7	6	—	—	6	6	6	6	6
Political Education	—	—	2	2	2	2	2	—	—	—	1	1	1	2	—	—	1	1	1	2	2	—	—	1	1	2	2	2
Science (including agriculture)	1	1	5	5	4	4	4	1	1	3	3	3	4	4	1	1	3	3	4	4	4	—	—	2	2	2	2	2
Geography	—	—	3	3	3	3	3	—	—	2	2	2	2	2	—	6	2	2	2	2	2	—	—	2	2	2	2	2
History	—	—	—	3	3	3	2	—	—	—	1	1	2	2	—	—	—	2	2	2	2	—	—	—	—	2	2	2
Domestic Science/Home Economics (optional for boys)																												
Arts and Craft	2	2	2	2	4	4	4	2	2	2	2	2	3	4	2	2	2	2	3	3	4	1	1	2	2	2	2	2
Physical Education	2	2	1	1	2	2	2	2	2	—	1	1	1	2	1	1	1	1	1	1	1	2	2	2	2	2	2	2
Music	2	2	2	1	1	2	2	—	—	1	1	1	1	1	1	1	1	1	1	1	1	2	2	2	2	2	2	2
Religion	2	2	2	2	2	2	2	1	—	1	1	1	1	2	1	1	1	1	1	1	1	2	2	2	2	2	2	2
Adult Education (only for teachers)	—	—	3	3	3	3	3	1	—	3	3	3	3	3	—	—	3	3	3	3	3	—	—	—	—	—	—	—
Agricultural Theory	—	—	—	—	—	—	—	—	—	—	—	—	—	—	3	3	4	4	4	4	4	—	—	—	—	—	2	2

Plus: self reliance every afternoon

Note: The source did not indicate the allocation of periods for Grade 6 between 1971 and 1974.

former levels, though Grades 3 and 4 continued with a reduced number of periods. Finally in 1980 it was decided to exclude English until Grade 3, and extra emphasis was given to Swahili and arithmetic.

A curriculum cannot be evaluated merely by looking at the titles of lessons. However, we can note that despite apparently radical changes in the overall direction of the education system, the balance has not changed very much. Even though 85 per cent of Tanzania's population lives in rural areas, and even though the government has announced bold objectives of self-reliance, agriculture has a very minor place in the curriculum. The emphasis on English has been reduced while that on Swahili has been increased, but the syllabus remains highly academic. The curriculum is still similar to that used during the colonial era, even though the objectives of education have changed significantly and enrolment rates are much higher. Carr-Hill comments that the main current concern of the ministry is to consolidate what is already being offered rather than to question what exists.[11]

Because few other countries have announced such bold changes as has Tanzania, the changes in their education systems might be expected to be even less noticeable. Indeed, most other school systems pay even less attention to agriculture. In part, the reasons for this were noted in Chapter 7, namely that schools are seen by many parents and pupils as ways *out* of the village rather than as agents for development of village skills.

Language in the curriculum

The topic of language in the curriculum is so important that it requires some further comment. Table 9.1 shows that Sierra Leone students were supposed to learn English even at the beginning of primary school, and African languages were not included in the syllabus. By contrast, the Grade 2 syllabuses for Swaziland and Uganda allocated more time to African languages than to English, and only in later grades was this situation reversed. In Tanzania, as we have mentioned, coverage on English was reduced in 1980 in order to give more time to Swahili.

The language issue has two main sides. Some governments argue that the official language (English, French or Portuguese) is needed for national unity and that for children to become fluent it is best for them to learn in that language from their first day of school. Some governments add that particular regions have so many vernaculars that it is impossible to select one which is spoken by all pupils and teachers. However an increasing body of research indicates that children who commence study in their mother tongues learn more efficiently, and later learn other languages more rapidly.[12] It may also be argued that use of vernaculars reduces the gap between schools and the communities, and strengthens indigenous cultures. Because of the force of the latter arguments, the trend is for African languages to be used more widely.

Nevertheless, even Tanzania continues to teach English in primary schools. Some people would argue that this policy is not necessary in a country in which a single African language is spoken so widely, and in which a very small proportion of children move from primary to secondary school. Moreover English is not being taught very well. Carr-Hill comments that 'not only is the teaching of English in the primary schools taking away valuable time from other, possibly more relevant subjects, it is not being taught sufficiently well for that small minority who do continue to secondary school'.[13] In these circumstances, it can be argued, Tanzanian children are getting the worst of both worlds. However a recent report has recorded that public opinion is overwhelmingly in favour of keeping English in Tanzania, even at the primary school level.[14] It therefore seems unlikely that the present balance between subjects will greatly change in Tanzania and similar forces operate elsewhere.

Further discussion on school syllabuses and timetables would require more space than is available, and we cannot explore the topic in great detail. Instead, readers are referred to Hugh Hawes' excellent book,[15] and the curriculum documents of their own countries.

Gender in the Curriculum

One important aspect of the hidden curriculum concerns the implicit role which textbooks assign to women and girls. Many textbooks, research suggests, focus more on males than females, and in the process reinforce the positive self-images of boys and the negative self-images of girls. Where books do focus on females, their images are frequently shaped by stereotypes, for example showing women in the home with babies rather than in offices running businesses. In this way, it is suggested, the textbooks reinforce male dominance in society. They encourage males to aspire to wage-earning, high status jobs, and they encourage females to aspire to domestic, low status jobs.

Although little research has yet focused on this topic in Africa, the nature of the issue is indicated by evidence from Papua New Guinea. Tables 9.3 and 9.4 show the results of Brown's study of the content of the secondary school social science textbooks. First she examined the pictures in the books to see how many showed males only, how many showed females only, and how many showed both sexes. Table 9.3 shows the bias of the pictures in the Grades 7–9 textbooks. Of the 398 pictures, 39.9 per cent showed males only whereas only 10.6 per cent showed females only. Table 9.4 shows the bias in the stories which involved people in the textbooks for Grades 7–10. In 70.5 per cent of the stories a male was the main character, whereas in only 6.5 per cent of stories was a female the main character. Brown also assessed the nature of the stories to see whether males were treated in a more favourable light. The small number of stories in which females were the main character were balanced, with half stressing positive characteristics and half stressing negative characteristics. However among the stories in which males were the main character, nearly twice as many stressed positive characteristics as negative ones. Brown concluded that the hidden message of the books was highly biased in favour of males.

Table 9.3   Content of pictures in the Papua New Guinean social science textbooks, classified by sex[16]

Grade	Male Only	Female Only	Mixed Group	No People	Total	N
Grade 7	40.4%	10.6%	23.8%	25.2%	100.0%	151
Grade 8	48.7%	13.5%	21.8%	16.0%	100.0%	156
Grade 9	24.2%	5.5%	16.5%	53.8%	100.0%	91
Grades 7–9	39.9%	10.6%	21.3%	28.1%	99.9%	398

Note: N = number in sample. The Grade 10 textbook had no pictures.

Table 9.4   Content of stories in the Papua New Guinean social science textbooks, classified by sex of main character[17]

Grade	Male Only	Female Only	Mixed Group	No People	Total	N
Grade 7	75.0%	10.7%	14.3%	0	100%	28
Grade 8	52.2%	4.4%	21.7%	21.7%	100%	23
Grade 9	100.0%	0	0	0	100%	2
Grade 10	100.0%	0	0	0	100%	8
Grades 7–10	70.5%	6.5%	14.8%	8.2%	100%	61

Schools may also have hidden biases in the subjects which boys and girls are encouraged to study. One international study has stated that:

All secondary education is moulded on [a] traditional image of women. Though boys and girls follow broadly the same curricula, the differences creep in as soon as vocational experience, guidance or training are involved. . . . For example, the omnipresence of domestic science as an optional or alternative subject in general education tends to accustom girls to the role of mother-wife-housewife instead of broadening their outlook. The existence of special courses for girls, implicit or explicit restrictions in the range of possible options and sexually biased admission criteria in technical and vocational education all tend to steer female students towards subordinate jobs that bear little relation to economic realities, give scant satisfaction and confine them to the service sector instead of encouraging social mobility and allowing them to enter one of the productive sectors.[18]

The study was based on six countries of which one, Madagasgar, was in Africa. Its general conclusion was that secondary girls tend to be steered into such subjects as domestic science, and to aspire to home duties and low status jobs rather than paid employment and high status jobs. This conclusion would seem to be applicable in most, if not all, the countries in Africa. The poor image of females projected by the hidden curriculum is probably one reason why so many females drop out in lower stages of the education system. In turn, the fact that they drop out makes it harder for them to compete with males for high status jobs, and perpetuates the vicious circle.

Examinations and the curriculum

We are all aware that exminations have a very powerful influence on the type of teaching and learning in the school system. Examinations are usually considered part of the official curriculum, even though some of their effects may be unplanned and may actually contradict other official policies. For example, governments may state that they wish pupils to have a broad general education and to develop enquiring minds while their examination systems may encourage rote learning and narrow foci.

Chapter 1 has already noted some changes in examination systems in Africa. It highlighted the creation of the West African Examinations Council, which serves the five English-speaking West African states, and the localisation of examination systems in other parts of the continent. It also pointed out that Cambridge University's external examinations are still used in several countries, and thus that some international connections remain very prominent.

Because of their importance to students' subsequent careers, examinations can have a powerful 'backwash' effect. Examinations for entry to universities influence the curricula of senior secondary schools; examinations for entry to senior secondary schools influence the curricula of junior secondary schools; and examinations for entry to junior secondary schools influence the curricula of primary schools. Although this distorts the education system, it has generally proved impossible to abolish examinations. This is chiefly because they are needed by decision-makers to determine who should continue to the next educational level, and because employers use examinations as an indicator of students' ability. Pupils are often so conscious of the need for success in examinations that they challenge their teachers if they think that the content of lessons seems to be straying from the syllabus.

The extent to which examinations can satisfactorily measure a pupil's achievements in school is widely questioned. First, examinations are usually restricted to academic skills and totally ignore the social side of school life – i.e. whether the children are polite, respectful to their elders, and so on. Second, although examinations are often intended to assess five or six years' work, the examinations themselves last only a few hours. As such, it is impossible for them to measure anything except a tiny fraction of what students have learned. Third, many examinations are restricted to multiple choice answers. The candidates are expected to choose from a range of options merely by shading a box. They can easily gain a few marks by guessing, and because they do not give written answers they do not demonstrate their fluency even in writing the language, let alone in speaking it.

The chief reasons for setting multiple choice questions are usually to make marking fast and reliable, and to make assessment more objective.

Essay answers take a long time to mark, and the grade which they are given is very much a matter of judgement. Some countries now have computer systems which count the number of correctly shaded boxes automatically, and which are very fast. Because multiple choice questions fail to test writing skills, however, some governments prefer to have at least some questions which require the students to express themselves.

In line with Bloom's well-known taxonomy of educational objectives,[19] examinations can be categorised according to their focus on knowledge, comprehension and application. These may be explained as follows:[20]

Knowledge questions require only recognition or recall of facts, generalisations or principles. For example, (from a Somalia geography paper):

An area well known for its Artesian basin and wells is:
a) The Kalahari
b) The great basin of Western U.S.A.
c) The Indo-gangetic plain
d) The central lowlands of Australia
e) The Pampas

In this question the candidates have to recognise the correct answer, and either they know it or they do not.

Comprehension questions on the other hand require more than recall and recognition, for candidates need to understand the meaning of concepts and symbols. Questions in this category include the translation of material from one form to another, and interpretation of maps, tables and graphs. For example, (from a Sierra Leone Verbal Aptitude paper):

Study this example of secret writing followed by its meaning, and use it to answer the question underneath.

Example: PDYBSQVTZTMFTQ
　　　　　iknowthesecret

The secret writing for 'know' is
a) DBSY
b) DSBT
c) BVST
d) DYBS
e) SYBD

Application questions require the ability to apply and use rules, concepts and principles in *new* circumstances. For example, (from a Kenya mathematics paper):

In a village there are 300 farmers who either keep livestock or grow one or more of the crops maize, cassava and beans.

50 farmers grow no crops
10 farmers grow all three crops
35 farmers grow beans and cassava
38 farmers grow maize and beans
15 farmers grow maize and cassava

105 farmers grow maize
141 farmers grow beans

a) Represent the information on a Venn diagram.
b) Determine the number of farmers who grow cassava only.
c) Determine the number of farmers who grow exactly two crops.

In this item candidates have to demonstrate and apply their understanding of how to represent new information symbolically through Venn diagrams, and then how to use that representation to derive conclusions.

Angela Little's study of 122 examination papers in the Gambia, Ghana, Kenya, Liberia, Tanzania, Sierra Leone, Somalia and Zambia found that the largest number of questions (42 per cent) were knowledge items. Almost an equal proportion (38 per cent) were application items, and the remainder (20 per cent) were comprehension items. However, there were wide variations between countries, between subjects and between levels. Subjects like English and mathematics usually had the highest proportions of comprehension and application questions.[21]

Perhaps surprisingly, Little also found that primary school leaving examinations had higher proportions of comprehension and application questions than did secondary school leaving examinations. This may partly be explained by the dominance of mathematics and English in primary examinations, but Little expressed concern that few items in the geography, history, biology, civics and religion subject areas tested anything except recall or recognition of facts. Her research raises questions about the extent to which education systems are related to the problems of the real world.

Although they involve less subjectivity in grading than essay questions, even multiple choice examinations can be very biased. Some people make the mistake of thinking that examinations can be neutral instruments for measurement just like thermometers or litre containers. A thermometer should measure the temperature of a liquid on the same scale, whether that liquid is sulphuric acid or ink. A litre bottle will measure volume with similar neutrality. Examinations, however, may be highly biased.

Some of the best work to expose the biases of examinations has been conducted by H.C.A. Somerset.[22] For example one mathematics paper for the old Kenyan Certificate of Primary Education (CPE) examination included the question:

Through what angle does the hour hand of a clock move from 9 am to 4.45 pm?
a) $7\frac{1}{2}$ degrees
b) $22\frac{1}{2}$ degrees
c) 45 degrees
d) 270 degrees

At first sight this might seem a fairly neutral question. However Somerset points out that children in urban and privileged schools have much more contact with clocks than do children in rural schools. Children in urban and privileged schools are also much more likely to understand idiomatic

English expressions. In this connection he asks: 'Which hand of the clock is the hour hand—the one which travels round the clock every hour, or the one which moves from one number to the next?'[23] He points out that even the *teachers* in low-cost schools could not have been relied upon to give the right answer, and that the question is therefore very unfair on their pupils.

Another question in the arithmetic paper required pupils to work out the cost of rice. Somerset demonstrated that urban children had an extra advantage because of their knowledge of what the price of rice should have been. Questions in the general knowledge paper were also commonly biased towards an urban environment. Somerset's research heightens awareness of the need for examiners not only to set questions which, if they are multiple choice, have only one answer and yet have good 'distractors' (the 'wrong' answers), but also to be aware of the biases in the questions themselves. It is quite possible to alter the balance by including questions on maize-meal as well as rice, or to ask questions about shadows thrown by the sun instead of about clocks. However, many examination setters fail to pay adequate attention to this point.

In conclusion, we may observe that the official and hidden curricula in African school systems are critical but neglected topics. Many governments in recent years have paid considerable attention to the quantity of education, but have given much less attention to what actually happens inside schools. One reason for this is political—that the governments want to provide schooling for as many people as possible, even if they have to make qualitative sacrifices. Another reason is conceptual: it is easy to measure the number of schools and the number of children inside them and thus to assess progress, but it is much harder to measure qualitative aspects of education. Despite this difficulty, this chapter has shown that it *is* possible to assess the curriculum and its impact. We hope that in the next few years much more attention will be paid to what children learn inside their schools.

Questions and project work

1 Make a list of the documents in your country which lay down the official curriculum.

2 Find out the official policy in your country on the language of instruction in primary schools. Discuss the arguments for and against this policy. In your discussion, address the questions of national needs, local needs, the abilities of teachers and pupils, the effectiveness with which pupils learn in vernacular and other languages, and the availability of textbooks in different languages.

3 Obtain the official regulations on the number of periods per subject and per grade in the primary schools of your country. Draw pie charts for Grades 1 and 6 similar to those in Table 9.1. Comment on what you have found.

4   Obtain copies of the examination papers in your country for *either* the last grade of primary school *or* the last grade of secondary school. Classify the questions according to whether you consider them to be testing knowledge, comprehension or application. Take note of the subject areas in which each type of question seems most common, and comment on your findings.

Notes

1   Ozigi, Albert and Canham, Peter *An Introduction to the Foundations of Education*. Macmillan, Lagos 1979, pp. 88–9.
2   Federal Republic of Nigeria *National Policy on Education*. Federal Ministry of Information, Lagos 1977; revised and re-issued 1981.
3   Republic of Botswana *National Policy on Education*. Government Printer, Gaborone 1977.
4   Federal Republic of Nigeria *Report of the Seminar on a National Policy on Education*, Federal Ministry of Education, Lagos 1977.
5   Unesco 'Wastage in Primary Education from 1970 to 1980'. *Prospects*, Vol. XIV, No. 3, 1984.
6   Republic of Ghana *Seven Year Development Plan 1963–70*, Office of the Planning Commission, Accra 1963, pp. 150–1; Republic of Ghana *Five Year Development Plan 1975–80*, Ministry of Economic Planning, Accra 1975, Part II, p. 294.
7   Fredriksen, Birger 'Universal Primary Education in Developing Countries: A Statistical Review'. *Prospects*, Vol. VIII, No. 3, 1978, p. 369.
8   Carr-Hill, Roy *Primary Education in Tanzania: A Review of the Research*. Swedish International Development Authority, Stockholm 1984, p. 41.
9   Hawes, Hugh *Curriculum and Reality in African Primary Schools*. Longman, London 1979, pp. 82–5.
10 Carr-Hill, op. cit., pp. 42–3.
11 Ibid., p. 45.
12 Bamgbose, Ayo (ed.) *Mother Tongue Education: The West African Experience*. Hodder and Stoughton, London 1976; Dutcher, Nadine *The Use of First and Second Languages in Primary Education: Selected Case Studies*. World Bank Staff Working Paper No. 504, Washington 1982.
13 Carr-Hill, op. cit., pp. 50–1. See also King, Kenneth *The Death of Education for Self Reliance in Tanzania?* Centre of African Studies, University of Edinburgh 1983, p. 11.
14 Criper, C. and Dodd, W.A. *Report on the Teaching of the English Language and its use as a Medium of Instruction in Tanzania*, Overseas Development Administration, London 1984.
15 Hawes, op. cit.
16 Brown, Marilyn 'Implicit Values in the Social Science Curriculum: Male and Female Role Models' in Bray, Mark and Smith, Peter (eds.) *Education and Social Stratification in Papua New Guinea*. Longman Cheshire, Melbourne 1985, p. 177.
17 Ibid., p. 178.
18 Dupont, Béatrice *Unequal Education: A Study of Sex Differences in Secondary-School Curricula*. Unesco, Paris 1981, p. 45.
19 Bloom, B. *Taxonomy of Educational Objectives*. David McKay, New York 1956.
20 Little, Angela 'The Role of Examinations in the Promotion of the "Paper

Qualification Syndrome" ' in International Labour Office *Paper Qualification Syndrome (PQS) and Unemployment of School Leavers*. Jobs and Skills Programme for Africa, Addis Ababa 1982, pp. 178–9.

21   Ibid., p. 180.

22   Somerset, H.C.A. 'Who Goes to Secondary School? Relevance, Reliability and Equity in Secondary School Selection', in Court, D. and Ghai, D. (eds.) *Education, Society and Development: New Perspectives from Kenya*. Oxford University Press, Nairobi 1974; 'Aptitude Tests, Socio-Economic Background and Secondary School Selection'. Paper presented to the Rockefeller Foundation Conference on Social Science Research and Educational Effectiveness, Bellagio (Italy) 1977; 'Examination Reform: The Kenya Experience'. Institute of Development Studies, Brighton 1982.

23   Somerset, 'Who Goes to Secondary School?' op. cit., p. 160.

Chapter 10

New ways and radical alternatives

This chapter looks at the ideas of some major educationists who have proposed radical alternative forms of educational development. The two individuals to which it devotes particular attention are Ivan Illich and Paulo Freire. It also looks at the use of technology in the classroom and the development of distance teaching. It concludes with a case study of an innovative teacher education programme in Zimbabwe. The innovations proposed by Illich and Freire and the development of new forms of education must be viewed in the context of the climate of the 1970s, and when we are looking ahead to the next century we should ask what their ideas have to offer to educational planners and practitioners.

The climate of the 1970s

By the end of the 1960s, the optimism of the beginning of the decade had begun to evaporate, both in industrialised and in less developed countries, and observers increasingly criticised the nature of the education systems. In industrialised countries, fundamental questions began to be asked about the relationships between the school system and such issues as the threat of nuclear weapons, the breakdown of the family, the growth of crime, abuse of drugs, and the economic exploitation of less developed countries by the industrialised nations. Radicals in Europe and North America viewed schools as agents of social control rather than instruments of liberation, and they were unhappy about the overall direction of changes in society.[1] These views, already sharpened by the Vietnam war, were voiced in such official documents as the 1969 Pearson Report which was called *Partners in Development*, the 1972 Faure Report which was called *Learning to Be*, and the publications of the Club of Rome which began in 1974 with *Limits to Growth*.[2]

In less developed countries the problems were perhaps rather different, but the questions in some places were equally radical. As in industrialised countries, the principal problems were non-educational: urban unemployment, rural-urban drift, regional inequalities, and the unequal development of nations in which, for example, Nigeria became richer as Ghana became poorer. As in industrialised countries, however, the education system was seen both as a dangerous mechanism which could increase problems and as a potentially valuable instrument for improvement.

Foremost among the African philosophers was President Nyerere, whom we have already mentioned several times in this book.[3] Radical forms of education were also introduced in the liberated zones in Mozambique and Guinea-Bissau, and in Ethiopia.[4]

Illich and Freire

Ivan Illich's powerful book, *Deschooling Society*, was first published in 1971.[5] In it, he put forward three main arguments. The first was that schooling was an infringement of liberty because children were forced to attend whether they wished to or not, and because the syllabus was both determined by others and rigid in its content and timing. Secondly, Illich argued that schooling increased rather than decreased social inequalities, for it pushed out children with unsupportive and poor backgrounds and favoured children from educated and affluent families. Thirdly, Illich argued that schools were instruments of economic and cultural imperialism. The curriculum was determined by the middle classes and only valued certain types of knowledge. Popular music, for example, is a passionate love of many young people, but has almost no place in official school curricula.

Illich's principal recommendation was to 'deschool' society. By this he meant the abolition of schools as we know them, in order to allow people to learn how, when and where they liked. He suggested that people should develop learning networks in which more knowledgeable and less knowledgeable people would be linked. Most of these networks would be informal, and would focus on such institutions as museums and libraries. However, Illich failed to provide a convincing alternative model, and in practice his solutions were very vague. They might be valuable for adults and post-primary students, but they seem too unstructured to be of much value to small children. Illich certainly made many people think, and perhaps his ideas have helped introduce some flexibility into both schools and adult education programmes. However, very few people agree that we should go as far as abolishing schools altogether.

Paulo Freire's ideas were rather different from Illich's, but also radical. Freire wrote in the 1970s with experience of education first in Brazil and Chile and later in Guinea-Bissau, and called for a type of education which would liberate the rural and urban poor.[6] He felt that teaching and learning should not be separated, and that 'those who are called to teach must first learn how to continue learning when they begin to teach'.[7] He stated that schools should not be places where knowledge is merely transmitted from teachers to students, but 'learning markets' where societies and their values would be constantly re-made. Instead of traditional relationships between teachers and students, Freire suggested, both should learn from each other and operate on a much more equal basis.

Freire was particularly concerned with adult education, and he pioneered new methods for teaching literacy. However, he was interested in literacy as a means rather than an end, and his final objective was social revolution. He wrote:

Literacy for adults, seen in the perspective of liberation, is a creative act. It can never be reduced to a mechanical matter, in which the so-called literacy worker (teacher) deposits his/her own words in the learners, as though their conscious bodies were simply empty, waiting to be filled by that word. Such a technique is mechanical and relies on memorizing; the learners are made to repeat again and again, . . . all together: la, le, li, lo, lu; ba, be, bi, bo, bu; ta, te, ti, to, tu, a monotonous chant which implies above all a false conception of the act of knowing. . . .[8]

Thus the subject matter of the literacy classes was at least as important as the ability to recognise letters and words. One of Freire's most famous books is called *The Pedagogy of the Oppressed*,[9] and the title reflects Freire's concern for radical social change. In his literacy classes participants learned about human rights, inequalities and land reform, and their lessons suggested ways to overthrow their oppressors. Not surprisingly, the authorities in Latin America were unenthusiastic about Freire's work.

On the other hand, some revolutionary regimes have been strongly interested in his work. In Africa, one of the clearest examples of this comes from Guinea-Bissau. Shortly after independence in 1974, Freire was invited to help guide the new education system and to help invigorate the adult education sector. His comments are contained in a well-known book subtitled *The Letters to Guinea-Bissau*.[10]

However, although one might sympathise with Freire's objectives, his projects have sometimes been disappointing. Even in Guinea-Bissau, according to one report:

The first alphabetisation [literacy] programme started first among the . . . Armed Forces in Bissau and in the interior. Also, in 1976, 120 members of the . . . youth movement were given training of a few weeks, in order to be monitors for alphabetisation. At the same time, 200 Lycées students were trained during the long holidays on a voluntary basis, to become cultural animators. The intention was that they would return to their home regions in order to initiate alphabetisation on a mass scale. The students were meant to work with the peasants during the day, and to animate culture circles including alphabetisation, health education and agricultural education during the evenings.

Of all these projects, only the alphabetisation in the armed forces was a success. Almost all the campaigns in the suburbs and in the countryside gave poor results in that only a minority of the circles managed to complete their intended programme, and only a very small fraction of the participants learnt how to read and write.[11]

The report blamed the poor response to the campaigns on failure to adequately mobilise the political party and mass organisations; the enormous difficulty of carrying out literacy in Portuguese, which was a foreign language for most of the participants; shortage of instructors and materials; and lack of motivation among the participants. In connection with the last point, many people do not see literacy as an essential skill in life. Moreover, many of the poor and oppressed are less interested in changing the social system than in rising within it.

Although Illich's proposals do not seem realistic and Freire's projects have not always been very successful, their views should not be ignored. They encourage us to ask the following questions about all levels of schooling:

1 Do schools educate or do they really indoctrinate?
2 Do we have too little formal schooling or too much?
3 Should there be a distinction between education for children and education for adults, or can the two be linked more closely?
4 Similarly, should there be a distinction between formal and nonformal education, or can the two be totally integrated?
5 Is the concept of a 'teaching profession' in tune with the needs of modern Africa? Or should *everybody* consider herself/himself both a teacher and a learner?

Even now, too many Ministries of Education concern themselves only with trying to run the existing system more efficiently, and fail to ask these fundamental questions.

Technology in the classroom

Recent years have also witnessed several major projects to use new technologies in education. In Niger, televisions were introduced in a few primary schools to enrich the nature of instruction. A larger and more ambitious project was later launched in Ivory Coast. Neither project has proved very successful, however, and important lessons should be learned from this.

The Niger project was launched in 1964. From the viewpoint of the Niger government, its main objective was to help achieve rapid primary school expansion. At that time only about 7 per cent of school-aged children actually attended school, and it was felt that a shortage of teachers was a major constraint on expansion. If televisions could be used instead of teachers, it was argued, rapid expansion would be possible. The scheme was also heavily supported by the French government, which wanted to find out first whether television could reduce drop-out rates and improve quality; second whether school leaver 'monitors' instead of teachers could be used to supervise children's learning; and third whether television could be used to teach French to children who had never spoken the language before coming to school. The architects of the project decided to use monitors instead of teachers because they wanted to save money. They also hoped that the monitors would be more flexible than trained teachers.[12]

For the first ten years the Niger project was restricted to 20 classes in Grade 1, and thus was very small. In 1974 the project was extended to another 100 classes, but it was still quite small, and it remained isolated from the main system. The project was launched with an initial capital budget of $1.5 million and an annual recurrent budget of $500,000, all of which was provided by the French government. The French also supplied 27 educators and 25 technicians, who for the first seven years were in sole charge of setting up both the new curriculum and the television programmes.[13]

The nature of the French involvement gives one clue why the project never really took off. Schramm points out that the project operated separately from the Ministry of Education, and that it was treated like a French experiment on Niger soil.[14] It therefore never became a 'mainstream' activity. Schramm also notes that teachers and parents were suspicious of the scheme, and that it was very costly.

On the other hand, the project did have some successful aspects. The television classrooms were popular among the children, who came to school even when they were ill and when the weather was bad, week after week, year after year. The monitors also worked well. The project supervisors said that it was easier to train monitors in the new curriculum and methods than to retrain traditional teachers. However, it is not clear that similar results would have been obtained if the project had been dramatically expanded. These successful results probably arose at least partly from the enthusiasm and intensive input of a team of educationists working in a small number of schools.

The Ivory Coast project was launched in 1969, was much larger, and also aimed to allow the government to achieve universal primary education. By 1975 educational television was available in some subjects in the six primary grades, and it was expected that all classes would be covered in 1985. This project also received considerable help from the French government, and gained additional assistance from Unesco, the World Bank, West Germany, Belgium and the United States. The total budget for the first five years was approximately $15 million.[15]

Unlike in Niger, the Ivory Coast project employed staff who were already teachers. A three year course (later reduced to two) was provided for teachers who were expected to become administrators, and instruction for classroom use of television was added to existing one-year teacher training programmes. Special one-month courses were offered to teachers who were to go into classrooms with televisions. The authorities argued that by putting their best teachers onto the television and broadcasting throughout the nation, they were both making effective use of scarce talent and setting good examples.

In 1981, however, the Ivory Coast project was abandoned. The reasons for this were partly technical and partly psychological. First, it was found that the televisions often broke down because of the harshness of the climate and attacks by rats and cockroaches. Electricity supplies were also a major problem, especially in rural areas which had to rely on generators and large batteries. Thirdly, the scheme ran into major financial difficulties, and finally it was never very popular with the teachers, some of whom felt that the televisions threatened their status and jobs.[16]

The experiences of these two projects therefore warn innovators not to be too ambitious. Educators should not abandon efforts to find new ways to teach, but the costly failure especially of the Ivory Coast project emphasises the need for realism when proposing solutions.

Distance education schemes

By contrast, several out-of-school distance education projects have been much more successful. Correspondence courses using the postal services are the most obvious examples of distance education, but other schemes use radio and television. Distance education schemes can be much more flexible than school-based education, for they can reach people all over the country. They can cater for people who had to drop out of the system when they were younger but who later wish to upgrade their qualifications, and by allowing people to study in their spare time they also allow them to continue working during the day. The Centre d'Enseignement Supérieur in Brazzaville (Congo), opened in 1962, was the first correspondence college to be established in Africa.[17]

Distance education schemes may be particularly valuable for upgrading skills of rural primary school teachers. The case study at the end of this chapter focuses on a Zimbabwean project to achieve this, and similar schemes may be found in many other countries.[18] By training or re-training teachers 'on the job', it is possible to improve the quality of education without taking the teachers away from their classrooms.

Distance education schemes may also provide another chance for young people who could not attend conventional secondary schools. Some schemes offer instruction in such specific skills as accountancy and book-keeping. Others lead to the same examinations as would be taken by full-time students in conventional secondary schools.

Developments in distance education have gone hand in hand with developments in technology. Radio seems to be more flexible than television, and is cheaper and easier to manage. A project in Somalia begun in 1974 had an estimated audienced of 1,255,000 adults, who were part of a major literacy campaign. Particular attention was focused on 50,000 nomads who joined settlement schemes between 1973 and 1976. The project suffered from a shortage of support materials and a lack of follow-up programmes, but it was at least partially successful.[19]

Criticisms of distance education schemes usually refer to the danger of creating two-tier systems in which the pupils still in the ordinary schools have an advantage over the others. Young *et al.* are therefore careful to point out that distance education is no substitute for more and better schools.[20] Rather than alternatives to schools, these projects should be seen as complements. It would seem that distance education can be particularly valuable when it is used to achieve a limited, short-term objective. The Zimbabwean case study at the end of this chapter gives one example of this.

Some advocates of distance education suggest that it can be relatively cheap. Tanzania's distance teacher training programme claimed that its costs per teacher trained were only one third of the cost of the equivalent residential programme,[21] and Taylor's study of a Bophuthatswana project pointed out that proportionate salary costs were considerably less than those of normal schools.[22] This is not always true, and it partly depends on whether the distance education projects are able to cover enough people to justify the initial investment in equipment, materials, course design and training. However, it is one reason why distance education has become an attractive alternative form of instruction.

Case study: ZINTEC—a Zimbabwean scheme for distance teaching

Zimbabwe attained its independence in April 1980 after a long and devastating war. The new government, determined to reform society and to response to popular aspirations, embarked on a programme of massive educational expansion. Primary school fees were abolished, schools which had closed because of the war were reopened, and new schools were constructed. Regions which had previously been neglected were given high priority, and provision was also made for the 300,000 children of primary school age who had gone to neighbouring countries during the war but who returned to Zimbabwe after independence. Table 10.1 indicates the extent of the expansion in the primary school sector.

Table 10.1   Primary schools and enrolments in Zimbabwe 1979–84

Year	Schools	Enrolment	% increase in enrolment
1979	2,401	819,686	–
1980	3,161	1,235,994	50%
1981	3,698	1,684,481	36%
1982	3,805	1,934,614	15%
1983	3,960	2,044,487	6%
1984	4,141	2,143,581	5%

Of course, such an expansion could not be achieved easily. One of the most difficult problems was to find enough staff to teach the children. It was necessary to recruit many people who were untrained, and their number increased from 6,000 in 1980 to 14,000 in 1981 and 27,000 in 1983. The fact that so many teachers were untrained threatened the quality of education, and required the Zimbabwe government to find an innovative approach. Their main solution was the Zimbabwe Integrated Teacher Education Course (ZINTEC).[23]

In the conventional system for training primary school teachers, students undertook a three year course. The Zimbabwe government felt that this process was too slow to meet the system's urgent needs. Moreover, most of the trainees' time was spent in colleges rather than in primary school classrooms, and the authorities felt that this system was rather irrelevant and inefficient. The ZINTEC model combined residential and distance learning in an attempt to provide a teacher-training system that was both rapid and effective. Five ZINTEC colleges were established, in each of the country's main regions.

Before students are recruited for the ZINTEC programme, they must work for at least one term as untrained teachers in registered primary schools. They should also have either five O levels or the equivalent Grade II certificate (six passses plus English).

After recruitment, the students first undertake sixteen weeks of intensive training at the college centre. During this period they participate in micro-teaching sessions covering at least one lesson per subject, receive instruction in practical subjects such as homecraft and agriculture, and learn about the philosophy, sociology and psychology of education. This short period of intensive training gives the students a sort of 'survival kit' for the future. Each college takes three groups of students per year, with about 200 students in each intake.

Following this initial training, students are sent to schools for three years. There, they continue their study of education theory through distance learning, and continue with supervised teaching. After two terms they should return to the college for a three week vacation course. During term-time they should also participate in weekend seminars and tutorial sessions with field tutors and district education officers. Each field tutor is supposed to be in charge of 30 trainees, though in practice the tutors have about 50 trainees.

After three years in the field, the students return to their colleges for a final 16 weeks. During this time they review and discuss their experiences, and prepare for their final exam.

The first group of students completed the ZINTEC programme in 1984, and the government was pleased with their results. The centre near Harare had a high drop-out rate because there were a large number of attractive opportunities outside the teaching profession. Elsewhere, however, financial inducement, coupled with a positive attitude towards the programme and a sense of dedication and patriotism, led to a high completion rate.

On the other hand, administration of the system was less satisfactory. Many of the staff recruited to run the scheme had no primary school experience themselves. There was also insufficient coordination between the different sections at headquarters and between the ZINTEC colleges and the regional centres. This caused inefficiency and waste of resources. In addition, organizational and administrative problems led to the collapse of the vacation courses and weekend seminars, and many of the training materials were said to be inappropriate to the students' needs.

ZINTEC is stil young, and deeper evaluation will not be possible for several years. In the meantime, we may observe that although it has suffered from some organizational problems, it is an imaginative programme which aims to meet the urgent needs of Zimbabwe's post-independence expansion. Such innovatory thinking, coupled with careful attention to the details of implementation, is urgently needed throughout the continent.

Questions and project work

1 Why did Ivan Illich wish to 'deschool society'? Explain the rationale behind his idea and what he wanted to replace schools with. Indicate whether you consider his proposal to be desirable, giving reasons for your answer. (Note: to answer this question you should look at Illich's book, in addition to reading the relevant section in this chapter.)

2 In the light of the work and views of Illich and Freire, comment on the view that the concept of a 'teaching profession' is not in tune with the needs of modern Africa, and that everybody should consider themselves both teachers and learners.

3 Discuss the view that recent attempts to introduce televisions into the classrooms of African schools have done more harm than good.

4 In the light of the experience of ZINTEC and similar schemes, comment on the view that traditional teacher training colleges should be abolished and that all teachers should be trained while they are already in schools, using distance teaching methods and occasional residential sessions.

Notes

1 See for example Goodman, Paul *Compulsory Miseducation*. Penguin, Harmondsworth 1971; Young, M.F.D. (ed.) *Knowledge and Control*. Collier Macmillan, London 1971.
2 Pearson, Lester B. *Partners in Development: Report of the Commission on International Development*. Praeger, New York 1969; Faure, Edgar *et al.* *Learning to Be: The World of Education Today and Tomorrow*. Unesco, Paris 1972; Meadows, D.H. et al. *Limits to Growth: A Report for the Club of Rome's Project on the Predicament of Mankind*. Pan, London 1974.
3 See especially pages 73–6.
4 Ganhao, Fernando 'The Struggle Continues: Mozambique's Rural Experience in Education'. *Development Dialogue*, No. 2, 1978; Searle, Chris *We're Building the New School!*. Zed Press, London 1981; Johnson, Anton *Education in Mozambique 1975–84*. Swedish International Development Authority, Stockholm 1984; Dias, Carlos 'Education and Production in Guinea-Bissau'. *Development Dialogue*, No. 2, 1978; Goulet, Denis *Looking at Guinea-Bissau: A New Nation's Development Strategy*. Overseas Development Council, Washington 1978; *Education in Socialist Ethiopia*. Ministry of Education, Addis Ababa 1984.
5 Illich, Ivan *Deschooling Society*. Harper and Row, New York 1971. See also Illich, Ivan *Celebration of Awareness: A Call for Institutional Revolution*. Penguin, Harmondsworth 1973; Macklin, Michael *When Schools are Gone: A Projection of the Thought of Ivan Illich*. University of Queensland Press, Brisbane 1976; and Martin, J.M. (ed.) *Innovations in Education: Reformers and their Critics*. Allyn and Bacon, New York 1975. For a list of Illich's other writings and of criticisms and commentaries, see Kallenberg, A.G. *Ivan Illich: A Bibliography*. Centre for the Study of Education in Developing Countries, The Hague 1977.
6 Freire, Paulo *The Pedagogy of the Oppressed*. Penguin, Harmondsworth

1972; Freire, Paulo *Cultural Action for Freedom*. Penguin, Harmondsworth 1972; Freire, Paulo *Education: The Practice of Freedom*. Writers and Readers Publishing Cooperative, London 1974.

7 Freire, Paulo *Pedagogy in Process: The Letters to Guinea-Bissau*. Writers and Readers Publishing Cooperative, London 1978, p. 9.

8 Ibid., pp. 72–3.

9 Freire, *Pedagogy of the Oppressed*, op. cit.

10 Freire, *Pedagogy in Process*, op. cit.

11 Carr-Hill, R. and Rosengart, G. *Education in Guinea-Bissau 1978-81*. Swedish International Development Authority, Stockholm 1982, p. 139.

12 Schramm, Wilbur *Big Media, Little Media*. Sage, London 1977, pp. 144–5.

13 Ibid., p. 143.

14 Ibid., p. 162.

15 Ibid., p. 144.

16 World Bank *The Ivory Coast: The Challenge of Success*. Johns Hopkins University Press, Baltimore 1978, p. 277; Great, John 'Primary Teaching by Television is Abandoned', *The Times Higher Education Supplement*. 8/5/81.

17 Kabwasa, Antoine and Kaunda, Martin M. (eds.) *Correspondence Education in Africa*. Routledge and Kegan Paul, London 1973, p. 114.

18 Greenland, Jeremy (ed.) *In-Service Training of Primary Teachers in Africa*. Macmillan, London 1983. Taylor, D.C. 'The Cost-effectiveness of Teacher Upgrading by Distance Teaching in Southern Africa', *International Journal of Educational Development*, Vol. 3, No. 1, 1983.

19 Young, M. et al. *Distance Teaching for the Third World*. Routledge and Kegan Paul, London 1980, p. 212.

20 Ibid., passim.

21 Greenland, Jeremy 'INSET in the New Commonwealth-Africa' in Thompson, A.R. (ed.) *In-Service Education of Teachers in the Commonwealth*. Commonwealth Secretariat, London 1982, p. 84.

22 Taylor, op. cit., p. 22.

23 This section is based on Sibanda, Doreen 'The Zimbabwe Integrated Teacher Education Course' in Greenland *In-Service Training of Primary Teachers in Africa*, op. cit.; Government of Zimbabwe, *Annual Report of the Secretary for Education for the year ended 31st December, 1983*. Government Printer, Harare 1984; and Mattaka, Stanley 'ZINTEC' in Gardner, Roy (ed.) *Improving Quality in Primary Education: Who Makes it Happen?* Department of Education in Developing Countries, University of London Institute of Education 1985.

Chapter 11

Education and the future

In this book, we have examined links between education and society on several levels. The first chapter looked at education in an international context. It noted that the dominant form of schooling in Africa was imported from Europe in recent centuries, and pointed out that education continues to play a significant role in international relationships, many of which operate to Africa's disadvantage. Secondly (in Chapters 2, 3 and 4), we examined links between education and society at a national level, paying particular attention to nation building, employment and social stratification. Thirdly (in Chapters 5, 6, and 7), we examined Islamic and indigenous forms of education, the local role of education, and its interconnections at the community level.

Chapter 8 approached the subject from a rather different angle, and examined the sociology of educational institutions. Both schools and individual classrooms, we pointed out, are themselves societies. Within each operates a series of written and unwritten rules which serve to maintain the societies and control their evolution along similar lines to those of wider societies. This final chapter draws together some of the strands analysed above. It relates individuals' aspirations concerning education and development to wider forces, and notes some directions of change. It also pays close attention to the prospects for educational reform, and discusses the extent to which it is possible either to change the school system without changes in wider societies, or to change wider societies without changing the school system.

Education in the 1980s

Both education and development, as we pointed out at the beginning of this book, are complex processes. Education embraces nonformal and informal learning as well as schooling, and development includes social as well as economic change. The breadth and complexity of each have become increasingly apparent to planners and practitioners over the last two decades. Arguably, there is still much that they not only do not know, but are also unaware that they do not know. However, more people see some of the weaknesses in their understanding of economic and social issues, and this, in an ironic way, might be considered some form of progress.

The United Nations characterized the 1960s as the First Development

Decade. It was a period during which most African countries gained political independence, and it opened with considerable optimism. It was expected that absolute poverty would be drastically reduced and perhaps eliminated in the foreseeable future, and that the less developed nations would rapidly catch up with the industrialized ones.

Table 11.1   Gross National Product per person (1980 dollars)[1]

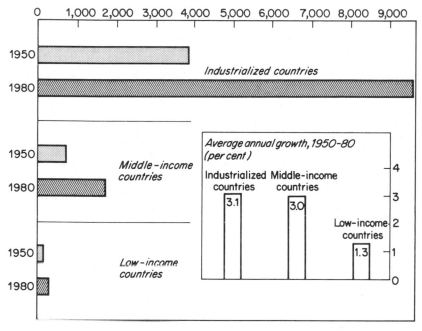

In the Third Development Decade of the 1980s, however, there is much less scope for optimism. Economic growth has not matched expectations, and, as Table 11.1 shows, the gap between rich and poor nations has widened. Some groups in Africa are actually poorer than they were 20 years ago, and the economies of some countries have continued to be manipulated by outside powers. In many cases political independence seems little more than a token.

For a few countries, the experiences of the last two decades have been more agreeable. Chief among them is Nigeria which, because of its petroleum assets, has emerged as a much more prosperous and influential nation. Gabon and Ivory Coast have also maintained high rates of economic growth; and with the termination of the guerilla war and the achievement of independence in 1980, Zimbabwe appeared set for a period of rapid development and prosperity.

However, the experiences of the majority of countries have been disappointing, and in some cases disastrous. The Ghanaian situation is among the latter, and little now remains of either the economic strength or the optimism of the late 1950s and early 1960s. The fate of Uganda has been particularly tragic, for the tyranny of Amin's government (1971–79) was followed by continued political strife, and a once prosperous economy was almost totally destroyed. Zambia's experience has been less dramatic, but is not unlike the majority. Its economy has been severely hit by falling copper prices, by its landlocked position within the continent, and by unfavourable international terms of trade. By 1981, it was reported, a peasant farmer in Zambia had to grow three times as much maize as he did at independence to buy the same shirt, blanket or hoe. Apart from areas in which missionaries were active, medical and educational facilities were as bad as, if not worse than they had been at the end of colonial rule.[2]

Furthermore, the economic position of the majority of African countries is more likely to get worse than better in the foreseeable future. The rate of population growth in Africa is not only the highest in the world but also, in contrast to other continents, is still increasing.[3] At present it is highest of all in Kenya, where it exceeds 4 per cent each year and is contributing to severe pressure on resources. By itself population growth in Africa should not be a problem, for overall densities are far below those of Asia and even Europe. However, population growth reduces income per head, and must be seen in the context of international distribution of resources, where the picture is also bleak. International terms of trade are already set against African countries and are expected to get worse. In the period 1977 to 1985, prices of goods imported by African countries were expected to rise by 149 per cent. The chief increases were in fuel (270 per cent), food (115 per cent) and capital goods (106 per cent). In contrast, export prices were expected to rise by an average of only 66 per cent. Prices of metal and mineral exports might have increased by 159 per cent, and those of agricultural raw materials by 121 per cent, but prices of food and beverages were expected to fall by 8 per cent.[4]

A similar pattern of optimism followed by more sober appraisal has been seen within the education sector. Educational targets set at the 1961 Addis Ababa conference envisaged achievement of universal primary education throughout the continent by 1980. Also by that date, the meeting planned that 30 per cent of the secondary-aged and 6 per cent of the tertiary-aged population should receive education.[5] A great deal was achieved, but because of the unanticipated population growth final accomplishments fell far short of the targets. It is now estimated that even by 1985 only 61 per cent of primary-aged children were attending school;[6] and although only 61 per cent of the adult population was estimated to be illiterate in 1980 compared with 81 per cent in 1960, the absolute number of illiterates in the continent was thought to have risen from 124 million to 156 million.[7]

This situation has been achieved after considerable expenditure of resources. For developing countries as a whole, total real public expenditure on education increased from $9 billion in 1960 to $36 billion in 1976 (in 1976 dollars).[8] This was equivalent to an increase from 2.4 per cent to 4.0 per cent of Gross National Product, and is a trend which, according to available information, has continued in the 1980s. Even though only a minority of the population receives anything more than a few years' education, in most African countries the education sector competes with defence for the largest portion of official budgets. Governments have been aware that they cannot even hope to provide education for the majority of their people without reducing unit costs, but this has proved difficult to do. Education is a labour intensive activity, and teachers' salaries represent the largest single item of expenditure. But in many countries teachers are already poorly paid, and if governments were to reduce their salaries further it would lead to more teachers abandoning the profession entirely.

Furthermore, over the last two decades, there has been increasing doubt about the usefulness of this expenditure. Education has been expected to achieve many objectives, which include promoting national unity, providing human capital for economic growth, improving social equality and permitting individual self-fulfilment. The experience of the last few years has shown that these goals are much more elusive than was previously assumed. As we have shown in this book, national unity, economic growth and social equality depend on a large number of factors other than education. Indeed, in so far as education consumes a considerable proportion of national resources that could otherwise be devoted to health, agriculture, industry and so on, it may actually preclude rapid advance.

The capacity of education to act as an independent variable has, we have pointed out, been overestimated. Instead of the anticipated fruits, many nations have witnessed increased political instability, large-scale unemployment, depopulation of the rural areas and overpopulation of the urban ones, very high drop-out rates within the education system, and reinforced social stratification. In several parts of the continent, a significant proportion of pupils who leave school after six or more years do so without becoming permanently literate in any language.[9] The first part of secondary education has therefore become remedial primary education, and the first part of tertiary education, remedial secondary education.

In presenting this bleak picture, we do not wish to deny the many achievements that have taken place. Chief among them is simply that African nations cater for as many pupils as they do. Indeed, in absolute terms, it must be pointed out, the continent-wide Addis Ababa primary school targets were achieved.[10] There have also been significant advances in textbook production, much of which is now written specifically for African conditions, and in the use of African languages for instruction.

However, we are suggesting that these innovations have been relatively modest. The Zambian government once compared the education system to a train which travels from the first grade of primary school to the last grade of university, but which, without stopping, ejects most of its passengers along the route.[11] Thus, although only a minute proportion of pupils will ever attend university, the curriculum all the way down the system is structured as if they all would. In all parts of the continent, school children study and take vacations in a pattern which bears no relation to the seasons or the demands of agriculture but instead is a colonial legacy originally designed to coincide with European timetables. In most Islamic areas, very little account is taken of the parallel and older system of Islamic education. And while the majority of people in African countries live in rural areas, only to a marginal extent do school curricula examine even the basics of agriculture.

Taken together, these arguments present a powerful case for educational reform. In the second section of this chapter we shall examine the potential for reform.

The potential for educational reform

Educational reform is a term that can be used to describe a wide range of activities. At a minor level, reform can imply curriculum adaptation or introduction of such bodies as Parent-Teacher Associations. More fundamental reform involves the restructuring of the entire education system, the economy and the society itself. It embraces changes in the nature of education and in the relationships between schooling and nonformal and informal learning, and usually has implications for the access of specific groups to power and wealth.

For obvious reasons, modest reform is easier to accomplish than fundamental reform. However, both encounter obstacles of three types, which we shall examine in turn. The first concerns limited capacity of and resistance from the education system itself; the second relates to resistance from influential sectors of society; and the third concerns the basic relationships between education and the economy.

Resistance from the education system

In most African countries a large proportion of teachers are inexperienced and underqualified. With reference to Nigeria's UPE campaign, Professor Babs Fafunwa remarked in 1974 that: 'it will be a disservice to the country if all we can think of in terms of UPE is to multiply the number of existing schools and carry on business as usual'.[12] Yet that is very much what happened, and one reason why it happened was that the education system was hardly able to do anything else. In 1976, the year that UPE was launched, only 40.9 per cent of Nigerian primary teachers were qualified, and in some states the proportion was much lower.[13] In Kano State, for example, only 13 per cent were qualified, and over half the primary teachers had only primary schooling themselves.[14] The majority of staff, therefore, lacked both the experience and the self-confidence required to embark on innovative techniques. Most of them relied on the methods and materials with which they had themselves been taught, and it would have been naive to have expected them to do otherwise. Similarly, the administrative system was so fully occupied with building, staffing and enrolment problems that few resources could be spared for more fundamental matters which, at least in the short term, would probably have brought even more upheaval. Thus, to a large extent the mere scale of operations for UPE precluded basic reform.

Other countries in Africa have not embarked on quite such major programmes, and the pressures on the system have not been so great as they were in this instance. However, all countries are trying to expand educational provision, and finance and other resource constraints are not the only obstacles to doing so. In the pressure for quantity, questions about the nature of education usually get pushed into the background. Two problems with in-service teacher training are firstly, that as teachers improve their qualifications they become eligible for higher salaries and unit costs therefore rise; and secondly, in-service training often qualifies the recipients to leave the profession and take jobs elsewhere.

Apart from the limited capacity for change within the education system, there is also a built-in resistance to change. We have suggested that schools tend to be too isolated from the communities in which they work. One might also suggest that ideally communities should be more involved not only in such matters as erecting buildings or raising funds but also in more fundamental forms of curriculum development and actual teaching. In the few places where this even begins to happen, it only does so because the educational authorities have been prepared to let it do so. More often, they resist what they see as incursions into their territory. Educationists and teachers prefer society to regard them as experts; they wish to be accorded authority and respect, and neither the administrator in the ministry nor the teacher in the classroom is usually very pleased when existing ways of operation are challenged.

One example in which the educational establishment obstructed reform is provided by the Zambian proposals. In 1976, the ministry in Lusaka produced an ambitious document which proposed much greater flexibility and participation in the system, which would both reduce unit costs and permit greater coverage of the school-aged population.[15] After extensive debate, however, the reforms were almost entirely swept aside. In 1977 a much less radical document was produced,[16] and, largely because the education profession resisted both the threat to its established position and the suggestion that it should work harder, the school system has continued to operate very much as before.[17]

Resistance from society

Fundamental reforms are often resisted by influential sectors of society, for while changes may be very desirable for the majority, they are usually to the detriment of a minority. In this case, we must realize that governments are composed of individuals who are themselves members of a social élite and may be unwilling to cede power to other groups. Indeed, in some cases so-called reforms are no more than ways in which the élite increase their power rather than the opposite.

This may be demonstrated very clearly by the Burundi example. In 1972, members of the Hutu ethnic group rebelled against domination by the minority Tutsi and killed 5,000 people before the army could restore control. Although the Hutu form 85 per cent of the population, effective power is, and always has been, held by the minority Tutsi. The short-lived rebellion was followed by brutal repression. Over 100,000 Hutu are thought to have been killed, and an equal number fled to neighbouring countries. The Tutsi were particularly keen to kill all educated Hutu, and it is estimated that in the University of Bujumbura, 120 of 350 students disappeared, while 60 were killed; in the Ecole Normale Supérieure, 40 per cent of 314 students disappeared; in the Ecole Technique de Kamenge, 170 out of 415 disappeared, and 60 were killed; in the Athénée de Bujumbura, 40 per cent of students disappeared; and in the Ecole Normale de Kiremba, 10 of 335 pupils were killed.[18]

Shortly after this bloody massacre, the Ministry of Education produced a so-called reform document.[19] It included general statements about the needs to relate educational to rural life, to reduce drop-outs, to involve the community and so on. But, as Greenland has shown, narrow educational matters had to be seen in a political context.

> Educational considerations counted for less than nothing during the repression . . . Soldiers would march into a lesson, possibly a 'civics' lesson, and order certain boys outside. Many such Hutu were clubbed to death before the lorry reached prison, all were dead and buried the same night. The most insignificant educational innovation is now suspicious to the Tutsi because it could allow the truncated remnant of Hutu to make progress, and it is suspicious to the Hutu because it might be a trick to reveal potential Hutu leaders of the future who will then be eliminated.[20]

The proposals to make Kirundi the medium of instruction in the primary schools, Greenland continued, was seen by the Hutu as a deliberate means not so much to make education more 'relevant', but to keep them in rural areas and prevent them from taking their place in the country's leadership. Inevitably, therefore, the reform document which may have looked sensible and desirable on paper, was more a means for a minority to maintain its stranglehold on the majority. 'Since guns matter more than textbooks, these valuable and logical reforms lost their educational significance for Burundi before they left the printing press.'[21]

The Nigerian case is less stark than that of Burundi, but provides another example of the way political factors may obstruct reform. A major change in educational thinking over the last two decades has been awareness that investment in primary education usually yields greater economic returns than does investment in secondary or higher education, and, in addition, may have the considerable social benefit of distributing resources more equitably.[22] This fact was explicitly recognized by Nigerian planners in the guidelines of the 1981–85 Development Plan.[23] In practice, however, the greatest educational investments in Nigeria have been in universities which, because of their high unit costs, have led to greater expenditure than was devoted to the entire UPE scheme. The six universities existing before 1975 had been increased to 13 by that year, numbered 19 in 1981, and were projected to reach 24 by the middle of the decade. In the mid-1980s a new government became more critical of the universities, but the sector still consumed a vast amount of money. This reflected the demands of a vocal section of the population. The governments of the late 1970s were more concerned with short-term political ends than with longer term economic or social ones, and their successors found it hard to take a different line.

This, indeed, is perhaps the most important reason for misdirection of resources, and constitutes the greatest obstacle to change. Taking an overall view of society, it is easy to identify Dore's diploma disease, the sickness we discussed earlier.[24] While we might disapprove of this situation, however, we must recognize that societies are composed of individuals, and that even while the overall view indicates misdirection of resources, individuals may not have the option of doing anything other than participate in it. A principal feature of African economies, we have noted, is a sharp divide between the rewards of the modern, formal sector and those of the traditional, informal and agricultural sectors. Access to the former is chiefly gained through educational qualifications, so that under the existing system individuals have a strong incentive to acquire as many certificates as possible. Indeed, to choose to do otherwise is to condemn oneself to a life of poverty and insecurity. The economic divide cannot be easily bridged, partly because the modern sector is linked to the world economy, which has its own standards, and partly because those who are gaining from the present situation strongly resist reform.

In other words, we are suggesting that although to some extent the education system shapes the attitudes of its participants, the reverse force is much stronger. The economy and society shape the education system, and it is impossible fundamentally to reform the education system without first reforming the wider economy and society. This is clearly demonstrated by the experience of the nonformal fashion of the 1970s, which it is worth recapitulating.

Faced with strong criticisms of the formal education system in developing countries, in the early 1970s a significant group of educators suggested a reform. The chief innovation they proposed was the development of nonformal education which, they argued, was sufficiently flexible to avoid most of the problems of the formal system. Nonformal education usually involved short programmes, provided specific skills, allowed for a wide range of age-groups, and could often operate more cheaply than formal education. As the decade progressed, however, the problems of nonformal education became more apparent. The most important of these was that, where nonformal schemes were alternatives to formal ones, they tended to be viewed as second-best options and had undesirable consequences of social stratification. The Rural Education Centres of Burkina Faso exemplified this, for although they provided skills which were apparently more related to rural life, the potential participants soon realized that formal primary education offered much greater opportunities for economic advance and entry to the modern sector. Consequently, only whose who were unable to enter primary schools attended the Rural Education Centres. Demand fell, and eventually the project withered away.[25]

By the end of the decade, therefore, many of those who had earlier been enthusiastic about nonformal education were becoming disillusioned. It is significant that the fashion was led by the international agencies, and it is worth noting that most national governments throughout the decade were aware that formal provision was more popular with their peoples.

Many officials paid little more than lip-service to nonformal education, or, if they gave it greater attention, considered it a type of education more suitable for other people's children than their own. By the end of the decade, the attention of the international agencies was reverting to formal provision and, if they were concerned with nonformal educationl at all, it was mainly as a supplement to or a part of formal provision.

The nonformal fashion was a major movement, which clearly showed the resilience of established institutions and processes. On a national level, the Tanzanian experience is also instructive, for there also major initiatives have been taken and have had significant results.

Some aspects of the Tanzanian education system were compared to those of the Kenyan system in Chapter 4. It will be recalled that after the 1967 Arusha Declaration, Tanzanian educators made major efforts to combat several undesirable colonial legacies. They sought to orient the schools to the villages, in which most people lived, rather than to the towns; they wished to encourage traditional values of cooperation rather than competition; and they introduced measures to evaluate students' attitudes as well as knowledge. However, the extent to which they have achieved this has been constrained by the attitudes of both the teaching profession and society in general. Parents had clear ideas about what they thought should happen in schools, and felt that heavy emphasis on agriculture and highly flexible classroom situations were not part of them. In the promotion examinations, only 0.1 per cent of the students who had failed on character assessment had not also failed on academic grounds, and had not therefore become 'safe' to fail. Pressure still to go from primary to secondary schools and thence to university manifested itself in the large number of private secondary schools which opened during the 1970s.

In consequence, even after many years of hard work from the educational authorities, the similarities of the basic Tanzanian educational structure to those in other African countries were still much greater than the differences. Children were still organized in classes according to grades in primary, secondary and tertiary institutions; they still wore uniforms and sat behind desks in neat rows while the teacher at the front wrote on a blackboard; the school year was still sharply divided into terms and holidays; and the school day was still divided into individual periods, the ends of which were generally signalled by the ringing of a bell.

The Tanzanian situation, therefore, provides a clear example of the ways in which the school system is shaped by the demands of society. It is no more than a contemporary example of a phenomenon that has existed for almost as long as the education system itself. As we noted in Chapter 4 and 9, the history of education is littered with efforts to introduce manual work and greater relevance into the curriculum, the majority of which failed because they did not meet the perceived needs and desires of their recipients.

Relationships between education and the economy

Fundamental educational reform may be obstructed by the needs of the economy and its links with the education system. It is here that the

Chinese experience is particularly instructive.

In 1966 the Chinese leadership embarked on a very far-reaching reform of the entire economy and society. It was called the Cultural Revolution, and was led by Chairman Mao. Its objectives were to eliminate the exploitation of the lower classes by the higher ones, which, Mao felt, was something which had not been achieved in the period since the communists took over in 1949, and to establish a socialist state. In the educational sphere, examinations were abolished since, the authorities argued, they encouraged competition, social division and rote learning of facts rather than education in the broad sense. The division between education and work was also to a large extent abolished. All students were forced to work and all workers forced to study. Finally, positions of influence in society were allocated less according to skills and more on the basis of attitudes.[26]

The Cultural Revolution was a very bold initiative, and went far beyond the more timid type of social and educational reform usually advocated in Africa. Its long-term results, however, have been disappointing. Official policies were maintained until 1976, but in that year Chairman Mao died. He was succeeded by the so-called Gang of Four, who maintained the same broad policies, but who a few months later were overthrown themselves. Two years of uncertainty followed, but in 1978 the leadership was taken over by Deng Xiaoping, who embarked on a reversal of Mao's policies. The economy, he said, had suffered acutely, and he referred to the Cultural Revolution as 'the lost ten years'. He therefore commenced what he called the 'four modernizations' of industry, agriculture, military strength and technology. To accomplish his aims, he pointed to education as a crucial component. However, in contrast to Mao he was more concerned with the skills that could be provided through education than with the attitudes. Consequently, the years that followed Deng's ascendancy to power saw a marked reversal of educational strategies. Examinations and competitive entry to post-primary institutions were reinstated. Curricula became more academic again, and practical subjects were relegated to the background. Grammar schools, and even private institutions, re-emerged, and officials openly sought first to restore the pre-Cultural Revolution position and then to continue along their former path.[27]

Increasingly there exists a pervasive world-wide economy and culture, of which, it can be argued, the school is a part. Commenting on international connections, Samir Amin has suggested that:

> Cultures are destroyed nowadays not by separation and isolation but by participation. Throughout the Third World we are witnessing a fantastic process of cultural destruction – the imposition of a model of consumption which is European and capitalist in origin, but completely degenerate, and reproduced in forms which are merely caricature. We have also seen that any country which has really tried . . . to change its internal social relationship has been forced to withdraw from the rest of the world.[28]

With over a billion people, China has more than twice the population of the whole of Africa. It was therefore able to close its doors to the outside world and embark on social and economic reforms in a way that is not possible for any African country. This makes the failure of its efforts even more significant, for if China, with its gigantic size and very strong political will, is unable to achieve reform, one must ask whether it is worthwhile for African nations even to contemplate such changes. In *The diploma disease*, published in 1976, Ronald Dore looked to China as one of the few places in which this disease might be cured.[29] Within four years he was forced to revise his option, and it is to be doubted whether the disease can ever be cured.[30]

Yet although the failure of the Chinese project leads to a pessimistic conclusion, African educators should still try to combat the defects of the education system. On a smaller scale, many measures can at least reduce educational and social problems, even if they cannot eliminate them altogether. Thus, even though Tanzania, like China, has encountered major problems in its educational reform, its efforts have not been entirely wasted. First of all, the Tanzanians have achieved widespread awareness of social problems and their causes, and this itself is an advance. Secondly, they have shown that there is at least some scope for local participation, for reducing inequalities and for relating education to life rather than merely pursuing certificates. They have shown that education for adults is, in some respects, at least as important as education for children. And in Tanzania, as in every African country, there are teachers, often in remote villages, who are active and thoughtful workers, listening to, cooperating with, and leading their communities to better things. Throughout the continent, many improvements in textbook provision and curriculum development have already occurred and can be extended. There is much scope also for administrative improvements and for support of teachers, and useful experimentation continues with radio and programmed instruction as alternative teaching mechanisms.

The nonformal fashion of the 1970s did lead to disillusion for many. Some in the West questioned the whole premise of international aid. P.T. Bauer and Basil Yamey, professors at the London School of Economics, argue that 'aid has done little or nothing to help the poorest people in aid-receiving countries'.[31] For them, aid increases the dependency of the so-called Third World on the First, bringing little real development and increasing North–South confrontation. Bauer goes further by saying that 'foreign aid is a process by which poor people in rich countries help rich people in poor countries'. Cynical and conservative he may be, but perhaps the world recession of the early 1980s has forced governments in both the industrialized and non-industrialized sectors to examine development projects and to ask the question 'will they improve the educational standards of those they are intended to help?'

However, it should not be suggested that the effort and resources have been wasted. We wish to stress again that education reflects society more than it shapes it, and that this has been realized too rarely both by educationists and non-educationists. The fact that many planners are now more aware of the resistance of education systems to reform is itself an advance, and may lead to education being placed more frequently in a wider socio-economic framework. It is only when we ask *why* the education system is expensive, irrelevant and inefficient that we can begin to find remedies for it. The question 'Why?' will lead to the question '*For whom* is it not meeting desired objectives?' The answer to this will probably be 'for the majority of the population'. But for a minority, the education system works very well. It allocates positions of responsibility to them, and maintains them and their families in those positions once they have arrived. Thus, only when the majority are in a position to, and see the need to, modify the power of the minority can we expect either fundamental social or educational change.

Questions and project work

1 Discuss, with examples, the suggestion that education reflects society more than it changes it.

2 'Despite many welcome changes in teachers and subjects taught, in goals and structures, there remains a discouraging, almost desperate, continuity between some of the current debates over educational strategies in Africa and those which filled colonial committee rooms and reports.' (Gifford and Weiskel) Comment on this statement, with reference to the educational history of your own country.

3 Critically examine the suggestion that, despite the reforms of Tanzania's education system following the Arusha Declaration in 1967, the similarities between the system now and before that date are greater than the differences.

4 Obtain copies of your country's former development plans and education policy statements. Take note of the sections which state intent to reform the education system. Assess the extent to which these reforms have or have not been achieved, and comment on the factors which permitted, encouraged or hindered this situation.

Notes

1 The World Bank *World Development Report*. Washington 1980, p. 34.
2 The *Guardian*, 2/2/81. See also International Labour Office *Zambia: Basic Needs in an Economy Under Pressure*, Addis Ababa 1981.
3 The World Bank, op. cit., p. 99.
4 The World Bank *Report*. Nov/Dec 1980, p. 1.
5 UNECA/Unesco *Conference of African States on the Development of Education in Africa: Final Report*. Paris 1961, Pt. II, p. 16.
6 Unesco *Trends and Projections of Enrolments by Level of Education and by Age*. Paris 1977, p. 20.
7 The World Bank *Education Sector Working Paper*. Washington 1974, p. 29; Unesco *Estimates and Projections of Illiteracy*. Paris 1978, p. 111.

8   The World Bank *World Development Report*, op. cit., p. 46.
9   See for example Bray, Mark *Universal Primary Education in Nigeria: A Study of Kano State*. Routledge and Kegan Paul, London 1981, p. 110; and Aryee, Georges A. 'Effects of Formal Education and Training on the Intensity of Employment in the Informal Sector: A Case Study of Kumasi, Ghana'. ILO Geneva 1976, p. 36.
10 Fredriksen, Birger 'Progress towards Regional Targets for Universal Primary Education: A Statistical Review'. *International Journal of Educational Development*, Vol. 1, No. 1, 1981, p. 7.
11 Republic of Zambia *Draft Statement on Educational Reform*. Ministry of Education, Lusaka 1976, p. 1.
12 *New Nigerian*, 7/8/74.
13 Federal Republic of Nigeria *Implementation Committee for the National Policy on Education Blueprint (Onabamiro Report)*. Federal Ministry of Education, Lagos 1979, p. 58.
14 Bray, op. cit., p. 75.
15 Republic of Zambia, *Education for Development*, Ministry of Education, Lusaka 1976.
16 Republic of Zambia *Educational Reform: Proposals and Recommendations*. Ministry of Education, Lusaka 1977.
17 See Garvey, Brian 'Educational Development in an Evolving Society: Zambian Education, 1964–1977' in Fincham, Robin and Markakis, John (eds.) *The Evolving Structure of Zambian Society*. Centre of African Studies, University of Edinburgh 1980; Alexander, D.J., 'Problems of Educational Reform in Zambia', *International Journal of Educational Development*, Vol. 3, No. 2, 1983.
18 Greenland, Jeremy 'Reform of Education in Burundi: Enlightened Theory Faced with Political Reality'. *Comparative Education*, Vol. 10, No. 1, 1974, pp. 57, 60.
19 République du Burundi *Réforme du Système de l'Education au Burundi*. Ministère de l'Education Nationale et de la Culture, Bujumbura 1973.
20 Greenland, op. cit., p. 61.
21 Ibid., p. 62.
22 See The World Bank *World Development Report*, op. cit., p. 49; Psacharopoulos, George. *Returns to Education: An International Comparison*. Elsevier, Amsterdam 1973; Psacharopoulos, George 'Returns to Education: An Updated International Comparison'. *Comparative Education*, Vol. 17, No. 3, 1981.
23 Federal Republic of Nigeria *Guidelines for the Fourth National Development Plan 1981–85*. Federal Ministry of National Planning, Lagos 1980, p. 70.
24 Dore, Ronald *The Diploma Disease*. George, Allen and Unwin, London 1976.
25 See Simkins, Tim *Non-Formal Education and Development*. Dept. of Adult and Higher Education, University of Manchester 1977, p. 35. See also King, Kenneth 'Minimum Learning Needs for the Third World: New Panacea or New Problems?' *Prospects*, Vol. VI, No. 1, 1976.
26 See Price, R.F. *Education in Modern China*. Routledge and Kegan Paul, London 1979, Chapters 1 and 3.
27 See Pepper, Suzanne 'Chinese Education after Mao: Two Steps Forward, Two Steps Back and Begin Again?' *China Quarterly*, No. 8, 1980; and Hayhoe, Ruth (ed.), *Contemporary Chinese Education*. Croom Helm, London 1984.
28 Quoted in Ocaya-Lakidi, Dent 'Towards an African Philosophy of Education'. *Prospects*. Vol. X, No. 1, 1980, p. 14.
29 Dore, op. cit.

30 Dore, Ronald 'The Diploma Disease Revisited'. *IDS Bulletin*, Vol. 11, No. 2, 1980. See also Unger, J. 'Severing the Links between Education and Careers: The Sobering Experience of China's Urban Schools' in Oxenham, John (ed.), *Education versus Qualifications?*. George, Allen and Unwin, London 1984.
31 See Bauer, P.T. and Yamsey, Basil 'Why we should close our purse to the Third World'. *Times*, 11/4/83; Bauer, P.T., *Equality, the Third World and Economic Delusion*, Macmillan, London 1982; Hurst, Paul 'Educational Aid and Dependency'. EDC Paper No. 6, University of London Institute of Education, 1984.

Index